THE HOLY SPIRIT
IN THE WORLD

A Global Conversation

Kirsteen Kim

Founded in 1970, Orbis Books endeavors to publish works that enlighten the mind, nourish the spirit, and challenge the conscience. The publishing arm of the Maryknoll Fathers and Brothers, Orbis seeks to explore the global dimensions of the Christian faith and mission, to invite dialogue with diverse cultures and religious traditions, and to serve the cause of reconciliation and peace. The books published reflect the views of their authors and are not meant to represent the official position of the Maryknoll Society. To learn more about Maryknoll and Orbis Books, please visit our website at www.maryknoll.org.

First published in Great Britain in 2008.

Society for Promoting Christian Knowledge
36 Causton Street
London SW1P 4ST

Cover art from "Pentecost" by Lucy D'Sousa-Krone, used with permission of Internationales Katholisches Missionswerk, e.V., Aachen, Germany.

Manufactured in the United States of America.

Library of Congress Cataloging-in-Publication Data
Kim, Kirsteen.
  The Holy Spirit in the world : a global conversation / Kirsteen Kim.
    p.   cm.
  Includes index.
  ISBN 978-1-57075-750-1
  1. Holy Spirit.   I. Title.
  BT121.3.K55 2007
  231'.3—dc22
                                      2007007821

British Library Cataloguing-in-Publication Data
A catalogue record for this book is available from the British Library

SPCK ISBN 978-0-281-05969-0

CONTENTS

PREFACE

Growing up in the British churches in the 1970s, the stirrings of the charismatic movement reached me and kindled a lifelong interest in the Holy Spirit. The first thing I understood of the theology of the Holy Spirit was that, when God calls us to follow Jesus, we are not simply expected to emulate the behavior of a distant historical figure by "being good," but we are offered the power to become like Jesus. The Spirit seemed to be an invisible energy and a kind of supernatural medium which connected me to God and my Christian friends. However, such a concept made little sense to many of those around me, who seemed to have given up belief in anything "spiritual." It also seemed foreign to the preaching in my Reformed church tradition.

However, in my formative years I was exposed to a number of different interpretations of spirit. There was the inner light for which the Quakers waited in their silent meetings, and at the same time the lively spirit that excited the dancing and aroused the passionate chorus-singing in the house church. I wondered how I could be sure that I was filled with the spirit, whether speaking in tongues was a necessary sign, and which gifts I had been given. Guidance through pictures and visions was given when spiritual people were praying, but according to one Pentecostal preacher, there was also a "lying spirit" that could make me behave deceitfully. At the Christian Union, they emphasized the sanctifying spirit that would save me for life after death, and the mighty spirit that gave the first Christians courage for evangelism, whereas at the Anglo-Catholic church, quite a different spirit seemed to waft through the incense—a mysterious and very holy spirit somewhere out there in the universe, rather detached from what was really going on. At some point I read John V. Taylor's *The Go-Between God* (1972), which connected the Holy Spirit with life and creation and opened up many new possibilities for thinking of the spirit as engaged with the world.

When I moved with my new husband to a new life in his home country of Korea, I was aware of ancestor spirits and spirits around the Buddhist temples. In the church—a Presbyterian church at that—there seemed to be an unlimited confidence in the availability of spiritual power to achieve goals and an inner yearning, expressed in agonized prayer, to have more of this power. At the seminary in the United States where we later went on to study, the talk was of spiritual warfare and the need to pray against territorial spirits, but there was also a course offered on "God the Holy Spirit" alongside those on God the Father and God the Son. Unable to take this option, I began to wonder about its content. In India, the spiritual power of

Hinduism was very evident not just in the temples but also in the streets and in politics. At the same time, in the seminary there was also the memory of the Indian revival and links with growing Pentecostal movements, which were very negative toward Hinduism. The students showed a great deal of interest in the spirit and spirituality, yet the Western textbooks said little that was relevant, and I felt ill-equipped to answer their questions. However, some Indian theologians seemed to be reflecting on God as spirit in a way that was positive toward Indian thought and movements. Intrigued, I gathered materials to follow this up in my doctoral thesis.

Back in Britain after ten years away, I was struck by a new openness toward spiritual experience of all kinds. Yet in academia the world seemed to be reduced to the material and the human, and theology was history. This book is the result of my endeavors to try to make sense of these varied experiences of the spirit, and of the meanings and meaninglessness of the concept. It is also the fruit of a hunch that, in the contemporary West, we may be able to put the gospel message across more meaningfully if we begin from the Spirit, rather than the historical Jesus. And after all, it is the role of the prevenient Spirit to prepare the world to receive Christ.

My interest in the Holy Spirit is not to suggest any lack of interest in Jesus Christ, but comes from a conviction that in a multi-cultural world there is more than one way of explaining his significance. It is not my intention to suggest a radical rethinking of the foundations of Christian faith, but to try to express the faith of the Bible in a way that may appeal to the hearts and minds of those with whom I grew up. This approach that begins with the Spirit—informed as it is by experience in Korea and India particularly—is one that I hope will have wider relevance to all those seeking to understand the presence and activity of God in the world.

I wish to acknowledge the help and support of a number of people in writing this book: first, my husband, Sebastian C. H. Kim, who has always encouraged me to study and write. Second, I wish to thank Israel Selvanayagam, the principal, and the staff and students of the United College of the Ascension, Selly Oak, Birmingham, which has been my home for the last five years, for their fellowship and challenging discussion. Third, I am indebted to the many scholars who are cited in the following pages for their stimulating work. I have been privileged to interact with many of them personally in Britain and Ireland, in India, in South Korea, and in the United States. I have also particularly gained from the networks of the British and Irish Association for Mission Studies, the International Association for Mission Studies, Churches Together in Britain and Ireland, and the World Council of Churches. Fourth, I particularly wish to thank Bill Burrows of Orbis Books for his enthusiastic interest in my work, and Jacques Matthey of the World Council of Churches for giving me several opportunities to develop it in ecumenical dialogue.

This book is dedicated to my parents, Neil and Gwyneth Freeman.

A testimony and prayer:

> I experience the Holy Spirit in the wind of God, the breath
> of Jesus Christ, the shared life of God's people.
> The Spirit leads me to Jesus Christ, and witnesses to him
> as the Son who reveals the Father in heaven, Creator
> of the Universe and Source of all—one God, three-in-
> one and one-in-three.
> Come, Holy Spirit!

Kirsteen Kim
Selly Oak, Birmingham, England
July 2002

Controversy at Canberra, 1991

At the opening event of the Canberra Assembly of the World Council of Churches, delegates were invited into the spirit-world of the native peoples of Australia. Aboriginal elders sought the permission of the spirits of the land, who, according to Aborigine traditions, had created it in the Dreamtime when the Mother of the earth had awakened them or set them free (Porter 1990). Then, at the first plenary, Professor Chung Hyun Kyung, a woman theologian from South Korea, dispensed with lectern, notes, and even shoes, appearing on stage as a Korean shaman in the midst of Korean—and some Aboriginal—dancers. This was the Seventh Assembly of the World Council of Churches (WCC), held in Canberra in 1991 under the theme, "Come, Holy Spirit, renew the whole creation."

As drums beat out the traditional Korean rhythm, Chung drew on the symbolism of her shamanist ancestors to address the conference theme. She led an exorcist's dance, invoking the Holy Spirit and the spirits of suffering and oppressed individuals, peoples and parts of creation—ranging from Hagar to Joan of Arc, the victims of Tiananmen Square, and the Amazon rain forest. These, she said, were spirits filled with *han*—a Korean word meaning resentment, bitterness, and grief. The spirits which trouble the living in Korea are the spirits of those who have died young, or in unhappy circumstances, or with unrealized expectations. The resulting *han* needs to be released and the problem solved through the intervention of the shaman (most of whom are women). Like a traditional shaman, Chung symbolically burned a piece of paper listing the names of the spirits, wafting the burning ashes up to heaven. She claimed that "these *Han*-ridden spirits in our people's history have been agents through whom the Holy Spirit has spoken her compassion and wisdom for life." In her presentation, the Holy Spirit was explained as identifying with these spirits, weeping with them and actively seeking their liberation in a greedy, divided world of death. The congregation was called upon to repent and follow the example of their Korean sisters in order to bring about the Spirit's "political economy of life," which is life-centered (as opposed to anthropo-centric), interconnected (as opposed to dualistic), and a "culture of life" (as opposed to the "culture of death" that Chung regarded as dominant in modern societies). Chung concluded with her intuitive image of the Holy Spirit as Kwan In—goddess of compassion and wisdom in the popular religiosity of East Asian Buddhism, whom she saw as a feminine image of Christ. She then urged all to join in the Spirit's "wild rhythm of life" (H. Chung 1991b).

Chung's performance was greeted with rapturous applause from those who admired her courage in daring to express her faith in such an unconventional and, as they saw it, indigenous way. For some the Canberra Assembly in general, and this presentation in particular, marked a watershed moment in which the churches of the "South" were at last able to liberate themselves from theological oppression (Van Butselaar 1998). At the same time, her presentation was immediately condemned by others, who thought she had stepped outside the bounds of Christianity and was engaging in syncretism. Lesslie Newbigin expressed the latter group's views when he warned that "there are many spirits abroad, and when they are invoked, we are handed over to other powers" (Newbigin 1994: 51). Emilio Castro summed up the ensuing debate as "concentrated on the issue of the action of the Spirit within and outside the church, and on the criteria necessary to recognize the presence of the Spirit" (Castro 1991: 163). Disquiet over Chung's presentation was such that a special plenary had to be arranged at which she defended herself robustly (Kinnamon 1991b: 16). Two groups— Orthodox and Evangelical—voiced their opinions about Chung's presentation, and other aspects of Canberra's treatment of the theme, in separate responses to the Assembly.

Chung's presentation was in complete contrast to the very traditional theological paper by Parthenios, Orthodox Patriarch of Alexandria and All Africa, that preceded it (Parthenios 1991). The Orthodox churches had long tried to combat what they termed the "christomonism" of the Western church, and to introduce a more trinitarian approach to the World Council of Churches. The Holy Spirit theme of the Assembly was in part a response to this pressure, but Chung's approach was entirely contrary to their intentions, so much so that Orthodox participants called on the Council to set theological criteria which would define the limits of diversity, and suggested that unless this question was addressed they would consider withdrawing from the Council. They expressed "alarm" at a lack of discernment in affirming the presence of the Spirit in human movements, without regard for sin and error; and they stressed the need to "guard against a tendency *to substitute a 'private' spirit, the spirit of the world, or other spirits for the Holy Spirit*" (italics original). In a clear allusion to Chung's presentation, the Orthodox found it impossible to invoke the spirits of "earth, air, water and sea creatures." Though stressing their respect for local and national cultures, they also emphasized that the theology of the Holy Spirit (pneumatology) is inseparable from christology and the theology of the Trinity (Reflections of the Orthodox participants 1991).

Evangelicals at Canberra also found it necessary to make a statement, which, while more positive in tone, echoed the Orthodox concerns. They called for a "high Christology to serve as the only authentic Christian base for dialogue with persons of other living faiths" and for clarity about the relationship between the christological confession of the World Council of Churches, the person and work of the Holy Spirit, and the agenda of the Council (Evangelical perspectives from Canberra 1991). For Evangelicals, the question of whether the Holy Spirit could be considered to be at work in the whole creation hinged on biblical interpretation: whether the "breath" or "wind" of God in the Old Testament is to be identified with the Holy Spirit that possessed the prophets, was at work in Jesus, and was poured out at Pentecost (cf. Hübner 1989: 324 and Schweizer 1989: 406–408). Evangelicals suggested that Chung was syncretizing Christian faith with paganism, to which she responded that syncretism was necessary in the interests of the marginalized (Kinnamon 1991b: 16). The Protestant churches of Korea, which are largely Evangelical, were dismayed that the first Korean to make a plenary presentation at a World Council of Churches assembly was not a senior pastor or theologian, but young, unknown, and female (Ro 1993: 54). Furthermore, her lack of distinction between the Holy Spirit and the spirits, and her shamanistic invocation of spirits, were unacceptable to many who had converted to Christianity from shamanistic belief. For Koreans and other Asians who were familiar with shamanism, the presentation's shamanistic gestures and allusions were much more than "artistic devices," and their use attracted much criticism (Fung 1993).

Part of the reason for the "Spirit and spirits" controversy that erupted at Canberra was confusion caused by the widespread use of the language of the spirit in a number of different mission contexts which were brought together intentionally at Canberra. First, the program for "Justice, Peace, and the Integrity of Creation" (JPIC), which had a major influence at Canberra (Report of Section I 1991; Report of Section II 1991), introduced concern for the environment onto the mission agenda of the World Council of Churches and stimulated eco-theology, including a desire to dialogue with and learn from the cosmic spiritualities of those living close to the earth. "Indigenous spiritualities," portrayed as "earth-centered" and "feminine," were presented as an alternative model to the "destructive," "masculine" theologies of colonial Christianity, symbolized in this context by the issues of aboriginal land rights and by the military action in the first Gulf War, which was being waged at the time. Eco-theology tended to recognize and affirm cosmic spirits, at least metaphorically, as expressions of the creative work of God in the world (H. Chung 1994). Second, under the influence particularly of the North American Walter Wink, liberation theologians were encouraged to be aware of the "powers"—understood as social structures—against which the mission struggle was to be waged. Applying the biblical terminology of spirits, demons, and angels to political powers and systems, Wink sought to "name" and "unmask" the powers in social structures, that is, to address the spiritual dimension of institutions by "engaging" their "fallen" spirits through nonviolent resistance in order to bring about their redemption (Wink 1984; 1986; 1992: 3–10). Other liberation theologians recognized a positive dimension of power in the power of the Holy Spirit of fire to refine and purify, and described the Spirit as the divine agent of social liberation (e.g. Casaldáliga 1990; Rayan 1979: title). In this way a connection was made between Spirit and "spirits," although it tended to be an adversarial one (see, for example, M. Thomas 1990). Third, like liberation theologians, many Evangelicals and Pentecostal-charismatics were using the biblical language of "the powers" or "evil spirits," but in a rather different sense (McAlpine 1991). The theology of "spiritual warfare," in which the power of the Holy Spirit is victorious over other spirits, was prevalent in the so-called third wave of the Pentecostal-charismatic movement, led by John Wimber (1985), Peter Wagner and others. This emphasized the traditional Pentecostal-charismatic healing ministry for individuals perceived as demon-possessed, but also broadened this ministry to deal with the "territorial spirits" which Wagner believed were assigned to every geopolitical unit in the world (Wagner 1989).

The leaders of the World Council of Churches had hoped that, by choosing a pneumatological theme for the seventh assembly, they would be able to liaise with the fast-growing Pentecostal churches, which were hardly represented in the Council membership, and with the charismatic movements that were influencing member churches. Few "classical" Pentecostals were actually present at Canberra and their voices were not much heard (Robeck 1993: 109,116–17), but there were delegates who belonged to new movements with a strong orientation to the Holy Spirit. The ease with which Chung summoned spirits alarmed those participants for whom spirits were a supernatural reality (Fung 1993: 61–62). Cecil M. Robeck Jr., a North American Pentecostal visitor to the assembly, reports another Pentecostal saying to him after Chung's presentation, "I was so afraid I sat shaking through the entire presentation, pleading the blood and interceding in tongues" (1993: 112). Furthermore, many of the delegates from countries that were not traditionally Christian, like Chung herself, brought with them different cultural perceptions of the Spirit and awareness of a spirit-world. In a preparatory paper, Joseph Osei-Bonsu from Ghana stated that many African Christians were more Spirit-centered than Christ-centered because of "the endemic and chronic fear of evil spirits" against which the Holy Spirit affords protection (1989: 459). On the other hand, there were those at Canberra who felt profoundly uncomfortable with the theme and even more so with discussion of spirits. A creation theology of the Holy Spirit was a new departure for many Europeans in the Reformed tradition. Heinz-Joachim Held, moderator of the Central Committee, is reported as admitting in a meeting of the Central Committee in 1990 that the idea of the Holy Spirit in the whole of creaturely reality was foreign to his tradition (Putney 1991: 609). Robeck recorded that many delegates from the "mainline" churches told him they were "frightened" by the idea of invoking the Holy Spirit because it was leading them into unknown territory (Robeck 1993: 116). That the reality and nature of other spirits was in question is reflected in the way the official report found it necessary to refer to them in quotation marks (e.g. Kinnamon 1991b: 15; World Council of Churches 1991d: 112; 1991e: 254).

Chung's presentation itself was ambiguous in its spirit-language. Indian theologian K. C. Abraham felt that Chung had been misunderstood because she "was not proposing a set of theological principles or doctrines." She and other "indigenous groups," he wrote, were "not making any truth claims, as we understand them," but sharing "symbols and rituals, which celebrate their earthly roots and the oneness of their humanity" (1991: 339; cf. Abraham 1994a). Nevertheless, though she was using the language of traditional Korean religious thought, both the Spirit and the spirits were clearly imagery for a socio-political message, and commentators were divided as to whether she respected the integrity of shamanistic spirituality. Looking at Canberra from the perspective of Chinese traditional religions, Raymond Fung accused Chung of either "spiritual *naiveté*" or else "manipulation and cynicism." He felt her "vague language" (such as describing the spirits as both "agents and icons" of the Holy Spirit) and "nonchalant attitude toward the spirit-world" were unacceptable in one who herself knew the experience of fear of the malevolent ancestor spirits from which she believed her Christian faith had liberated her (1993; see H. Chung 1988). The apparent demythologization of the Spirit and spirits appeared disrespectful of the very peoples she was trying to represent. On the other hand, Tso Man King, also Chinese, perceived that Chung was respectful of spirits, saying that she indeed had an "Eastern" approach to the spirits in keeping with her Korean ancestry, in that "when Dr. Chung called upon the spirits of the martyred, her intention was to honor them and to stand in solidarity with them, as well as with the suffering people in the world" (1991: 359).

As the discussion shows, there were many at Canberra from varied traditions who were using the language of Spirit and spirits. The difficulty was the wide range in understanding of what was meant by "spirit." Underlying cultural differences fueled the controversy at Canberra, and this led directly to a decision to devote the next few years to the study of gospel and cultures, culminating in the World Council of Churches' Conference on World Mission and Evangelism in Salvador, Brazil in 1996 (Duraisingh 1995: 203). Whilst this was undoubtedly a wise step, the change of topic meant few explicit links were made in subsequent discussions back to the questions raised at Canberra about theology of the Holy Spirit. Furthermore, the divisiveness of Chung's presentation made pneumatological discourse, particularly relating the Spirit to the spirits of the world, too sensitive for Council discussions, although the need for such discussion was clear (Hollenweger 1997: 383).

The potential of the language of Spirit and spirits for mission theology deserves further exploration for a number of reasons. First, the fact—evident at Canberra—that spirit language is shared between Christians of very different theological persuasions makes it a vehicle of ecumenical discussion. Furthermore, the fact that the language of the spirit-world is found in the Bible makes it part of the shared heritage of *all* Christians. Second, not only is it part of the biblical tradition, but the language of the spirit-world as it emerged at Canberra would seem to have potential for a theology of pluralism, as suggested by Justin Ukpong, a Nigerian Catholic, in his preparatory article for the Canberra Assembly, "Pluralism and the problem of the discernment of spirits" (1990). Ukpong recognized a multiplicity of both good and bad spirits in the world, even in the biblical material (: 80). Third, at Canberra the representatives of almost all strands of Christian tradition applied the language of Spirit and spirits to the full range of ecumenical concerns (see Kinnamon 1991). The language of spirits was applied to social, economic and political movements and forces, both destructive and constructive. Spirits were also connected with matters of the human heart, giftedness, morality and evangelism. In its emphasis on the natural world, the JPIC movement drew attention to the forces or spirits of creation, expressing solidarity with them. The language of Spirit and spirits was also applied to unity, dialogue and reconciliation, themes which have been further developed since then.

It was clear at Canberra that interest in the Holy Spirit does not necessarily lead to interest in other spirits or use of spirit-world language. Not all the papers produced around Canberra had other spirits clearly in view. The other plenary presentation by Parthenios, Patriarch of Alexandria and All Africa, made only passing reference to "the spirit of evil" from whom the Holy Spirit delivers us (1991: 33). From the Catholic Church, Philip Rosato discussed "the mission of the Spirit within and beyond the Church" as teacher, unifier, liberator and vivifier, without finding it necessary to use the language of the powers (1990). Nor in his portrayal of the Spirit's work in creation, *Spirit of Life* (1992 [1991]), published in the same year as the Assembly, did Jürgen Moltmann show interest in other spiritual forces. Nevertheless, we have noted that there were those among the Pentecostals and liberation theologians who stressed spiritual warfare or socio-political struggle against structural forces, and therefore regarded awareness of other spirits—chiefly evil spirits—as adding an essential dimension to the understanding of the Holy Spirit. And there were others like Chung and Ukpong whose cultural background meant that the language of spirit was inextricably associated with a world of many spirits, both malicious and divine. The Canberra debates opened up a wide range of applications for pneumatology, and also gave spirit-language a pluralistic character (for further discussion see K. Kim 2004c).

The controversy that arose around the conference theme—"Come, Holy Spirit, renew the whole creation"—at the seventh assembly of the World

Council of Churches in Canberra, Australia in 1991 was evidence of the varied understandings of "spirit" and of the Holy Spirit's relation to the world. By examining some of these understandings within their cultural contexts, and by following subsequent international debate, this book is intended to highlight the issues involved in any theology of the Spirit in the world and to sketch emerging perceptions that are challenging the shape of traditional European theology. The book concludes with a reflection on the World Council of Churches' world mission conference in Athens in 2005, for which the organizers dared to choose a theme reminiscent of the Canberra Assembly, while significantly different: "Come, Holy Spirit, heal and reconcile." The conference showed the extent to which debate and other factors had moved mission theology of the Holy Spirit forward, and raised the possibility of conciliation around a topic that was once so controversial.

CHAPTER 1

The Spirit in the World:
Church, Believer, "Everywhere"

The Western Church has been reopening the files on the Holy Spirit, thanks to its encounter with the theology of the Orthodox churches, growing awareness of the theological significance of diverse spiritual traditions, theological reflection on movements of the Spirit for liberation, and especially the recent rise of Pentecostal theology. The "flood" of writing on the topic referred to by Jürgen Moltmann in 1991 has by no means abated. However, as Moltmann lamented, much of the discussion only retraces old ground and does not question the foundation of Western pneumatology (Moltmann 1992 [1991]: 1). What is needed is a new paradigm of the Holy Spirit in the context of globalization and post-modernity. The clash at the Canberra Assembly of the World Council of Churches between traditional Christian pneumatologies—Orthodox and Western—and theologies of the Holy Spirit using indigenous spiritual traditions may be the stimulus that is needed to reformulate theology of the Holy Spirit for a world of many spirits.

The Holy Spirit in Post-modernity

Such a new paradigm must begin by giving substance to the meaning of the word "spirit." Under the influence of modern rationalism and materialism, the category of spirit—well-recognized in traditional societies—underwent a sustained onslaught, such that the term became meaningless to many in Western societies. Popular use was relegated—along with the word "ghost"—to the realms of the psychological and the paranormal. Cultural understanding of "spirit" is linked with pixies, fairies and demons in the fantasy world of wizards and witches, remembered in fairy tales and resurrected for the purpose of entertainment in books like the Harry Potter series. The rise of New Age spirituality renewed interest in the term in materialistic and individualistic ways, so that in the contemporary West, "spirit" has become a catchword for marketing anything cool—including cigarettes, clothing, health cures—and "spirituality" is a politically correct means of self-expression. In such a climate, the biblical term "Holy Spirit" is divested of its profound scriptural meanings; it has lost its cosmic dimensions, and its connection with God the Father and Jesus Christ is very unclear.

The Holy Spirit was until recently the Cinderella of theology: as the Third World is marginalized and ignored, so it was with the Third Person of the Trinity. The interest of modernity was very much in God the Son. Scientific concerns meant that God the Son was often reduced to the historical Jesus, and so the connection between the Father in heaven and the earthly Son became increasingly tenuous. Though it remained possible in modernity to defend God the Father as representing some kind of transcendence, scientific materialism struggled even more to find a place for God the Spirit. If the Spirit was discussed under the heading of "Trinity," it appeared as metaphysical speculation and, as such, largely irrelevant to life on earth. So the Spirit was assigned to the realm of values, or to the human mind, or religious experience, and the link to divinity was obscured. Popular movements of the Holy Spirit attracted scholarly attention, beginning with the work of Hermann Gunkel (1979 [1888]), but they were reduced to the level of religious phenomena and appeared increasingly personal or communal, and therefore of little relevance to wider society. It is striking how little attention Christian theologians paid to such movements until recently.

In this context it is appropriate—and indeed a missiological necessity—that we re-examine what the Bible and Christian tradition reveal about the Spirit and other spirits, particularly as they are involved with the world. Biblically, the terms "Holy Spirit" and "Spirit of God" are ways of talking about God's presence and activity in the world. These are informed by the cultural use of "spirit" in biblical times to refer to life, breath and wind. The meaning of these terms was also understood against a background of awareness of a spirit-world, which we find in many biblical stories. This book is an attempt to make the Holy Spirit meaningful in the contemporary West by delving further into the biblical material, and by examining how some Christians in other parts of the world understand the Holy Spirit in the light of their distinctive cultural understandings of "spirit." The steps toward a mission theology of the Holy Spirit will be informed by these explorations, and by recent conversations between the various contextual theologies of the West, of Eastern Orthodoxy, of India, of Korea and of other places. Through these conversations on the subject of pneumatology, the churches enrich one another's understanding (K. Kim 2004b).

These discussions suggest that the development of pneumatology in the contemporary West will be less concerned about the essence and divine origin of the Spirit and more about the Spirit's mission in and to the world. The interest today is not so much in philosophy as in the practical questions of how and where the Spirit is to be discerned. In a society taken up with a desire for experiences of all kinds, pneumatology has great potential relevance. It also has the capability to broaden the contemporary penchant for experience beyond desire for individual fulfillment and temporal satisfaction. However, if it is to relate to contemporary society, pneumatology must recognize the Spirit's work beyond the boundaries of the church or the Christian heart. Furthermore, a theology of the Spirit for today must take into account the other spirits encountered in an increasingly plural world. It must raise awareness of, and help us respond to, the many different world-views and belief systems that we encounter today. Finally, it must offer guidance for Christians on which modern-day powers to support and which to resist, and how to do so ethically and effectively.

In an era in which history is frequently revised, and therefore historical "facts" are often challenged as a basis of belief, Christian apologetic cannot rely on establishing the historical truths about Jesus. And where meta-narratives are regarded with suspicion, theology must distinguish itself from ideological systems. Any attempt to share the gospel in a Western context will founder if it relies on convincing people of the historical facts of Jesus' life, death and resurrection, or of the certainty of judgment, or of the absolute reliability of the Bible as a prerequisite to faith. Discussion of shared life-experience and of personal spirituality is likely to prove a wiser starting point. However, any theology of the Spirit that relates only to matters "spiritual"—in the sense of that word that is disconnected from historical realities—will not be Christian. Pneumatology must relate to economic injustice and the experience of oppression and marginalization that is the experience of so many in the world today. It will have to both reflect the experience of globalization and also challenge it by attention to local realities and particular stories (Selvanayagam 1998). It is my hope that this book will point toward a theology of the Spirit in the world that discerns and affirms local expressions of the Spirit's presence, and also furthers a worldwide "fellowship of the Spirit."

This agenda for a mission theology of the Holy Spirit is ambitious and long. It cannot all be accomplished in the pages of one book, but it is hoped that this will at least be a beginning. As a preparation for what follows, we will undertake two brief surveys: first of theological understandings of the presence and activity of the Spirit in the modern and pre-modern West, and second, in the next chapter, of the biblical material relating to the Spirit.

Roman Catholic, Protestant and Secular Pneumatologies

If the question, "Where is the Holy Spirit to be found?" is put to a member of a local church in the West, it will usually elicit one of three answers: "in my heart," "in the church," or "everywhere." The answer "in the church" can be traced back to Augustine in the fifth century, who was particularly interested in the nature of the unity of the Trinity and relations within the Godhead. Observing the biblical evidence that the Spirit is both the Spirit of the Father and the Spirit of the Son (Jn 16:13; Mt 10:20; Rom 8:9, 11;

Gal 4:6), he surmised that the Spirit is the "unity," "commonness," or "communion" between the Father and the Son, the "bond of love" (1991: 209—*The Trinity*, book 6, chapter 7). This image was carried through into medieval Catholicism in an emphasis that the Spirit proceeds from both the Father *and the Son*, and led to the *filioque* clause ("and the Son") being added unilaterally to the creed by the West. Whereas Western theologians saw the *filioque* as protecting the New Testament message that God's Spirit is the Spirit of Jesus Christ, Eastern and other theologians have seen an unbalanced emphasis on divine unity rather than Trinity and a subordination of the divine Spirit to Christ, which is not justified in trinitarian theology (see chapter 4). British Reformed theologian Alasdair Heron summarizes the effect of the *filioque* on Western pneumatology: "No longer does he [the Spirit] 'blow where he will'; rather, 'it goes where it is sent'" (1981: 113).

Augustine also taught that the love, or *communio*, within the Godhead was imparted in Christ to the church. This love, which Augustine so closely identified with the Holy Spirit (cf. 1 Jn 4:7, 12, 13, 16; Rom 5:5), was the most excellent spiritual gift (1 Cor 13) and therefore the most important characteristic of the church. In the same vein, he described the Spirit as the equivalent of the soul of the church (1993: 276—Sermon 267 on the day of Pentecost, part 4). Although Augustine did not entirely equate the Spirit, love and the church, this description was used in later periods to domesticate the Spirit to support the claims of the Roman church over against others. The result was an alternative Trinity of God-Christ-Church, and the restriction of discourse about the Spirit to discussion of the mystery of the triune God (Heron 1983: 87–98; cf. Kärkkäinen 2002: 46–48). The Holy Spirit therefore became a technical theological term not in common parlance, except in stylized form in the blessing and the baptismal formula, "In the name of the Father, the Son and the Holy Spirit." Thus the Holy Spirit tended to be reduced to "a category from above the Church, authenticating and approving what the hierarchy does" (Kavunkal 1998: 420).

Latin theology, following Augustine, began with the unity of God, and not the Trinity. Anselm, the father of scholasticism—the medieval flowering of Roman Catholic theology—did not refer to the Holy Spirit at all in his history of salvation or theology of redemption, but only within his speculation about the inner life of God (Burgess 1997: 29–35; see also Congar 1983: III 96–102). Consequently, in christology, little importance was attached to the presence of the Spirit in Jesus; the emphasis was on Jesus' gift of the Spirit to the church. As the central power of the papacy was increasingly asserted, Roman Catholic ecclesiology was developed along juridical rather than charismatic lines. The first systematic treatises on the church passed over its pneumatological aspects "practically in silence" (Le Guillou 1975: 208). Between the Council of Trent and the Second Vatican Council, in reaction to heretical and reformation movements,

personal religious experience was discouraged by the church and accommodated on the periphery by the religious orders and their practice of mysticism or "spirituality." In his book *The Holy Spirit and Liberation*, José
Comblin sums up the situation when he complains that, though the mission
of the Son was recognized in the incarnation, the mission of the Spirit
became little more than "a literary device to express the actions of the one
God" in and through the church. He sees the results of this neglect of the
Spirit in the world in the contemporary disjuncture in soteriology between
an ahistorical doctrine of justification and a secularized theory of liberation,
and in the separation in christology between "Jesusology"—or the study of
the historical Jesus—on the one side and the Christ "mythology" born of
scholasticism on the other (1989: 13–17).

From his thorough study of pneumatology in medieval Roman Catholic
theology, Stanley M. Burgess finds many examples of scholars and saints
who "had something significant to say about the divine Third Person," such
as Bernard of Clairvaux, Bonaventure and Thomas Aquinas. However, he
concludes that those who treated the Holy Spirit "as their primary theme"
often came from two groups. "The first were those who argued the Roman
Catholic case for the *filioque* against Eastern Christians, insisting that the
Spirit proceeded from the Father and the Son. The second included a variety of fringe elements, each of whom believed that the Holy Spirit in some
ways intervened in human affairs, superseding established Roman practices
and beliefs" (1997: 2). The first group aimed to enhance christology (and
the Roman Church) by in some way subjecting the Spirit to Christ, while
members of the second group were regarded as heretics and seen as a threat
to the church; neither group, therefore, led to significant development of
pneumatology. In systematic theology, the biblical role of the Spirit was
taken over by matters of ecclesiology, or displaced into other aspects of theology, including the doctrine of grace (Wainwright 1997: 289) and the theology of the Virgin Mary (Johnson 1992: 129). For many Catholics in the
period between the Middle Ages and the Second Vatican Council of
1962–65, it must have been as if the words "I believe in the Holy Spirit; the
Holy Catholic Church . . ." in the third article of the Apostles' Creed identified the two.

The Protestant reformers repudiated the association of the Spirit with the
Catholic hierarchy, and concentrated instead on the illuminating role of the
Spirit in the interpretation of Scripture and the sanctifying role of the Spirit
in the life of the believer. In general, where Catholicism focused on the presence and activity of the Spirit in the institutional church, Protestantism has
looked to personal spiritual experience, and its theology of the Spirit has
concentrated on the individual heart and life. Heron argues that the reformers were well aware that the fundamental insights of the Reformation—justification by faith and the authority of Scripture—were necessarily bound
up with the Holy Spirit (1983: 99). Luther revolutionized the medieval

understanding of the historical outworking of God's grace through the church when he reinterpreted justification as the direct intervention of God on behalf of the sinner, mediated and appropriated only by the immediate activity of the Spirit of God. In other words, justification is accompanied by sanctification when God's Word comes to the believer through faith, which is itself a gift of the Spirit (: 100–102). For Calvin, the union between Christ and the believer, which lies at the heart of his theology, is brought about by the Spirit. Calvin gave a systematic priority to the activity of the Spirit in the individual Christian life and this was to set the tone for future Protestant thinking about the Spirit (: 102–105). Regarding Scripture, Luther gave a central role to the Spirit in conveying the Living Word through the reading of the Bible. The Bible cannot be understood without the Spirit, and the Spirit's "inner witness" is to none other than the Word in Scripture. Calvin's perspective was similar but expressed in terms of his theology of unity: the Spirit that unites us to Christ also enables the reception and appropriation of the Bible (: 105–106). Therefore, in the emerging Protestant theology, the Spirit was seen in two ways: as Enlightener, who inspires Scripture and interprets it, and as Sanctifier, who brings about faith and empowers the new spiritual life (: 99, 106).

Later Protestant theology has not always preserved the explicit pneumatology of the reformers. The emphasis on individual relationship with God has resulted in a tendency to reduce the Spirit to "an element within our own personal psychological, intellectual or spiritual history" (Heron 1983: 108–111). The reliance on *sola scriptura* has led to a suspicion of later doctrines, including the Trinity; to a questioning of the personhood of the Holy Spirit; and to Unitarianism (: 111–12). On the other hand, there have also been Protestant movements in which the theology of the Spirit—or one aspect of the Spirit—takes center stage. A pneumatological foundation was implicit in certain Protestant doctrines and their associated movements, such as "sovereignty" in the Puritan movement, the inspiration of Scripture among the Reformed churches, the doctrine of grace in the Wesleyan-Methodist revival, "holiness" in the Holiness churches, the "inner light" of the Quakers, the requirement of adult baptism in the Baptist churches, teaching about "gifts" of the Pentecostal-charismatic movement, and the emphasis on "experience" of liberal theology (cf. Heron 1983: 112–17). However, none of these movements developed an explicit pneumatology that challenges the classical Western model. In both Catholic and Protestant thought, the work of the Holy Spirit appears limited to either the Christian—or at most the Western—community, or to personal Christian faith.

In the modern period, the meaning of "Spirit" was reinterpreted in terms that were increasingly secular. Heron has traced three different modern theologies of the Spirit that reflect the differing starting points of the great trio of Kant, Schleiermacher and Hegel, associating the Spirit with the practical, the psychological and the philosophical, respectively. The "practical" or Kantian understanding sees the Spirit "as a cipher for the realm of moral and spiritual values." It begins with the ideal figure of Jesus Christ as reconstructed in the nineteenth century. "Spirit" is understood primarily in relation to the human consciousness, and the Spirit of God tends to be domesticated in the highest human religio-ethical ideals of the kingdom of God and "the brotherhood of man." The liberal theology of Ritschl, with its focus on love, popularly expressed by Adolf Harnack, is the chief example of this (Heron 1983: 112–13). The "psychological" approach, which has its origins in the Reformation and in Schleiermacher's work, also owed much to Kierkegaard's reaction against idealism, and viewed the Spirit from an interior, pietistic or subjective standpoint that connected the Spirit primarily with the self. This view has its origins in the New Testament experience of the Holy Spirit and its antecedents in the Old Testament prophetic tradition, and identifies the Spirit with individual experience or the experience of the community. Whereas Schleiermacher took a communitarian approach, others—such as Wheeler Robinson—took an "in my heart" view, understanding the social or historical experience of the Spirit as a corollary of individual experience (Heron 1983: 99–114, 137–40; Robinson 1928: 2–3, 20, 44–45, 147–49. Cf. Stendahl 1976: 78–96). The "philosophical" interpretation originated in Hegel's use of the term "Spirit" (or "Mind," *Geist*) as the fundamental category of ultimate reality and offered a dynamic vision linking the Spirit with the entire history of the universe. It picked up the Old Testament concept of the Spirit in creation and Greek philosophical ideas of *pneuma*, and related the Spirit to cosmic forces, issuing in evolutionary and process theologies. "Philosophical" theologies consider the Spirit in such general terms as "being," "existence," "historical dialectic," "life" or "progress" (Heron 1983: 99–116, 137–40; Robinson 1928: 20–21).

Each of these approaches represented a secularization of the concept of "Spirit" by identifying the Spirit's presence and activity irrespective of the boundaries of the church. The philosophical interpretation particularly contributed to the popular view that the Spirit is "everywhere" as part of the processes of creation and evolution. On the other hand, the modern views also tended to tie the Spirit to Western civilization as representing the best ethical standards, the most developed consciousness, and the highest reaches of human development. It was not considered whether the movement of the Spirit was also evidenced in the cultures of Asia, Africa and Latin America. Now that the West no longer represents the "center of gravity" of Christianity, and the integrity of other religions is increasingly respected, pneumatologies based on such an ethnocentric assumption are open to serious question.

Hendrikus Berkhof connected the tendencies of Catholicism and Protestantism to either "institutionalize" or "individualize" the Spirit, respectively, with the Apostles' Creed, which includes under the phrase "I believe in the Holy Spirit" the category of ecclesiology—"the holy catholic church and the communion of saints"—and also the category of salvation (or sanctification)—"the forgiveness of sins, the resurrection of the dead and the life eternal" (1965: 33). Without implying that salvation is individual or that this is all that can be said about catholic and protestant pneumatologies, it is tempting to make a further link between the creed and the pneumatology of the Orthodox churches. As we shall see in chapter four, Eastern Orthodox pneumatology makes a strong connection between the Spirit and creation, understanding the Spirit as "the Lord, the Giver of Life." The Orthodox churches also locate the Spirit "everywhere," drawing attention to the Spirit's presence and activity in the world, but this differs significantly from the modern liberal interpretation.

Before that discussion, and without prejudicing what is to follow, it is necessary in chapter two to review the biblical material relating to the Spirit. This will be done with post-colonial awareness that biblical scholarship is not without vested theological and ideological interests. The aim of the chapter is to open up the possibilities for understanding "spirit" biblically, rather than to close these off by starting with a particular theological position. Chapter three will treat twentieth-century Western figures who have developed mission theology of the Spirit: first, several missiologists who have made connections between missiology and pneumatology, and second, some theologians who have considered the involvement of the Spirit in the world. Our study of Indian Christian pneumatologies in chapter five will reveal a predominant cultural awareness of a Universal Spirit in the very creation itself, which sheds a different light on some of the biblical material and challenges the Western paradigm, particularly with regard to the Spirit's work in history, cultures and religions. Korean Christian theologians—the subject of chapter six—are wrestling with questions of power against a background of spirit-religion as well as Buddhism and Confucianism. They have experienced the Holy Spirit in the encounter with political powers, as well as in Pentecostal-charismatic phenomena, and read the biblical material and Christian history in a way particular to their context. In chapter seven, we will look at some of the developments in mission pneumatology since the Canberra Assembly of 1991 and highlight Indian and Korean perceptions in a global conversation about the Spirit in the world.

CHAPTER 2

The Spirit in the Bible:
Pentecost, Christ, Creation

We turn now to examine the occurrence and meaning of "spirit" in the biblical record. The intention in this chapter is not to construct a biblical theology of the Spirit. If this could be done without any cultural, social or theological bias, there would be little point in continuing this book. We will highlight references to the word "spirit" in the original texts, being as comprehensive as possible but reserving judgment on the more contentious issues of interpretation, and being content at this stage simply to map out the material Christian theologians have to work with in constructing a mission theology of the Holy Spirit. Many of the texts and patterns of meaning noted here will be referred to in later chapters.

There are three basic starting points for interpretation of the references to the Spirit, which yield significantly different pneumatologies. The first, the "pentecostal," begins with the out-pouring of the Holy Spirit at Pentecost. The second, "catholic," view starts with the Holy Spirit's involvement in the life and ministry of Jesus Christ. And the third, "orthodox," perspective goes back to the Spirit's role in creation as the hermeneutical key. In the first interpretation, attention is drawn to the sudden appearance of the Holy Spirit on the day of Pentecost, when the fearful and uncertain disciples were gathered in an upper room praying. The Spirit came in from outside as a roaring wind and flames of fire, and enabled them to speak in other languages. Filled with the Holy Spirit, Peter immediately went outside to testify before a crowd composed of representatives of many nations, who heard the message of the resurrection of Jesus Christ and responded by repentance, baptism, and joining the community. This event was simultaneously the birth of the church—the fellowship of the Spirit—and the beginning of Christian witness in the power of the Spirit, which carried the gospel from Jerusalem through Judea and Samaria and across the world, as told in the rest of the book of Acts. In this story, the work of the Spirit is most evidenced in the Gentile mission of the Apostle Paul and in the life of the congregations that he founded. In the "pentecostal" view, the Holy Spirit bursts onto the scene as a new and powerful force that becomes characteristic of the Christian mission. The Spirit is experienced in forgiveness, healing, guidance and empowerment as the church grows and spreads across the world.

Sometimes the impression is given in the "pentecostal" perspective that this grand entrance is the first appearance of the Holy Spirit in Scripture, and that the Spirit comes on stage only after Jesus has gone off. However, closer examination of the Lukan record shows that this is not the case: the Holy Spirit is first mentioned with reference to John the Baptist (Lk 1:15). The "catholic" interpretation pays greater attention to the role of the Spirit in the life and ministry of Jesus Christ, and tends to view the mission of the church as a consequence of this connection. It begins with the Annunciation, when Mary is told that she will conceive a child "by the Holy Spirit," or with Jesus' baptism in the River Jordan, when the Holy Spirit descended on him like a dove. Jesus is seen as the source of the Spirit, which he promises will be sent from the Father. The disciples receive the Spirit directly from the risen Christ, who breathes the Spirit into them. In this way the Spirit appears as a presence within them, which binds them to Christ, rather than as a force from without. In the Johannine corpus, the Spirit is associated with unity and love (as Augustine noted), rather than with power. This produces a great deal of interest in the indwelling of the Spirit, and the intimate way in which the Spirit as Paraclete expresses the abiding presence of Christ with the disciples after Jesus has gone to the Father. The indwelling of the Spirit is also described by Paul as "the Spirit bearing witness with our spirit that we are children of God" (Rom 8:16), and so believers are encouraged to walk according to the Spirit, live according to the Spirit, set the mind on the Spirit, live by the Spirit, be led by the Spirit, and pray in the Spirit (Rom 8:4, 5, 6, 13, 14, 26).

Reading the Bible from the "orthodox" perspective, beginning with the Spirit moving over the waters at creation (Gen 1:2), adds a material and creative dimension to the Spirit's work, and broadens its scope to include the whole created order, as we shall see in later chapters. It draws attention to the continuity between the Testaments and to the fact that the Spirit was already known before the incarnation of Jesus Christ and before Pentecost. In this survey, we will trace references to "spirit" in the Bible from Genesis onwards, withholding for the time being discussion on the questions raised by these three approaches.

The Spirit as *Rūach*: Wind, Breath, Air

The Hebrew word *rūach*, translated "spirit," means "blowing," as in wind or breath, and came to mean divine power, including the power of life itself (see Dunn 1978: 689–709; Heron 1983: 3–60).[1] It occurs in the Bible nearly four hundred times, but with a variety of meanings. Considering the wide

---

[1] I am indebted to Dr. Renato Lings for help with questions on the Hebrew text.

variety of settings from which the material in the Hebrew Bible arose, it is likely that a number of different cultural understandings of "spirit" are represented. However, in the Septuagint, or Greek translation of the Hebrew Bible, the Greek word *pneuma* is almost always used as a translation for *rūach*, and so takes on a very similar range of meanings. The early Christian writers were therefore able to bring together all the varied nuances of *rūach* to inform their understanding of the Spirit that they experienced. This means that it is important to examine what was available to them from the tradition, not in order to suggest a unified Old Testament theology of the Spirit, but to better understand the meaning of the Spirit in the New.

Rūach occurs right at the beginning of the Scriptures as we have them, in Genesis 1:2, when the Spirit or "wind" of God is described as moving or hovering over the face of the waters at creation. "Wind" is the most common meaning of *rūach*; because it is unseen, it was understood to be caused directly by God (cf. Gen 8:1; Am 4:13; Ps 104:4). The breath of God is creative of life (Ps 33:6) and also destructive, "the blast of God's nostrils" being used to describe God's contempt and anger (Ex 15:8; 2 Sam 22:16; Job 4:9). In Genesis 2:7 God breathes into Adam to constitute him as a living soul. Though the word used here is *nᵉshāmâ*, this is a synonym of *rūach*; *rūach* is often used in the sense of "breath of life," for example in Genesis 6:17. In a vision of Ezekiel (37), the dry bones in the valley come to life as a result of God's *rūach*. The psalmist praises this creative and life-giving role of God's *rūach*, on which the creatures of the world are dependent (Ps 104:29–30; Job 34:14–15; cf. Eccl 3:19), though idols lack it (Jer 10:14). The two terms appear in parallel in Isaiah 42:5, where the Lord "gives breath (*nᵉshāmâ*) to the people upon [the earth] and spirit (*rūach*) to those who walk in [the earth]." Job sums this up: "The spirit (*rūach*) of God has made me, and the breath (*nᵉshāmâ*) of the Almighty gives me life" (33:4).

As life-force, *rūach* varies in intensity: Pharoah's spirit was "troubled" (Gen 41:8) and Job's was "broken" (Job 17:1). It may be used to denote self-expression in the sense of "plan" (Isa 19:3) or behavior—for example, humility (Prov 16:9), pride (Eccl 7:8), patience (Eccl 7:8; cf. Prov 14:29), steadfastness (Ps 51:12), or submission (Ps 51:17). In these senses it may have a similar meaning to the words "soul" or "mind." *Rūach* can denote the life-force of an individual (e.g. Judg 15:19) or group (e.g. Num 16:22), but it is essentially from God. In about one hundred passages, it is expressly called "the Spirit of God," or of Yahweh, and it may be contrasted with the flesh (Isa 31:3). So the Spirit is a gift (Eccl 12:7; Ezek 11:19; 36:26), a point which is emphasized equally in the New Testament (Acts 2:38; 8:20; 10:45; 11:17; Heb 6:4; Jn 4:10; 7:39).

The Spirit is given to leaders such as Moses, Joshua, Samson, Saul and David to empower them for powerful tasks, and sometimes withdrawn from them (Num 11:17; 27:18; Judg 13:25; 1 Sam 16:13–14; cf. Mk 12:36). *Rūach* is described as the source of creativity (Ex 31:3) and exceptional ability (Dan 6:3), but it is most closely associated with the gift of prophecy. The verb translated "to prophesy" refers to "spirit-wrought ecstasy" (see, for example, Num 11:25–27), and so the Spirit of God is understood to be the inspiration of the prophets (Zech 7:12). When the Spirit came upon them, they prophesied (Num 11:29), and they spoke the word of the Lord by the power of the Spirit (2 Kings 2:15; Isa 61:1). The view of the prophets as endowed with the Spirit is confirmed in the New Testament (Mt 22:43; Mk 12:36; Acts 1:16; 4:25; 28:25). Furthermore, the prophets looked forward to an outpouring of the Spirit in the last days. Isaiah expected this would lead to fruitfulness, justice and peace, and indeed national deliverance by the Spirit as in the past (32:15–20; 63:11–14). Joel had a vision of the Spirit coming on "all flesh" (those of low social status—servants and women—are particularly mentioned), leading to prophecy, dreams and visions (Joel 2:28–29). Ezekiel looked forward to God putting "a new spirit" (or "heart") within the nation of Israel, reviving them from the dead and causing them to live according to the Covenant (11:19–20 inter alia; 37:1–14). This new life of abundance and obedience will come about through the Son of David, the Messiah, the Servant of the Lord, who will be specially ordained by God for this task and who will extend salvation to all nations (Isa 11:1–8; 42:1–4).

Symbols of the Spirit: Word, Water, Fire

As we have seen, the root meaning of *rūach*, "blowing," leads to an association of the imagery of wind, breath and air with God's Spirit. This association continues in the New Testament with the word *pneuma* (Dunn 1978: 689–709; Heron 1983: 3–60): the Spirit blows where it wills (Jn 3:8), and at Pentecost the Spirit comes like a wind (Acts 2:2). There is also a connection of wind with the dove, which was the sign of the Holy Spirit when it was seen to descend on Jesus at his baptism in the River Jordan (Mk 1:9–11; Mt 3:13–17; Lk 3:21–22; cf. Jn 1:29–34). Birds make invisible air currents visible, and the "hovering" of the Spirit over the waters at creation implies a bird (Gen 1:2). Birds are traditional messengers of the divine because they come down from heaven and rise up there again. Like the angels—also winged in popular imagination—they are thought to be messengers of God. The meaning of *rūach* as breath is also reflected in the use of *pneuma* to refer to the breath of life (Lk 8:55; Acts 17:25; Rev 11:11; 13:15), and when Jesus breathes the Spirit into the disciples (Jn 20:19–23; cf. 2 Thess 2:8).

The Second Person of the Trinity is often described as the Word of God, and the Third Person as the Spirit of God, but if the unity and the interpenetration of the three persons is not appreciated, this may lead to a counter-scriptural wedge being driven between the concepts of word and spirit. In

Scripture and in common parlance, "word" or "speech" is very closely related to "breath." At creation, as the Spirit of God was moving over the waters, God spoke (Gen 1:2–3). As the Psalmist says, "By the word of the Lord the heavens were made, and all their host by the breath of his mouth" (Ps 33:6). The Spirit of God inspired the words of the prophets, and the word of the Lord in the scriptures is inspired by God, literally "God-breathed" (2 Tim 3:16). The most immediate results of the blowing of the Spirit at Pentecost were that the disciples began to speak (in other tongues) and that Peter spoke to those assembled in Jerusalem. This raises the possibility that the Word or *Logos* of the prologue of John's Gospel could also be understood in terms of the Spirit of God. Both were "in the beginning . . . with God" and involved in the work of creation (Jn 1:1; Gen 1:1–2). In this case, the development of the doctrine of the Trinity may have rigidly separated what were originally more fluid terms. This is an awkward question, for it would play havoc with that doctrine if Jesus Christ were to appear as the incarnation of the Third Person (Heron 1983: 157–59). There is a sense in the Bible in which "God is Spirit" (Jn 4:24), and, furthermore, Paul finds a confluence of the power of God in the Jewish tradition and the wisdom of God in the Greek tradition (1 Cor 1:24). On the other hand, word and spirit are not identical in Scripture, and the Spirit is not the only, or even the primary, way of describing God's involvement with the world.

It is often noted that there is a link between "spirit" and "wisdom" (*chokmâ* in Hebrew and *sophia* in Greek) in the Bible. In the "wisdom literature" of the Old Testament, "the idea of Wisdom operates . . . in a fashion not unlike *rūach* and other terms elsewhere in the Old Testament which link God and man" (Dunn 1998: 34). Wisdom has a cosmic and creative role and is with God from the beginning (Prov 3:19; 8:22–31; Ps 104:24). Wisdom is the giver of life (Prov 4:13; 8:35) and of the prophetic word of justice (Prov 8:20) (Johnson 1992: 94). The wisdom of Daniel is much admired by Nebuchadnezzar, who understands this wisdom to be due to the presence of the "spirit of the holy gods" in him (Dan 4:8, 9, 18; 5:11, 12, 14). In the New Testament, Stephen is described as "full of the Spirit and of wisdom" (Acts 6:3, 10). Paul mentions that the Spirit gives wisdom and knowledge (1 Cor 12:8; Eph 1:17), and this of a higher form than merely human wisdom (1 Cor 2:4, 13). But *pneuma* and *sophia* are brought even closer together in descriptions of the universal significance of Jesus Christ, who is not only born of the Spirit but is also the personification of wisdom, sharing wisdom's divine origins (1 Cor 1:24, 30; Col 3:16; cf. Jn 1:1, 14; Col 1:15). Indeed, as we have seen, wisdom and spirit are all joined in Christ because, logically, there is and can only be one Lord and one mediator between God and man (1 Tim 2:5) (Dunn 1978: 325; Heron 1983: 37).

In addition to wind, the Spirit is also related to other traditional elements of creation. Throughout the Bible, the Spirit is closely associated with fire and with water, both in their constructive senses of peace and well-being, and also in the sense of purification, purging and destruction (e.g. Isa 30:27–28). The fire of sacrifice purifies and wafts the elements up to heaven (Deut 4:11), and the fragrance of the burning incense is smelt by God (Ex 30:8). The outpouring of the Spirit in the last days will be attended by portents of "blood, fire, and columns of smoke" (Joel 2:28–30; Acts 2:19). It will be a theophany much like Moses' encounters with the Lord in the burning bush and on the mountain (Ex 3:2–6; 19:16–19; 20:18). Like the Spirit, fire also gives light for guidance, for enlightenment and as a witness (e.g. Neh 9:12; Jn 1:9). Light is a power that banishes darkness (Jn 1:5; 1 Jn 1:5–7). The Lord led the people across the desert with a pillar of fire by night and of cloud by day (Ex 13:21–22). God sends "fire from heaven" as a sign of divine power over enemies (Gen 19:24; 2 Kings 1:10–14; Lk 9:54; Rev 20:9), and also of divine presence and acceptance (1 Chr 21:26; 2 Chr 7:1). John predicted that Jesus would baptize "with the Holy Spirit and with fire" (Mt 3:11; Lk 3:16). And at Pentecost the Spirit came not only as "a sound . . . from heaven like the rush of a mighty wind," but also as "tongues as of fire," which were a sign of the Spirit's appearance (Acts 2:2–3).

The fire and light of God is also God's glory (shĕkînâ; cf. Ex 24:15–17; Isa 60:1, 19), and on several occasions glory appears as a synonym or counterpart of "spirit" (Dan 5:20; 2 Cor 3:18; Eph 1:17). The root meaning of shĕkînâ is "dwelling"; that is, the glory of God refers to God's dwelling among human beings. This was centered in the ark of the covenant (1 Sam 4:22), and later in the "holy of holies" in the temple (Ps 26:8). The glory of God was with the people throughout their wanderings, and it therefore represents some instances of the New Testament usage of "spirit" for God's presence better than rūach does (Moltmann 1992: 47). Shĕkînâ became the typical representation of the Spirit of God in post-biblical Jewish tradition (Johnson 1992: 85). The prophets looked forward to the revelation of God's glory to all flesh (Isa 40:5), and God's glory was seen to be revealed in the conception of Jesus Christ, his revelation, his passion, and the turning of the Gentiles to Christ (e.g. Lk 1:35; 2:32; Jn 12:23; Col 1:27).

Peter describes the Spirit as "the Spirit of glory and of God" (1 Pet 4:14). Moses hid from the glory of God in the cleft of a rock (Ex 34:29–35). Moses' experience led Elijah to expect that when God came, it would be in a strong wind, or an earthquake, or a fire, and so Elijah also hid—although in his case God spoke in "sheer silence" (1 Kgs 19:11–12). As a result of his encounter on the mountain, Moses reflected God's glory in his face (Ex 34:29–35). Jesus was similarly transfigured on a mountain (Mk 9:2–8), and his disciples saw "the light of the knowledge of the glory of God in the face of Christ" (2 Cor 4:6). Jesus Christ was born in the power of the Holy Spirit (Lk 1:35) and the shepherds saw the glory of the Lord shining around them (Lk 2:8–15). John describes Jesus' coming as light and glory (Jn 1:4–5, 9, 14). In the Spirit, we behold the glory of the Lord and are changed from one degree of glory to another (2 Cor 3:17–18; Rev 1:10–16; cf. Isa 6:1–5). It is well to remember that throughout the Bible, "power" and "glory" are often synonyms for the Spirit (e.g. 1 Pet 4:14) (Ridderbos 1975: 539). Furthermore, the writer of Hebrews 6:4–5, who struggles to find enough words to describe the status of believers, suggests light, gift, word and power as parallels of "Holy Spirit."

Water is another image for the Spirit in Scripture. Water and the Spirit are closely associated as the starting point for creation (Gen 1:2), and both are necessary for new creation or rebirth (Jn 3:4–6). So the Spirit goes together with the waters of baptism in Jesus' case (Mk 1:9–11 and parallels), and in the case of the believers (Acts 19:1–6; cf. Ezek 36:24–38). Baptism is a cleansing process and the Spirit also purifies (Ps 51:1–2, 6–7, 10–12). The Spirit is "outpoured" like water or rain, which streams through the land and brings revival (Isa 32:14–18; 44:3–4; Joel 2:28–29). The "living water" that the Messiah brings is the Spirit. It wells up in the desert and it comes from the rock, which is Christ (Isa 12:3; Jn 4:7–15; 7:37–39; Ex 17:1–7; 1 Cor 10:1–4). This is no ordinary drink; it is new wine (Mt 9:17) that is saved till last (Jn 2:1–11), and which fortifies people and causes them to behave in new ways (Acts 2:15). The Spirit or wine is also the blood of Christ (Lk 22:20; 1 Cor 11:25). On the cross, water and blood flowed out together from Jesus' side (Jn 19:34); this is described also as the sacrificial blood of the one who offered himself to God through the eternal Spirit (Heb 9:14). The Spirit, the water and the blood together bear witness that Jesus is the Son of God (1 Jn 5:6–12).

"The Spirit gives life" (2 Cor 3:6) and is represented by the elements necessary for life: air, fire and water in all their raw power, and also in their capacity to sustain abundant life. Our survey of the interplay of these different images with the concept of "Spirit" in the Bible demonstrates that a biblical theology of the Holy Spirit involves more than a study of the passages in which "the spirit" is explicitly mentioned. The theology of the Holy Spirit is a study of God's involvement with the world. The Spirit represents the presence of God, which is throughout the whole creation (Ps 139:7), and the mighty involvement of God in earthly affairs (Isa 63:10–14; Job 26:12–13). The New Testament also bears witness to God's involvement in the world by the Holy Spirit. This involvement is focused in Jesus Christ and those who are in him, and yet it holds out hope for the whole creation, as the Spirit bears witness (Rom 8:1–27).

The Spirit as *Pneuma*: Power, New Life, Freedom

The Hebrew word *rūach* and the Greek *pneuma* carried different cultural connotations. Between the Testaments, *rūach* as used in Palestinian Judaism was predominantly associated with prophecy and it also became more strongly focused in the expectation of the Messiah. Perhaps under the influence of Zoroastrianism, the Qumran scrolls have a distinctive teaching on two spirits, "the spirit of truth" and "the spirit of falsehood," which are locked in conflict. These different spirits predestine people to walk in opposing ways. In Hellenistic Judaism, the *pneuma* generally carried a positive meaning—the word *daimon* being generally used for evil spirits—and was often equated with God's Spirit and with wisdom. This led to a strengthening of the Spirit's association with creation and the conception of *pneuma* as God's universal creative power (Heron 1983: 23–38).

Pneuma occurs at least 250 times in the New Testament as a reference to the Spirit of God. On about forty occasions, *pneuma* is applied to evil spirits of some kind. On about forty other occasions, "spirit" is identified as referring to "the human spirit" or at least the dimension of the human being that interacts with the divine or "the breath of life" (Dunn 1978: 693). In English, it is necessary to differentiate between "spirit," "Spirit" and "the Spirit" because of our system of capitalization, which was not a feature of the original Greek, and there are also differences in the use of the definite article between the two languages. In some cases such a distinction seems clear, such as Romans 8:16, "it is the Spirit himself bearing witness with our spirit." However, there are other more ambiguous examples, such as Mark 14:38: "the spirit indeed is willing, but the flesh is weak," Luke 1:80: "the child grew and became strong in spirit," or John 4:23: "worship the Father in spirit and in truth" (for further examples see Dunn 1978: 694). There are therefore biblical difficulties in trying to draw clean lines between the Spirit of God that comes from outside and the inward human response, or the more general spirit of life.

Luke's Gospel in particular takes up the prophetic expectation of a new era of the Spirit. In Luke, the incarnation is seen to take place within the ongoing mission of God through the Holy Spirit—from the annunciation of Jesus' birth (1:35). Jesus was confirmed as Son of God by the Spirit (3:22), led into the wilderness by the Spirit (4:1–2), returned to Galilee "in the power of the Spirit" (4:14) and was anointed by the Spirit to preach good news to the poor (4:18). Jesus' mission in Luke is a struggle aided by the ministry of angels and opposed by other spirits, which apparently defeat him when he "gave up the spirit" and died (23:46). However, there are greater powers at work than the disciples and onlookers imagine. Jesus is raised from the dead and commands his disciples to wait for the promised "power from on high" in the form of the coming of the Spirit, who will empower them "to be my witnesses in Jerusalem and in all Judea and Samaria and to the end of the earth" (Lk 24:49; Acts 1:8). This promise of the Spirit of mission was fulfilled when the Spirit came upon the disciples at Pentecost as wind and fire, and like wine (Acts 2:1–4, 15). In his speech, Peter envisages the exalted Jesus himself as pouring out the Spirit, which he had received from his Father (2:33). The Spirit also comes in the same way on Samaritan converts (8:14–17), the household of Cornelius (10:44–47) and some Ephesians (19:6). The main role of the Spirit is to inspire prophetic witness to Jesus Christ. This is evidenced by the space given to Peter's sermon on the day of Pentecost and the other speeches in Acts. Throughout Luke's account, the Spirit is said to guide the activities of the Apostles (6:10; 8:29; 10:19; 11:12; 13:2, 4; 16:6–7; 19:21; 20:22), several of whom are described as "full of the Spirit" (4:8; 6:3–5; 7:55; 8:29, 39; 11:24; 13:9). In this way, Luke portrays the mission of the church as a participation in the ongoing activity of the Spirit of God, of which the incarnate life and death of Jesus Christ is the focal point and defining expression, inaugurating a new outpouring of the Spirit.

The Gospel of John also lays particular stress on the doctrine of the Holy Spirit, but is more concerned with the Spirit's presence than the Spirit's activity. The story begins with the revelation of Jesus to John the Baptist, who recognizes Jesus as the Son of God because he sees the Spirit descend on him (1:29–34). Jesus tells Nicodemus that he must be born again of the Spirit in order to enter the kingdom of God (3:5). He tells the Samaritan woman that God is spirit, and is to be worshipped in spirit and in truth rather than through any particular religious system (4:23–24). Jesus teaches that the Spirit is like the wind, unpredictable and not subject to human control (3:8), that the Spirit is like living water, which flows out of the heart of the believer, and that the Spirit is truth (14:17; 15:26; 16:13). The giving of the Spirit to the disciples is contingent on Jesus' glorification (7:39), and so the gospel is infused with the expectation of the Spirit who will accompany the disciples in the next stage of their lives, when they are sent as Jesus was sent (20:21). John devotes several chapters (14–16) to the Paraclete—or Counselor, Advocate or Comforter—who is the Spirit (14:17), and who will abide with and in the disciples. The "other Paraclete" (14:16), whom only the disciples can receive, will take Jesus' place when he is no longer with the disciples (16:7) and remain with them forever (14:16, 17). The Paraclete proceeds from both the Father and the Son (15:26; 14:16, 26; 15:26; 16:7). The Spirit or Paraclete will teach the disciples all things (14:26) and lead them into all truth (16:13), speaking as directed by Jesus (16:13–15), and bearing witness to and glorifying him (15:26; 16:14). The Spirit will remind the disciples of the truth of what Jesus taught (14:26) and announce the future to them (16:13), while convincing the world of sin, righteousness and judgment (16:8–11). The other gospels do not distinguish two separate events of Commission and Pentecost as Luke does. According to the writer of John, when the resurrected Jesus sent his disciples in mission, he breathed the Holy Spirit into them, which gave them power to forgive sins (20:21–23). For John, Jesus is the source of the regenerative Spirit of God who will accompany and indwell the disciples in their mission. It is fitting therefore that in the prologue to the Gospel of John Jesus Christ is presented as the heir of all God's involvement with the cosmos—life, light, word, glory, grace and truth (Jn 1:1–18).

The characteristic interest in the indwelling of the Spirit and the description of the Spirit as "the Spirit of Truth" in John's Gospel are both emphasized further in the first of the letters ascribed to John. The Spirit is the sign
of Christ's abiding presence (1 Jn 3:24; 4:13), but it is important to "test
the spirits" (4:1) in case they are false or the spirit of the Antichrist, and not
the Holy Spirit from God, who is the spirit of truth and confesses Jesus
Christ (4:2, 3, 6; 5:7). The Revelation to John was given "in the Spirit"
(1:10)—a state which enabled John to see heaven and other scenes otherwise hidden (4:2; 17:3; 21:10)—and represents "what the Spirit says" (2:7;
etc.). The book closes with an invitation from the Spirit and the Bride (the
church) to freely take "the water of life" (22:17).

The other two gospel writers do not choose to develop an explicit pneumatology as a way of explaining the involvement of God in the mission of
the disciples. Matthew's Gospel shares with Luke many of the same references to the role of the Spirit in the life and ministry of Jesus: Jesus' conception by the Spirit (1:18–20), the descent of the Spirit as a dove (3:16),
Jesus being led by the Spirit into the wilderness (4:1), the Spirit's anointing
to prophetic ministry (12:18), and casting out demons by the Spirit (12:28).
The writer includes, in common with the other synoptic writers, the reas-
surance that in the time of trial, "it is not you who speak, but the Spirit"
(13:20); however it cannot be said that Matthew develops a pneumatology
of mission. The Spirit is not mentioned explicitly in connection with the life
of the church or the disciples, except in the baptismal formula, "in the name
of the Father and of the Son and of the Holy Spirit" (28:19), which forms
part of "the Great Commission." Whereas in Luke mission comes to the
disciples as a promise—"You will be my witnesses"—that is fulfilled in the
experience of the Spirit (Lk 24:46–49; Acts 1:8; 2), in Matthew mission is
a command to make disciples (28:16–20) by the particular actions of baptizing and teaching. Jesus' promise of his ongoing presence with the disciples in mission, the very last verse of the book (28:20), can be read
pneumatologically, but this is not the way the gospel writer chooses to
express it.

Similarly, Mark does not refer to any occasion in which the Spirit came
on the disciples. Apart from the baptism and leading into the wilderness
(1:8, 10, 12), Mark's application of the word *pneuma* to Jesus' ministry
is confined to evil and unclean spirits (for which the other gospel writers
prefer to use "demon"), or to the human spirit. The Markan version of
the Great Commission passage appears only in the disputed longer end-
ing of Mark (16:15–18), though its emphasis on the distinction between
belief and unbelief and on the signs and wonders that accompany the disciples' mission are compatible with the mission theology of the gospel as
a whole. The Commission in Mark has a distinctively "charismatic"
nature, and the characteristics of mission have much in common with the
acts of the Holy Spirit as described by Luke. However, as in Matthew so

in Mark the experience of Pentecost appears to be implicit in the assurance of Jesus Christ's presence with his disciples that is attached to the Commission (Mk 16:20), rather than in any developed pneumatological explanation.

In contrast, in the Pauline epistles what is distinctive about the Christian community is the Spirit of Christ, which Christians are given as a foretaste, a guarantee or a down-payment of what is to come (2 Cor 1:22; 5:5; Eph 1:13–14; Rom 8:23). As in the book of Acts (10:47; 11:17; 15:8), the admittance of Gentiles to the community was on the basis that they too had received the gift of the Spirit in the same way as the Spirit came upon Jews (Gal 2:7–9). So Paul argues that it is the indwelling of the Spirit that defines the community—not outward signs of the flesh (Gal 3:3; Rom 8:9). "Spirit" is almost synonymous with "grace" in the sense of God's action in reaching out to human beings to establish relationship with them (Rom 3:24; 1 Cor 15:10; 2 Cor 6:1; Gal 1:15; Eph 2:8) (Dunn 1978: 701). Whereas it is only in Galatians and Romans that Paul uses the legal term "justification" to describe the "crucial transition" of entry to Christian faith, the term "gift of the Spirit" is used to describe the same event throughout Paul's writings, and this seems to be "common ground" with all the communities to which he wrote (Dunn 1975: 419–425). For the apostle Paul, the new life made possible by the death and resurrection of the Lord Jesus Christ is lived "in the Spirit," and life "in the Spirit" is characteristically "Christ-ian," so that "in the Spirit" and the other frequently used phrase "in Christ" are flip-sides of each other (Rom 8:9–11; Heron 1983: 46).

In Paul's theology of the Spirit—which is the most developed in the New Testament—being "in the Spirit" is decisively different from being "under the law" or "in the flesh" (Rom 7–8; 1 Cor 2–3; 2 Cor 3; Gal 3–5), not in the sense of being an alternative way of life, but rather an altogether higher quality of living. Paul several times refers to the spirit of human beings in a way that apparently refers to their spiritual or higher nature (Rom 8:16; 1 Cor 2:11; 5:3–5; 7:34), and to human beings being made up of body and spirit (1 Cor 16:18; 2 Cor 7:1; 1 Thess 5:23), which means therefore that the dead are spirit (e.g. Lk 24:37, 39). For Paul the Spirit is the Spirit of love—the highest and abiding gift of God (Rom 5:5; 15:30; 1 Cor 13; Phil 2:1)—which implies the need for growth toward maturity through various trials and tribulations. The Spirit can be used to account for almost every aspect of the work of God in Christ, including the cosmic process begun in him (Rom 8:18–25; Eph 3:7–21); the salvation and liberation he achieved (Rom 8:2, 5; Gal 4:6–7; Eph 3:4–6); the intimate relationship with the Father that he makes possible (Rom 8:15; Gal 4:6; Eph 2:17–18); the sanctification of believers as temples of the Spirit (1 Cor 3:16–17; Gal 5:22–23); the gifts made available, without favoritism, in him (1 Cor 12:4–11; Rom 12:6–8; cf. Heb 2:4); and the unity and peace he came to bring (Eph 4:3; Rom 8:6; 14:17; Gal 5:22).

The Spirit as *Pneuma* and *Rūach:* Continuity and
Discontinuity between the Testaments

James Dunn, a British biblical scholar, sees the First Letter of Peter as
"typical" of the New Testament understanding of the Spirit: "the Spirit
of prophecy (1:11), the inspirer of mission and the power of the gospel
(1:12), the power that sets men apart for God (1:2) and transforms them
into the image of God's glory through suffering and persecution (4:14),
the mode of existence in the life beyond death (3:18; 4:6)." The question
of the relationship between the Pentecostal Spirit (*pneuma*) and the *rūach*
of what Christians call the Old Testament has prompted much discussion,
connected as it is with questions of Christian claims to uniqueness, Jewish-
Christian relations, and Christian distinctiveness. At one end of the spectrum, the Swiss theologian Eduard Schweizer argues that Old Testament
references to the breath or wind of God in creation must be sharply distinguished from the Holy Spirit that came upon the godly (at Pentecost)
from outside the creation. He sees the language of the Spirit in the Old
Testament as analogous to the new creation, but discontinuous from it
(Schweizer 1989: 406–15). In his book on the Holy Spirit, C. F. D. Moule
is of the opinion that in the New Testament, Christ and the Logos are cosmic in scope but the Spirit is not (Moule 2000 [1978]: 19–21). At the
other end of the spectrum are those, like Jürgen Moltmann, who emphasize the continuity between the testaments, as expressed in the understanding that the Spirit is "the Spirit of life," which helps to overcome
"the false alternative between divine revelation and human experience"
(Moltmann 1992: 5–10).

Biblical scholars agree that there is no passage in the New Testament in
which the Spirit of God appears as working in the entire creation. However,
in the Old Testament, both the role of the Spirit in bestowing life and the
Spirit's involvement in creation are beyond dispute, and these are therefore
implicit in the New Testament (Hübner 1989: 332–33). It is not possible to
drive a wedge between the Spirit in the Old Testament and New Testament,
for, as we have seen in Luke's history, it is the prophetic Spirit already
known from the Old Testament that is active in bringing about the birth of
Jesus and is later poured out at Pentecost (cf. 1 Pet 1:11). Furthermore, the
sovereignty of the Spirit, who comes from God, is clear in the New
Testament: the Spirit blows where the Spirit wills (Jn 3:8), and is poured out
on Jew and Gentile alike (Acts 11:15–17). Though Paul's pneumatological
concern is chiefly with the unity of the Spirit and the spiritual life, neither
the gifts of the Spirit that he lists (including service, teaching, giving) nor
the fruits of the Spirit (love, joy, peace, etc) are the monopoly of Christians
(Rom 2:7–8, 10–11). What is clear in the New Testament is that the Spirit

of God, who is present and active in all creation, is focused in Jesus Christ, and concentrated in—but not limited to—his followers, who live in the Spirit. There is a discontinuity between the life and ministry of Jesus Christ and the bestowal of the Spirit on the disciples, which is clearly the result of Jesus' passion. The Spirit comes in a new way in the New Testament and is sent from Jesus Christ as well as from God. In this respect, the Holy Spirit in the Christian Testament becomes clearly defined by the character, life and spirit of Christ.

The question of the gender of the Spirit in Scripture, to which feminist theologians particularly have drawn attention, has been avoided until now, as it is a complex issue that is best addressed in full awareness of all the biblical material. The grammatical gender of *rūach* is feminine, *pneuma* is neutral, and the Latin *spiritus*, from which the English word "spirit" is derived, is masculine. In gendered languages, the grammatical gender of a word may not carry much significance, as any student of French or German can observe. However, the argument made from the imagery and functions of *rūach* (and *pneuma*) that "spirit" is a feminine concept in Scripture should be given credence. The Spirit's activities of creating new life, bringing to birth, nurturing life, grieving, instructing and inspiring (but not from a position of public leadership) are all characteristic of traditional women's work. Furthermore, a number of images of the spirit support this suggestion; these include: the bird brooding over the waters and the dove at Jesus' baptism (Gen 1:2; Mk 1:9–11 and parallels); the mother giving birth (Ps 139:13; Jn 3:5–6); the Paraclete, or Counselor, who is to be with the disciples in a supporting role, such as that played by a traditional wife or mother (Jn 14:15–17, 26; 15:26; 16:17–11), speaking not on her own authority but on that of the Father (16:13–14), and playing the role of midwife in what is essentially an experience of childbirth for the disciples (Jn 16:20–22); the *shĕkīnâ* or indwelling glory of God—another grammatically feminine noun with feminine connotations; and *sophia* or wisdom—feminine in all three languages and consistently personified in Scripture as female (see above) (Johnson 1992: 83–103). All this builds a convincing case that it is not inappropriate in English to refer to the Spirit by the pronoun "she." However, to label the Spirit as exclusively female, though tempting as a corrective, may suggest awkward and unintended implications for the understanding of God as Trinity, and may do damage to theological understanding, as the traditional labeling of the persons as male has done. Feminist theologians have rightly drawn attention to a legitimate biblical understanding of God in terms of female characteristics, overturning centuries of misunderstanding in the West. This applies to the whole of the Godhead and not only to one person. For this reason, I consider it best to avoid using any pronoun for any Person of the Trinity.

The Holy Spirit and the Other Spirit(s):
Cooperation, Confrontation, Consummation

The epithet "holy," which is used of "spirit" three times in the Old Testament but becomes characteristic in the New, has a double significance. First, it shows that the Spirit is from God—that is, divine. Holiness (deriving from a root meaning "separate") is one of the foremost characteristics of Yahweh (Lev 11:44–45). Second, "holy" distinguishes the Spirit of the Lord from all other spirits. In the Old Testament evil is described as a spirit sent from God (e.g. 1 Sam 16:14–23; Isa 29:10; 1 Kings 22:21–22). Though not found in the Hebrew Bible, the plural of *rūach* came to be used in the intertestamental period as a collective term for heavenly beings (Dunn 1978: 693). Similarly, *pneuma* and its plural are used to describe beings and powers other than the Spirit of the Lord, the Spirit of God, or the Spirit of Jesus Christ. Opinion was divided in those days, as it is now, about the existence of transcendent reality and a world of spirits. According to Acts 23:8, "the Sadducees say that there is no resurrection, nor angel, nor spirit; but the Pharisees acknowledge them all." Judging by the complexity of their language, most of the biblical writers seem not to have a simple two-part cosmology of God and world, but a differentiated vision of a hierarchy or community of beings, forces and powers.

There are more than forty references in the New Testament to "evil spirits," "unclean spirits" and "demons" (Dunn 1978: 694). These occur mainly in the synoptic gospels and Acts (e.g. Mt 8:16; Mk 1:23, 26–27; 9:25; Lk 4:36; 11:24, 26; Acts 19:12–13, 15–16; also 1 Tim 4:1; Rev 16:13–14; 18:2). It is interesting to note that there is no such reference in John's Gospel, which has a somewhat different worldview involving universal concepts rather than cosmic forces. In the Old Testament, evil spirits may be referred to as "from the Lord," as in the case of Saul (1 Sam 16:14; 19:9; cf. 2 Sam 24:1; 1 Chr 21:1). This is not the case in the New Testament, where the emphasis is on the power of the Spirit of God, acting through Jesus and other agents, over demons and evil spirits. It is "by the Spirit of God" that Jesus cast out demons (Mt 12:28; though note Lk 11:20, where "finger" is used in place of "Spirit"). This was an indication that the end-times of final victory over evil were beginning in Jesus' ministry (e.g. Mk 3:23–27; Lk 10:17–18; 11:19–20). There is reference to a ruler of demons, the spirit or god of this world, known as Beelzebul or Satan (e.g. Mk 3:22; Lk 10:17–20; Rev 12:7–17; cf. Job 1:6, etc.), and also to the spirit or god of this world who is not to be confused with the Spirit of God (1 Cor 2:12; 2 Cor 4:4; Eph 2:2) and to a "spirit of error" (1 Jn 4:6). However, not all spirits referred to in the New Testament are evil or unclean or false. A dead person can be referred to as a spirit (Lk 24:37, 39; Heb 12:23; 1 Pet 3:18–19).

Angels are described as "ministering spirits" (Heb 1:14); there are the spirits of the prophets (1 Cor 14:32; Rev 22:6); and it is possible to receive good guidance from a spirit (Acts 23:9). Paul and John particularly mention the need to discern the spirits to distinguish good from evil (1 Cor 12:10; 2 Cor 11:4; 1 Thess 5:19–22; 2 Thess 2:2; 1 Jn 4:1, 3, 6) (Dunn 1978: 695; Ukpong 1990: 80–81).

Discussion about spirits cannot be divorced from consideration of other unseen powers that are alluded to in the New Testament. In the Hebrew Bible it is sometimes suggested that Yahweh is not alone in heaven, but that there are other gods over whom he is pre-eminent (Ps 82:1; 86:8; 89:6–7; 138:1; Job 1:6), though the worship of such gods is, of course, idolatry. Other gods are contemplated in Paul's discussion of the question of meat offered to idols, where it is made clear that, for himself and those he has instructed, there is only one God, but this may not be the case for others (1 Cor 8:4–7). There are also "principalities" and "powers," "the world rulers of this present darkness," "the spiritual hosts of wickedness in the heavenly places" (Eph 6:12), the beast (Rev 13:1–7) and other powers mentioned in the book of Revelation. There are references in Paul to a spiritual struggle (Eph 6:10–18; 2 Cor 10:4–6), and other injunctions to resist the devil (Jas 4:7; 1 Pet 5:8), but there are also other legitimate authorities established by God with whom Christians are urged to cooperate (e.g. Rom 13:1–8) and angels who exercise God's power (Rev 8:7–10:11). Whatever the nature of the powers, attention is given in Scripture to "naming," "unmasking" and "engaging" them by discernment and resistance (Wink 1984; 1986; 1992).

The principalities and powers are overcome and disarmed in Christ by a greater power (Col 2:15). However else the Holy Spirit is understood in the Bible, the Spirit represents the power of God, who is present and active in the world (Lk 1:35; Acts 1:8; 2 Tim 1:7). However, those who look for power must not think that the Holy Spirit can be harnessed for control by human beings, because the Spirit remains a gift of God (Acts 8:18–20). Blaspheming against the Holy Spirit is the only sin that can never be forgiven (Mk 3:28–30; Mt 12:31–32; Lk 12:10). Lying to the Spirit or tempting the Spirit was the fatal fault of Ananias and Sapphira (Acts 5:3, 9). To set oneself up against the power of God is perhaps what the writer of 1 John refers to as the only "mortal sin" (5:16), because it is to cut oneself off from salvation. So the believers are warned not to resist, grieve, quench or outrage the Holy Spirit (Acts 7:51; Eph 4:30; cf. Isa 63:10; 1 Thess 5:19). Biblically, the sovereign Spirit of God cannot then be reduced to the power of the human spirit or to the power within the Christian community; the Spirit is free and abroad in the whole creation. It is for human beings to discern the Spirit and submit to the Spirit's power.

CHAPTER 3

The Spirit of Mission:
Impulse, Guidance, Power

Theology, Missiology, and Pneumatology
in the Twentieth-century West

For much of the twentieth century in the West, theology of mission and systematic theology were at opposite poles of the theological spectrum. Systematic theology was a cerebral exercise at the center, and theology of mission—if it was considered at all—was understood as consisting of the practical outworking of theological theory on the periphery, where church met world. In his monumental study *Transforming Mission* (1991), David Bosch charts a movement of mission theology from the periphery to the center of the theological curriculum (: 489–96). Painted with a broad brush, this transformation was the result of the confluence of two movements: the rethinking of mission (to the rest of the world) that became necessary in the "post-colonial" period, along with the realization that the West could no longer be regarded as "Christendom," and was itself in need of evangelization. The combination of theological reflection on mission practice and missionary concern in theology stimulated the "emerging ecumenical missionary paradigm" described by Bosch (: 368–510) and also referred to as *missio Dei*. In this chapter we will examine some of these developments in the West through the lens of pneumatology, looking separately at the two trajectories of missiology and systematic theology. It should be noted here that a full appreciation of *missio Dei* as a way of understanding the Spirit in the world, and also of the questions it raises, is not possible without consideration of the contribution of Eastern Orthodox theology, which is the subject of the next chapter.

Missiologies of the Spirit: Mobilization, Motivation, Range

The Covenant drawn up by a broad grouping of Evangelicals concerned for "world evangelization" at Lausanne in 1974 represents a revivalist view that focuses on the power of the Spirit to mobilize for mission and make evangelism effective. The reflections on the Holy Spirit occur under the heading, "the power of the Spirit." Its narrowly "pentecostal" reading of the scriptures is evidenced by the positioning of this paragraph near the end of the document, immediately before the statement on the return of Christ. The Holy Spirit thus appears as the added ingredient that is necessary to bring about the goals of Christian mission. This is what the content also implies. It begins by stating a belief in the power of the Holy Spirit rather than in the person of the Spirit. It goes on to mention the futility of mission enterprise without the witness of the Spirit and the Spirit's role in making the whole church missionary in nature. "Worldwide evangelization," the paragraph states, "will become a realistic possibility only when the Spirit renews the Church in truth and wisdom, faith, holiness, love and power." Therefore there follows a prayer for revival in the church to bring about obedience to the gospel in "the whole earth" (Lausanne Covenant: paragraph 14). Whilst this statement is well supported by biblical texts, it lacks a developed pneumatology of mission. It reads as if the Spirit realizes a work of mission, the goals and methods of which are determined by other—non-pneumatological—criteria. In the light of criticism of the Western missionary enterprise from within the movement, and also by those who were on the receiving end of it, in the twentieth century there began a quest for the integrity of mission. Something of this was reflected in the Second Lausanne Congress in Manila in 1989, which was concerned with "the whole gospel," "the whole church" and "the whole world" (Douglas 1990), but without any significant pneumatological development.

The modern missionary movement, of which Evangelicals are often uncritically proud, was dominated by a European sense of responsibility for the world and obligation to proclaim the message Europeans had received. This was expressed in the use of the "Great Commission" to justify and motivate mission. "The Great Commission" meant the command of Jesus Christ to his disciples after his resurrection to take the gospel into all the world. The scriptural reference was usually Matthew 28: 19–20, "Go therefore and make disciples of all nations, baptizing . . . and teaching . . . ," but Mark 16: 15–18, "Go into all the world and preach the gospel to the whole creation . . ." was also in view. Bosch, together with many other historians of mission, credits William Carey with initiating this paradigm in 1792 (1991: 340–41), but these same verses were already in use nearly one hundred years earlier by Thomas Bray, founder of two Anglican agencies (see Society for the Propagation of the Gospel 1703).

By the end of the nineteenth century, religion in both the United States and Britain was characterized by revival movements and future expectation. There was a widespread belief that this age was the last, or penultimate, in a series—the age of grace, or of the Holy Spirit, as distinct from the previous ages of the law—which gave a sense of urgency to world mission (cf.

Bosch 1991: 314). Such awareness was prevalent in the Anglo-Catholic Tractarian movement (1833–1845; see Manning 1865) as well as in the Evangelical movement, which was influenced by the dispensationalist theology of John Nelson Darby (1800–1882) (see Gordon 1893). This view came to a peak at the world missionary conference in Edinburgh in 1910, where the driving figure behind the conference, John Mott, expressed his belief that the Western churches were now resourced to bring about "the evangelization of the world in this generation" (1910: 10–11). Later Pentecostal groups tended to incorporate dispensationalist beliefs, with slight modification, and many also believed that the special outpouring of the Spirit in the Pentecostal movement was the "latter rain," which would bring forth an abundant spiritual harvest (Kay 2004). From the start, Pentecostal believers were active in spreading the message near and far, looking to the power of the Spirit to enable them to perform the signs and wonders they expected would accompany their mission (Anderson 2004a: 206–207).

However, critical reflection on their involvement in the transformation of lives and societies through the modern missionary movement, together with a heightened pneumatological awareness due to revival movements, led missionaries of widely differing theological traditions to rethink the link between mission and the Holy Spirit, and also the dominance of Matthew 28 in missionary motivation. Bosch (1991: 40) notes that two twentieth-century missionaries in particular, Roland Allen and Harry Boer, both questioned the emphasis on the exterior command and drew attention to the inward work of the Spirit in mission, thereby connecting the mission enterprise with the spirituality of the missionary. They stimulated the emergence of a radically different mission pneumatology from the triumphalism of Edinburgh 1910.

Roland Allen, who was a priest in the Anglo-Catholic tradition, and a missionary in China of the Society for the Propagation of the Gospel in the early years of the twentieth century, criticized the attitudes of his fellow missionaries. He accused them of racial and religious pride, and of an unwillingness to trust those whom he referred to as "the natives" to find their own way and run their own churches. This, he said, was why colonial churches were so dependent and uniform, and not rooted in the countries to which they had been introduced. Allen identified the reason for these problems of modern missions as a lack of awareness of or trust in the work of the Holy Spirit in mission. He put this down to a superior attitude, which meant that missionaries were imposing their own agenda and were unable to believe that the same Holy Spirit that inspired and guided them was also at work in their converts. The obligation laid upon Christians by the Great Commission was not, in Allen's opinion, the most desirable impulse for mission. Comparing contemporary missionary methods with those of Paul, Allen argued that obedience to the command led to inflexibility and paternalism on the part of the missionaries and brought slavery instead of liberty and empowerment to the converts. Believing that "the Spirit is prior to the letter," Allen put the work of the "Spirit of love, which eternally desires and strives for the welfare of all," before the Great Commission in missionary motivation (1962 [1912]: 141–50; 1964 [c1910]: 31–33).

Half a century later, theologian-missionary Harry R. Boer also asked what stirred the earliest church into mission, and concluded that neither in Acts, nor in Paul, was the Great Commission appealed to as a justification for the Gentile missionary enterprise. Though they were of very different denominational backgrounds, Boer—a North American Calvinist —was inspired by Allen's earlier work. He found no scriptural justification for the dominance of the Great Commission in modern missions. In a study of Luke-Acts, Boer further noted that the giving of the Great Commission did not immediately initiate the (world) missionary enterprise. He went on to show that "there is a surprising and unanimous testimony in the New Testament to the relationship between the Spirit poured out at Pentecost and the witness of the Church." Boer argued that the meaning of the Great Commission for mission, and its powerful place in the life of the mission-ary community, must be understood as derived from the Pentecost event. In Luke's Gospel, mission comes to the disciples as a promise—"You will be my witnesses"—that is fulfilled in the experience of the Spirit (Lk 24: 46–49; Acts 1:8; 2), whereas in Matthew's Gospel the famous Great Commission is a command to make disciples (Mt 28:16–20). In Boer's estimation, it is the awareness of the presence of the risen Christ—in the form of the Spirit— with his disciples in mission that transforms mission from legalistic obedi-ence into the innate behavior of all Christians (Boer 1961: 15, 112, 47). Both Boer and Allen saw the Great Commission as descriptive of the nat-ural consequences of Pentecost, rather than as prescriptive, a command to action. They understood the Holy Spirit to be the motivator of Christian mission, which now appeared to be an instinctive response to the internal prompting of the Spirit, rather than obedience to an external command. They believed that mission according to the Spirit would be much closer to the New Testament ideal than mission under law. As Allen explained, mis-sion is the work of the Spirit and "the Spirit is a missionary Spirit"; mission is a spiritual activity, written on the heart (Allen 1964 [c1910]: 33–36, 16–17). Or, to put it another way, mission is the outworking of a mission-ary spirituality.

In the light of work by Allen and Boer and other reflections on the bib-lical texts, Bosch suggests a reappraisal of Matthew 28: 16–20. Among his observations are that the clause "I am with you always" is not subordinate to the command; in fact, it is the other way around: "because Jesus contin-ues to be present with his disciples, they go out in mission." Bosch also emphasizes the context of the weakness of the disciples, and the fallacy of disconnecting the Great Commission from the moral and ethical teaching that defines the meaning of true discipleship in Matthew's Gospel and that is crystallized in "The Great Commandment" (Mt 22: 37–40) (Bosch 1991: 74–83). Turning to Luke-Acts, Bosch draws the same conclusions when he summarizes Luke's missiology of the Spirit in three terms: the Spirit initiates, guides and empowers the disciples' mission. The Spirit is the catalyst and impulse of mission at Pentecost and subsequently at each decisive point of the story in Acts. The Spirit also guides the apostles in the conduct of mission. At the beginning they wait on the Spirit to come and lead them, and later the Spirit directs them through prayer, visions and dreams. At Pentecost the Spirit came upon the disciples as "power from on high"; this was manifested in the boldness of the witness (Bosch 1991: 113–14). This boldness due to the Spirit is reflected in the phrase which has become characteristic of Bosch's work "bold humility" (or "humble boldness"), which he used to express the link between dialogue and witness that has been recognized in the post-colonial era (Bosch 1991: 489; cf. Saayman and Kritzinger 1996: title).

Bosch's characteristically "pentecostal" approach (see chapter 2) to the biblical material on the Spirit is revealed when he declares: "The Spirit is the risen Christ who is active in the world." This is related to his Evangelical background and his interest in Lukan eschatology, on which he did his doctoral study under Hans Conzelmann. The way Bosch's book is constructed reflects his view that mission is a distinctively New Testament concept (Bosch 1991: 17, 40). Bosch's interest is in the role of the Holy Spirit in Christian missionary work, rather than in reflections on the Spirit in the world. The point of his extensive reflections on the (synoptic) gospels is to connect the church's mission with that of Jesus Christ, which helps him establish the humble ethos and ethical concern of mission, opposing those who, in his view, reduce salvation to a vertical relationship with God and mission to church growth. However, he does not reflect specifically on the presence and activity of the Spirit in the mission of Jesus himself, so his reading of the Bible cannot be said to be "catholic" in the sense above (chapter 2). Nor does Bosch's missiological framework, which begins from the New Testament, allow for an "orthodox" reading or the development of a creation theology of the Holy Spirit. These omissions seem to be related to the way in which Bosch's "ecumenical consensus" appears as a Western perspective (K. Kim 2000), an issue to which we will return later (chapter 7).

Bosch's "emerging paradigm" reflects the growing awareness that mission is God's work, not ours, which was expressed in the term *missio Dei*. The concept was first articulated at the Willingen (Germany) meeting of the International Missionary Council in 1952. This was in the context of European soul-searching after the Second World War and its retreat from Empire, in which the theology that most spoke to the prevailing mood was that of Karl Barth. An interim report included in the conference volume, *Missions under the Cross*, stated:

The missionary obligation of the Church comes from the love of God in His active relationship with [humanity] . . . By the Holy Spirit the Church, experiencing God's active love, is assured that God will complete what He has set His hand to in the sending of His Son. This is the hope with which the Church looks forward to the goal of its existence, which in fact sets the Church marching onwards. In this sense "mission" belongs to the purpose of the Church (International Missionary Council 1953c: 241).

With the emergence of *missio Dei*, "[t]he church changes from being the sender to being the one sent" (Bosch 1991: 370). Though Bosch does not discuss the Johannine mission paradigm, its influence—particularly Jesus' words in John 20:21: "As the Father has sent me, even so I send you"—is clear, both on Bosch and on the paradigm as a whole. The church is sent in the power of the Spirit, and therefore the Spirit is the Spirit of mission. That God's mission is accomplished by the Spirit's presence and activity in the world is also implicit in the theology of *missio Dei*, though it is not always stated explicitly as it was at Willingen, for reasons that we will explain.

In his book *The Open Secret* (1995 [1978]), Lesslie Newbigin, missionary and ecumenist, set forth his theology of mission on a trinitarian basis and within a *missio Dei* framework. His chapter on the Third Person (1995: 56–61) is entitled "Bearing the Witness of the Spirit," and describes the Spirit as "the active agent" or "real agent" of mission, showing how, according to Luke, the Spirit "leads the way" in mission. The thrust of the chapter is to demonstrate, by emphasizing the sovereignty of the Spirit, that the Spirit "rules, guides, and goes before the church" in mission. This stress on the "prevenience" of the Spirit is intended to discourage triumphalism in mission and to point to the weakness of the church as merely an instrument of the living power of the Spirit: "Mission is not just something the church does; it is something that is done by the Spirit, who is himself the witness, who changes both the world and the church, who always goes before the church in its missionary journey" (: 56). Newbigin is also challenging the domestication of the Spirit in the church. Though Newbigin does not countenance the Spirit at work where the church is not, he emphasizes that mission "remains the mission of the Spirit" and that the Spirit acts to convert the church as much as to convert any Gentile (: 58–59). His insistence that "[t]he church is witness [only] insofar as it follows obediently where the Spirit leads" (: 61) suggests that the scope of the Spirit's work goes beyond the boundaries of the church in mission. Even in conservative circles that make a sharp distinction between the church and the world, the prevenience of the Spirit is recognized. It is the work of the Spirit to convict the world and to bring about repentance. It is also the Spirit's work to forgive and convert. As the Lausanne Covenant states, "The Father sent his Spirit to bear witness to his Son; without his witness ours is futile. Conviction of sin, faith in Christ, new birth and Christian growth are all his work" (Lausanne Covenant, paragraph 14).

Another pioneering work that probed the link between the Holy Spirit and mission is John V. Taylor's imaginative book, *The Go-Between God* (1972). Taylor, an Anglican missionary statesman, used his own experience as a missionary in Africa, as well as the work of African theologians, to analyze African traditional thought and discover what he called its "primal vision." He stressed a "sense of cosmic oneness" inherent in primal religion, and the sense of divine involvement in all creation as a power-force, despite the perceived remotenesss of the "High God" (1963: 62–63, 72–73, 83–92, 201). The primal vision and Tillich's awareness of the "Spiritual Presence" in cultural life lay behind Taylor's pneumatological reflections. Taylor began from the position that "the Spirit who is central to Paul's theology is the same being whom the Old Testament knew as the Spirit, or Breath, of God" (1972: 6); that is, he took an "orthodox" approach to the biblical record. He then explained the Spirit as "the go-between God"; that is, "the elemental energy of communion itself, within which all separate existences may be made present and personal to each other"—a description which was intended also to include a scientific understanding of the Spirit's work in matter (: 17–19). He regarded Jesus as distinctive in having a new mode of relationship with the Spirit, which Christians share. However, the unique presence of the Spirit in Christ "is not enclosed, either in Christ or in his church, but exists between the Christians and those who meet them" (: 180–82, 83). Taylor observed: "If we want to understand in a fresh way what it was that possessed Jesus at his baptism, and what it is we also need before we can engage in Christian mission, we have to probe into the meaning of the ancient images—the breath of life, the hovering wings, the unpredictable winds, the fire in the mouth" (: 7). This led him to define mission as essentially "continuing the work of creation" in cooperation with the Creator-Redeemer, and to give it the broadest possible scope, encompassing all creation and all creativity (: 36–40). Taylor advocated a mission of Christian presence that is defined by "Christians being present" in the midst of the world's life rather than engaging in any particular activity (: 223–44).

Though *missio Dei* led to a broadening of the scope of mission, as the mission of Jesus and his concern for the poor were taken into account as models for mission, Taylor's all-encompassing definition did not meet with universal approval. For one thing, as has often been said, "If everything is mission, then nothing is mission"; for another, such universal work of the Spirit seems to threaten the distinctiveness of Christian faith and mission. Bosch opposed the modification of *missio Dei* by the Dutch missiologist Hans Hoekendijk in the World Council of Churches in the 1960s, which followed much the same logic. Hoekendijk implied that because God's concern is with the world, the church is no longer necessary or useful. Bosch prefers to focus on the Spirit of mission rather than the mission of the Spirit because of his fears that the latter leads to the secularization of Christian faith. Recognition of the work of the Spirit in the world directly, as it were—that is, without being mediated through the church—was to Bosch nonsensical because it is through the tradition of Christian faith and the Christian community that we understand the Spirit (Bosch 1991: 382–85, 391–92). For his part, Taylor insisted on the uniqueness of the Christian experience of the fullness of the Spirit, as well as on the continuity between *rūach* and *pneuma*. Like Bosch, he upheld the church, but suggested it might be better "if we thought more of the church being given to the Spirit than of the Spirit being given to the church" (Taylor 1972: 83–84, 133). Bosch quotes Taylor approvingly because of Taylor's emphasis on the Spirit and the church as missionary (Bosch 1991: 378), but uneasiness was to continue about Taylor's suggestion that God's mission, beginning at creation, is larger than that of the church.

Catholic mission theology was greatly influenced by developments in Protestant thinking (Bevans and Schroeder 2004: 289–90). The encyclical *Redemptoris missio* of Pope John Paul II (1990) reflected concern about the same issue of the work of the Spirit in the world. The relevant chapter is headed, "The Holy Spirit: The Principal Agent of Mission." The title indicates that it takes a predominantly "pentecostal" approach, as the following quotation shows:

> The mission of the Church, like that of Jesus, is God's work or, as Luke often puts it, the work of the Spirit. After the resurrection and ascension of Jesus, the apostles have a powerful experience which completely transforms them: the experience of Pentecost. The coming of the Holy Spirit makes them *witnesses* and *prophets* (cf. Acts 1:8; 2:17–18). It fills them with a serene courage which impels them to pass on to others their experience of Jesus and the hope which motivates them. The Spirit gives them the ability to bear witness to Jesus with "boldness." When the first evangelizers go down from Jerusalem, the Spirit becomes even more of a "guide," helping them to choose both those to whom they are to go and the places to which their missionary journey is to take them. The working of the Spirit is manifested particularly in the impetus given to the mission which, in accordance with Christ's words, spreads out from Jerusalem to all of Judea and Samaria, and to the farthest ends of the earth (John Paul II 1990: paragraph 24).

There is little attention in that chapter to what we have called the "catholic" reading, beginning with Jesus' mission; but there is a discussion of creation theology of the Spirit under the sub-heading, "The Spirit Is Present and Active in Every Time and Place." The encyclical also affirms that "[t]he Spirit manifests himself in a special way in the Church and in her members." *Redemptoris missio* recognizes that the Spirit is present and active in individuals, society, history, peoples, cultures and religions, and also states that "whatever the Spirit brings about in human hearts and in the history of peoples, in cultures and religions serves as a preparation for the Gospel." It refuses to separate "the universal activity of the Spirit" from "his particular activity within the body of Christ." This amounts to claiming that the church, "to which Christ gave his Spirit," is at the center of the Spirit's work in the world (John Paul II 1990: paragraphs 28, 29). This seems to lack the humility of the *missio Dei* formulation, in which the church's identity is contingent on its participation in God's mission: "By the Holy Spirit the Church only continues to live as the Church when it is the place at which God's love, active in the death of Christ, is both sent forth into the world by witness and re-presented to God by worship" (International Missionary Council 1953c: 241). Again, the interest is in the Spirit of mission rather than the mission of the Spirit.

Theologies of the Spirit in the World: Above, Beneath, Between

In his 1963–64 Warfield lectures on the doctrine of the Holy Spirit, Dutch theologian Hendrikus Berkhof linked the neglect of the Spirit to the neglect of mission in systematics. He complained that, due to the paucity of reflection on mission—that is, theology's lack of orientation to the world—theology has been "static and introverted" and missed "the great movement of the Spirit" that is mission, which is logically prior to the church, and of which the church exists as an instrument (1965: 30–41). His proposal that mission was the Spirit's primary work led Berkhof toward an interest in the Spirit's wider work in the world. He broadened the scope of his study to include the Spirit in relation to creation, liberation and consummation (: 94–108). Despite the widening of the Spirit's work beyond what directly contributes to conversion, Berkhof's definition of mission is limited to Christian activity in other parts of the world; this is reflected in his perception of the movement of the Spirit in the world, which is focused on the post-Pentecostal witness of the apostles to the ends of the earth. That is, he tends to reduce the Spirit to "the name of the exalted Christ acting in the world" (Heron 1983: 168; Moltmann 1992: 13). Nevertheless, Berkhof's dynamic conception of the Holy Spirit showed that there could be a pneumatological connection between the domestic concerns of sanctification and ecclesiology and missiological interest in God's concern with the world outside the Christian community.

In this section, we will look at three German theologians whose work was profoundly influential in the twentieth-century European struggle between transcendence and immanence in theology in the context of modernity (see the analysis of Grenz and Olson 1992). The work of Karl Barth,

Paul Tillich and Karl Rahner illustrates three distinct ways in which the
Spirit was related to the world in systematics. Barth is credited with originating the idea of *missio Dei* when he stressed that mission "is not a matter of human goodwill and reparations, but a matter of divine purpose and
confirmation," and reminded missionaries that "the term *missio* was in the
ancient Church an expression of . . . the divine sending forth of the self, the
sending of the Son and the Holy Spirit to the whole world" (quoted in
Thomas 1995: 105–106; see Bosch 1991: 389; Bevans and Schroeder 2004:
290). His idea, mediated to students of mission by Karl Hartenstein, set mission firmly within the trinitarian framework with which he began his systematic thought. As Berkhof remarked, Barth stood alone in treating mission
under systematics (1965: 3). In Barth's theology, which is outlined in his
1935 *Credo*, mission was transformed from an activity of the church to an
attribute of God through God's Holy Spirit. According to Barth, just as the
revelation in Jesus Christ was through the Spirit, so is the ongoing work of
reconciliation: "the revelation of the Father in the Son is the revelation
through the Holy Spirit. We say exactly the same thing when we say that
the reconciliation of the world to God in Christ is the reconciliation through
the Holy Spirit" (1962 [1935]: 130). Barth described the Holy Spirit as "the
love of the Father to the Son, of the Son to the Father," which was expressed
in God's sending of Jesus Christ into the world and which continues to be
shared with humanity in the church, the forgiveness of sins, resurrection and
eternal life. The power of the Holy Spirit is nothing less than God's power;
this is made visible in the fact of Christian belief (: 136).

As a result of his re-reading of the Church Fathers, Barth reversed the
order of Western theology since the high Middle Ages by beginning with the
Trinity (Jenson 1997: 32). This led him to his rediscovery and reappraisal
of pneumatology, which he regarded as a "crucial question," and yet which
became one of the most debated aspects of his thought (Barth 1962 [1935]:
134; Jenson 1997: 33). In his polemic against contemporary liberal theology, Barth decisively rejected any association of the Spirit with the human
search for or approach to God, whether practical, psychological or philosophical (see chapter 1). As far as he was concerned, the holiness of the
Spirit signified that the Spirit is the Spirit of Jesus Christ and comes from
above. "Therefore what is spoken of [in the doctrine of the Holy Spirit] is
the concern of *God* for man, not the reverse" (1962 [1935]: 128). For
Barth—reacting against liberal theology, which he saw had so inculturated
the gospel as to fail to distinguish the gospel of Jesus Christ from national
interest—the Holy Spirit could not be in any way associated with human
religiosity, values or spirituality in any form, nor with the spirit of the age,
nor with evolutionary progress. He declared that "We have sufficient in the
Spirit" and that "none of these other spirits, whatever name they bear,
makes us accessible" to God's revelation and reconciliation (: 134). Barth
feared that the confusion of the Spirit of Jesus Christ with any other (nec-

essarily inferior) spirit would lead to conclusions that were contrary to the gospel: "It is rather the evil secret of all other spirits, of all world-spirits, from the lowest to the highest, that at best they make us put our trust in works" (: 134–35). Similarly, he was worried that the category of "Spirit" could be used "to supplement and enrich the revelation that took place in Jesus Christ under the title 'Spirit' with divers alleged truths drawn from nature and history, gained through reason or experience or even through immediate illumination," which he believed was contrary to scripture (Jn 16:14). He saw a clear distinction in the Bible between the Spirit of God and the Word of God, which was fully revealed in Jesus Christ (: 132–33). For Barth, the revelation in Jesus Christ was not only sufficient, it was also complete: "the revelation of the Spirit can add nothing to the revelation in Jesus Christ." He regarded the Holy Spirit as the one and only Spirit of Jesus Christ, coming from him alone and leading to him and nowhere else (: 135).

Barth described pneumatology as pointing to the subjective side of the divine revelation, where christology pointed to the objective side of the same revelation. Both Jesus Christ and the Holy Spirit speak "emphatically and completely" of God Himself (1962 [1935]: 129–30). But instead of treating them as complementary revelations, Barth tended to subordinate the Spirit to Christ in his description of the Spirit as "the Spirit of the *Word* of God" (: 134–35). For this reason he staunchly defended the *filioque* clause in the Nicene Creed along traditional Western lines. This meant that the Spirit appeared as a mode of operation of Christ in the world rather than as a distinct person of the Trinity. "When Barth *uses* the doctrine of the Trinity to solve theological problems, what actually appears and functions is regularly a doctrine rather of binity" (Jenson 1997: 34). Barth's pneumatology was caged in by his Christology, to the extent that "his achievement is not so much an original exposition of the third article of the creed as a detailed description of the Christian's subjective appropriation of the second article"; he failed to produce a dynamic doctrine of the Spirit (Rosato 1981: 181, 187; Ritschl 1981: 46–65). In Heron's opinion, Barth's approach does go beyond earlier "purely noetic or applicative understandings of the Spirit's work." He "depicts the Spirit as the living power of the risen Christ," but he does not go so far as to recognize that "Jesus is not only the giver but also the *receiver* of the Spirit" (1983: 167–70, 126–27). This limitation prevented Barth from appreciating any wider work of the Spirit in creation beyond the Christian revelation; this is one reason why the application of his theology to other religions, for example, was with decidedly negative effects (as shown by Kraemer 1938: title). Whereas his insistence on the otherness of the Spirit led to a theology that clearly distinguished the Spirit of Christ from other rivals—a stance that many agree was justified in the critical times in which he wrote—it has not always proved helpful in more pluralistic contexts. In Barth's work, the only other spirits at work in the world appear to be opposed to the Spirit of God and of Jesus Christ, and so the

Spirit's activity seems antagonistic to understandings of truth and ways of life that are not of the Christian tradition.

Barth's compatriot and contemporary, Paul Tillich, took a polar opposite approach to religions and culture, attempting to mediate between faith and current intellectual and social life by developing a theology of culture. Tillich's declared starting point was not divine revelation, but the human condition with its "ultimate concern." However, he found answers to cultural queries in the Christian faith. Contrary to Barth, he recognized experience as a source of theology, but only a dependent source. Though he regarded the source of all religious experience as the "Spiritual power" within "man," he also believed that "only if his spirit and the divine Spirit in him were one could his experience have revealing character," and generally (with the exception of Jesus Christ) he finds this not to be the case (1951: 46). In this way, Tillich's work provided a foundation for the development of pneumatology and Spirit christology in a way in which Barth's did not, whilst also establishing a normative relationship between the Spirit and the Spirit of Christ. Tillich insisted that a religious term like "Spirit" could not be discussed without relation to cultural understandings of the term (though these should not be allowed to define its meaning) (: 54–55).

In his systematic theology, Tillich identified five biblical religious symbols which he saw as correlating with basic human questions: the symbol "Spirit" was presented as an answer to modern questions of ambiguity in morality, culture and religion. Tillich also divided his theology into a trinitarian structure dealing with the "essential nature," the "existential disruption" and the "actuality" of life (see Kelsey 1997). His pneumatology is represented by the last of these, and covers the "Spiritual Presence" and "Kingdom of God"—the first treating the topic synchronically (or contemporaneously) in cultures and the second diachronically through history—and "Eternal Life," the conquest of all ambiguities (Tillich 1963). Though he chose biblical symbols, Tillich expressed his theology in philosophical rather than biblical terms.

Tillich understands life to be the process of the "actualization of potential being," that is, the uniting of the essence and existence of being, its power and meaning. Life has three "dimensions" (not to be thought of as "levels"): inorganic, organic and spirit. He wishes to reinstate the word "spirit" (with a lower-case "s"), which he sees as either corrupted, confused or discarded in contemporary discourse, to denote the dimension of life actualized only in human beings. It is not to be confused with self-expression, nor with a "spiritual world" of (naturalized) essences, nor with "spirits" in a ghostly sense, none of which constitutes life (1963: 11–30). In the dimension of the spirit, Tillich defines morality as the self-integration of life, culture as the self-creativity of life, and religion as the self-transcendence of life. It is within religion that "the quest for unambiguous life" begins, but the answers transcend any particular religious form or symbol (: 30–110). For

Tillich, "spirit" provides the necessary symbolic material to understand the religious symbols "divine Spirit" or "Spiritual Presence." The relation between Spirit and spirit is that "the divine Spirit breaks into the human spirit" and "drives the human spirit out of itself" (: 111–12). Tillich describes this event as "inspiration" or "infusion"; it is an ecstatic experience but it does not disrupt the structure of the centered self (: 113–20), and it is always mediated through the language of the revelatory tradition in which it occurs (: 127–28). The Spiritual Presence is manifested in faith and love (: 129–38), and creates the New Being, which Tillich believes is anticipated in all the religions (: 138–44).

Tillich recognizes a Spirit christology in the synoptic gospels, in which Jesus was recognized at baptism as one whose "human spirit was entirely grasped by the Spiritual Presence"; this makes him the Christ, "the decisive embodiment of the New Being for historical mankind" (1963: 144). This, however, implies the manifestation of God in his Spiritual Presence before and after Jesus Christ in history (or before and after the historical encounter of the subject with Jesus Christ): "The assertion that Jesus is the Christ implies that the Spirit, which made him the Christ and which became his Spirit (with a capital 'S'), was and is working in all those who have been grasped by the Spiritual Presence, before he could be encountered as a historical event" (: 147). However, "the exact relation of the Spirit of Jesus as the Christ and the Spirit working in those who are grasped by the Spiritual Presence after his manifestation to them" is a question which Tillich sees discussed (and answered) in the fourth gospel, in the distinction between Logos and Paraclete, so that "Every new manifestation of the Spiritual Presence stands under the criterion of his manifestation in Jesus the Christ" (: 148).

Because Tillich believed the secular "is open to the impact of the Spirit without the mediation of a church" (due to the freedom of the Spirit), he recognized the possibility of "latent Spiritual Community." Such communities, which might or might not be religious, are where the power of New Being is evident but Christ is not yet encountered. These he regarded as examples of the divine Spirit's wider creativity in humankind (1963: 246–47). However, he understood these as preparation for the encounter with Christ, not as manifesting the Spiritual Presence. He continued to maintain the ultimacy of Christ as the supreme manifestation of the divine Spirit that cannot be qualitatively surpassed (: 149–55).

Tillich's association of Spirit with spirit in the sense of the human dimension of life led him to connect Spirit with human creativity in culture rather than with biological life. However, he also recognized that "the multidimensional unity of life implies an indirect and limited influence of the Spiritual Presence on the ambiguities of life in general"; this is he saw most clearly in healing, which he described as bringing self-integration of the centered life (1963: 275–77). With regard to the "divine life" of the Trinity, he described "Spirit" as the religious symbol standing for the "dynamic unity" of the "Abyss"—the mystical expression of the depth of divine life—and the "Logos," which expresses the meaning and structure of the divine life philosophically. Since Tillich famously describes God as "ground of being," the Spirit as an "element" in the ground of being comes, as it were, from below rather than above (1951: 155–59). Another striking difference between the approaches of Barth and Tillich is Tillich's preference for the term "presence" and Barth's for "action" or "activity," when describing the role of the Spirit. "Presence" for Tillich is certainly dynamic, but it denotes the power of New Being itself, whereas Barth's concern has more to do with the application of the work of salvation, which is achieved by Christ.

Despite his insistence on christological criteria, many have questioned "whether [Tillich's method of correlation between faith and culture] does not finally result in translating the content of Christian faith without remainder into the deepest convictions of the secular culture it attempts to address" (Kelsey 1997: 100). Heron is suspicious that Tillich's conception of the Trinity "does not turn on [Jesus Christ]," but on "God as 'Spirit' and therefore as 'Life'" (Heron 1983: 161, 144). It is true that Tillich's pneumatology is in some ways a culmination of his whole system, and that the Spiritual Presence is central to his aim of constructing a theology of culture, because it justifies his concept of correlation. In Tillich's system, the Spiritual Presence provides or is the vital connection between the ground of being and the revelation in Jesus Christ, between divine essence and human existence, between the Christian message and the human situation, between *kerygma* and *apologia* (see Tillich 1951: 3–8). Taylor quotes Tillich as suggesting (perhaps wishfully) in 1963 that the concept of the divine Spirit could reconcile his theology, which starts with man, with the theology of Barth, which approaches man "from the outside" (Taylor 1972: 6).

As Jürgen Moltmann explains, the reaction of Barth and other dialectical theologians against liberal optimism and self-righteousness meant that for much of the twentieth century, Protestant pneumatology was caught in the perceived dichotomy between the Divine Spirit and the human spirit, the transcendence of the Spirit and the Spirit's immanence (Moltmann 1992: 5–8), usually indicated by preference for the terms "Holy Spirit," or simply "spirit" (with a small "s" or a capital "S"), respectively. Tillich tried to overcome this divide by connecting the Spirit with life as well as revelation. As we have seen in Barth and Tillich, the question of the scope and nature of the Holy Spirit's presence or activity in the world has implications across the whole range of theological thought; it also lies within an uncomfortable theological borderland between what is regarded as conservative and what is liberal.

In the Roman Catholic Church, Karl Rahner endeavored to bridge the gap between neo-scholasticism and modernizing movements in Catholic theology, and in so doing opened up possibilities for the development of pneumatology. Like Barth, he insisted on the realism of theological thought, but like Tillich, he found that the concept of the human spirit was necessary for understanding the divine Spirit (Di Noia 1997: 121; Heron 1983: 144). Rahner's theology, which has a highly developed theology of the Spirit, was to be extremely influential in the Second Vatican Council (1962–65), and at the same time he challenged the Council to be open to the Spirit, which "can never find adequate expression simply in the forms of what we call the Church's official life, her principles, sacramental system and teaching" (Rahner 1971: 75). Though Yves Congar is usually credited with re-founding Catholic pneumatology on the basis of the Council documents (Congar 1983), he focused on the Spirit in the church and in the heart, whereas Rahner's pneumatology could be said to be more ground-breaking in its clear orientation toward the world beyond the church.

Rahner adopted a "transcendental" method of theological investigation, for which the soul's experience in prayer was paradigmatic (Di Noia 1997: 119). He began his theology from human experience, rather than the natural order, and proposed the "supernatural existential"; that is, he saw human openness to the divine as evidence of God's historical calling of "man" to himself in Christ. In other words, human beings are naturally oriented toward the divine because they are created in readiness to receive God's self-communication (Rahner 1968 [1939]: xliv). His first significant book was entitled *Spirit in the World*, where "spirit" did not refer to the Holy Spirit but defined "man." Rahner distinguished the human spirit, which is directed toward God, from the Holy Spirit that can enable human transformation by divine grace. Conversely, the transcendental revelation alone cannot reveal the inner reality of God, which needs to be discovered through experience and is always greater than the human mind can comprehend: "In order to be able to hear whether God speaks, we must know that He is; lest His word come to one who already knows, He must be hidden from us." Thus Rahner describes the human person, as spirit, as "the mid-point suspended between the world and God" (1968 [1939]: 406–408).

In this way, "spirit" indicated the continuity that Rahner sought to affirm between nature and grace, or the supernatural. The same motive lay behind his famous assertion of the identity of the immanent Trinity and the economic Trinity (see, for example, 1975b: 1766); in other words, that the trinitarian relationship in the Godhead and the joint engagement of the three persons in bringing about salvation are one and the same. His intention was to stress the relevance to human life of the doctrine of the mystery of the triune God. Rahner found this mystery had been obscured and reduced to the baptismal formula, ever since Augustine's insistence on the unity of all three persons in bringing about salvation, as well as his "psychological" explanation of God as Trinity. Rahner grounded the doctrine of the Trinity in the biblical testimony to, and the human experience of, the missions of the Son and the Spirit: "without being identical, they form together the one divine self-communication" (1975a: 1761).

Rahner agrees with Augustine in characterizing the mission of *Pneuma* as love, in the New Testament sense of *agape*, and that of *Logos* as knowledge, in the sense of lived truth or fidelity. However, he broke with dominant Catholic thinking since the Council of Trent in interpreting grace as the action of the Spirit of God in history to bring about the divinization of the world, which is experienced by man as spirit (Rahner 1975a: 1760; Comblin 1989: 16–17). Rahner's genius was to connect Spirit with spirit, bringing together the theology of the Magisterium with the spirituality cultivated in the religious orders, and describing the experience of the Spirit as the source of theology. So he stressed the charismatic nature of the church, urging the hierarchy to recognize and use the gifts of the members. His pneumatology encouraged openness to other Christians in ecumenism and also toward believers in other faiths, whom he famously or infamously described as "anonymous Christians," when they respond to the self-communication of God in the Spirit (cf. Kärkkäinen 2002: 111–117). Rahner directly contradicted Augustine when he insisted on the possibility of salvation for all, on the grounds that "the world is drawn to its spiritual fulfillment by the Spirit of God, who directs the whole history of the world in all its length and breadth towards its proper goal"; though he continued to claim that the actuality of salvation "comes entirely through Jesus Christ," and therefore, he reasoned, looks for its fulfillment to the church (in the Catholic tradition) (1979: 200, 204). Rahner's inclusivism has been justly criticized as patronizing to those of other faiths, but at the same time it laid foundations for Catholic initiatives in interfaith dialogue on the grounds of the universal activity of the Spirit beyond the boundaries of the church. It is also true that, though he did not mean to confuse the human spirit with the Holy Spirit, there was a certain hybridization in Rahner's thought between the spirit of modernity and the Spirit of God (Welker 1994: 260).

Heron helpfully compares the pneumatologies of Barth and Rahner graphically: "Rahner works 'up' and 'in' from 'spirit in the world' to God's concrete revelation in the world in Jesus Christ," whereas "Barth travels 'out' in the light of that revelation and traces a movement 'down' in the Spirit, by which man is constituted as body and soul." For Rahner "man" is spirit, but for Barth "man" receives spirit. Whereas Barth's position makes clear that spirit signifies a relationship, not just an orientation, his emphasis on the initiative of God in the relationship tends to deny what Rahner emphasizes, which is the human response (Heron 1983: 143–44). The theologies of Barth, Tillich and Rahner are not arbitrary; each developed in dialogue with the dominant voices of their particular contexts. They have a great deal in common: they all see the Spirit as coming in some sense from "outside" and all reject pantheistic understandings. They all see the mission of the Spirit as integrally related to the mission of Jesus Christ, but whereas in Barth the one appears entirely dependent on the other, both Tillich and Rahner draw attention to the freedom of Spirit. This means they have an openness to cultures and religions that Barth's theology lacks; on the other hand, Barth has an incisive critique of cultures. In their differences the three are perhaps best seen as complementary. For Barth, the Spirit is the one who brings about confession that Christ is Lord; for Tillich the Spirit is evidenced in the creative fruits of human culture, and for Rahner in the charismatic gifts in the community. Their visions of the mission of the Spirit could be characterized as "above," "beneath," and "between": Barth emphasizes the sending of the Spirit from on high in revelation, Tillich the presence of the Spirit in the spirit-dimension of life, and Rahner the mediating role of the Spirit connecting human experience and God's self-communication.

The Spirit in Ministry and Mission

Despite the inspiration that these theologians have provided for theology of mission by their discussion of the relation of the Spirit to the world, we can agree with Berkhof that all three theologies in themselves lack a sense of the dynamic movement of the Spirit in the world. In Barth, the Spirit is confined to explicitly Christian confession; in Tillich, the emphasis is on presence in the world rather than movement; and Rahner is concerned with the Spirit's role of drawing the world into the church rather than the sending of the Spirit into the world. All three theologians reflect the concerns of settled ministry in an established church, rather than the mission context of Allen, Boer, Bosch, Newbigin, Taylor and *Redemptoris missio*. Though they are not limited to this, their theologies center on the contemporary appropriation in the church of the historic Christ-event, rather than on the ongoing encounter with Christ in the wider world. Because of this theological tendency, Western development of mission pneumatology has largely taken place on the edges of the church, and has not been integrated into systematic or dogmatic theology. The Spirit of mission has been separated from the Spirit of ministry, and an integrated understanding of the mission and ministry of the One Spirit has not yet been developed. In the next chapter we turn our attention to the East to consider how the Orthodox churches have related the Spirit to the world.

CHAPTER 4

The Mission of the Spirit: Unity, Creation, History

The Trinity, the Spirit, and the Eastern Orthodox Churches

The crowds in Jerusalem on the occasion of Pentecost (Acts 2:5, 9–11) came not only from points west of Jerusalem, but from all directions—east, north and south as well, indicating the spread of Christianity in the first centuries into Asia and Africa as well as Europe. Centers of the faith were established in the early period in Jerusalem, Antioch, Alexandria, Constantinople and Rome. The Patriarch of Rome was given primacy by the other patriarchs in the sense that he was first among equals. For the first four centuries, the five patriarchs and other representatives of the worldwide church (including from an early period the archbishops of Cyprus and Sinai) met in several ecumenical councils, where they developed together statements of belief, or creeds, that have come to be seen as classical expressions of Christian faith. However, though they continued meeting until the eighth century, the churches in the eastern part of the Greco-Roman Empire and beyond were gradually becoming estranged from those in the West, as a result of the separate development of Latin and Greek cultures. A major indication of this estrangement was that the tripartite statement of belief in the Father, Son and Holy Spirit formulated at the Councils of Nicea and Constantinople (CE 325 and 381) was given a central place in Eastern Christianity and became definitive of orthodoxy, whereas the Roman Church did not incorporate it into the celebration of the mass until CE 1014, preferring to use the Apostles' Creed and the Athanasian Creed (see Vischer 1981c: 4–5).

As the church in the East continued to spread geographically and diversify culturally, it became increasingly difficult to maintain common formulations of doctrine and practice among the Orthodox churches. At the Council of Ephesus (CE 431), the Persian or East Syrian (also known as Nestorian) churches, which later spread into India and China, could not agree with Greek formulations of the relationship between the human and divine natures of Christ. Further disagreement on this issue at the council of Chalcedon (451) led to the separate development of the monophysite churches in Africa (Egypt and Ethiopia), (West) Syria, and later of Syrian Christians in India. Through the mission activity of the Orthodox churches that developed from the Greek tradition of the Byzantine Empire, self-governing national churches arose in Russia, Greece, Romania, Georgia and Bulgaria (see Burgess 1989: 1–19; Vischer 1981c: 3–10). The Orthodox churches thus comprise Eastern Orthodox (Chalcedonian) and Oriental Orthodox (non-Chalcedonian) churches, but these have more in common with one another than they have with either the Roman Catholic Church or with the Protestant churches that arose out of it, even though the Western representatives were in agreement at Chalcedon.

The Spirit in East-West Relations: Life or Love?

The patriarchs of Rome—or popes—increasingly tended to assign themselves universal jurisdiction and act unilaterally, until eventually in CE 1054 the Latin and Greek churches excommunicated each other. The major theological point of difference was about the relation of the persons of the Triune God, and in particular the unilateral addition by the West of the phrase "and the Son," or *filioque*, to the Nicene-Constantinopolitan Creed in 589. The section of the creed in question refers to the relationship of the Spirit, the Third Person of the Trinity, to the Father, the First Person, which is expressed in terms of procession. The original formulation, which is still used in the East, is worded simply: "[the Spirit] proceeds from the Father." But in the West this section of the creed reads "[the Spirit] proceeds from the Father and the Son" (for the texts see World Council of Churches 1991a: 10–12). The longer version was formulated out of Western concern to make clear the interrelatedness of the Spirit and the Son, which is not otherwise stated in the creed (Vischer 1981c: 11). However, it can give the impression that the source of divinity is not the Father alone, and suggest the dependence of the Spirit on the Son. Over the centuries, theologians of the Orthodox churches have repeatedly accused the Western churches of neglecting pneumatology, and Western theology of subordinating the Spirit to Christ. Whether *filioque* is a reason or a symptom, there is a significant difference between Eastern and Western understandings of the Godhead.

There are two main distinctions to be drawn between Eastern and Western approaches to the Trinity. First, Western trinitarian doctrine, as developed by Augustine and the Scholastics, aimed to solve metaphysical questions about the nature of God in God's self, *ad intra*. Eastern concern, on the other hand, has been mainly with explaining the way in which the members of the Trinity work together *ad extra* to bring about the salvation of the world. Heron remarks that Western medieval thought interiorized the Spirit as the inner love of the Trinity, whereas in the East the emphasis was on the Spirit as life breathed out to the world (Heron 1983: 87–88). Second—and as a consequence of the first distinction—whereas Western thought stressed the unity of the Godhead—the three-in-one—Orthodox thought paid greater attention to the distinctions between each "hypostasis," or "person," of the Trinity. Augustine, in the West, made little distinction between the inner triangular relations of God (the immanent Trinity) and the way God acts in the world as Trinity (the economic Trinity) because he saw both as a unity. On the other hand, Athanasius and the Cappadocians in the East stressed that believers cannot know God's substance—they can only participate in God's energies—and therefore they concentrated on the unique roles played by Father, Son and the Spirit in bringing about divinization (Ritschl 1981: 54–61). At the same time, Orthodox theology balances its distinctions between the persons of the Trinity with an emphasis on their reciprocal being in each other, which is referred to as *perichoresis* or circumincession; that is, "no member of the Triune God functions without the involvement of the other Two" (Burgess 1989: 1–2). The Father is the origin and cause; the Son is generated by the Father and the Spirit proceeds from the Father, as two distinct movements. Thus each gift of God is *from* the Father, *through* the Son, *in* the Holy Spirit (Keshishian 1992: 41–42).

Augustine sought to use the Trinity to defend the divinity of Christ against the Arians, who rejected this doctrine. In so doing, he and his successors in the West emphasized the Father-Son unity and tended to describe the Spirit as what unites them, "the bond of love." Irenaeus, on the other hand, was responding to Gnostics, whose negative view of the world led them to deny that it was created by the Father of Jesus Christ; thus he stressed that God is both Redeemer and Creator through the Son and Spirit, and encouraged the association of the Spirit with life. Irenaeus' description of the Son and Spirit as the "two hands" of the Father became the basis for Orthodox theology of the Trinity (Ritschl 1981: 54–61). Awareness of these twin dimensions of God's work—the "double economy" of Son and Spirit—has allowed Eastern theology to develop both christology and pneumatology as distinct disciplines or perspectives in theology, while stressing their necessary interconnectedness, whereas Western theologians have preferred to develop doctrines of Father and Son and discuss their relationship under the heading of Trinity. Thus West and East have designated the Spirit "love" and "life," respectively.

After many centuries of isolation from one another, Orthodox leaders entered into discussions with Western churches, beginning in the late nineteenth century with Anglicans, and actively supported movements toward church unity. It was the Ecumenical Patriarchate in Constantinople in 1920 who first suggested a "League of Churches," and Greek-speaking churches joined the World Council of Churches at the first assembly in 1948. As a result of Orthodox criticism of what they saw as a one-sided emphasis on

christology and neglect of pneumatology in the West, which they felt
reflected a weakness in trinitarian foundation, the Council added the words,
"to the glory of the one God, Father, Son and Holy Spirit" to its confession
of faith in 1961. The Moscow Patriarchate joined the Council that year, and
other Orthodox churches (both Eastern and Oriental) joined in succeeding
years (see Sabev 1982; Special Commission on Orthodox Participation in
the WCC 1999).

One of the most vocal critics of Western "Christomonism" was the
Russian theologian Vladimir Lossky, who argued that the theological differences between East and West were rooted in the creedal belief in the
Spirit's procession from the Son (1957: 56). The suggestion of Lossky and
others was that the one-sided nature of Western theology should be coun-
terbalanced by the development of pneumatology, and that the Orthodox
should contribute their pneumatology to ecumenical discussions (Zizioulas
1985: 124–26). This they did to an extent that was almost "pneumato-
monistic." Since the *filioque* was the main doctrinal point of contention, the
commission on Faith and Order of the World Council of Churches spon-
sored two conferences in 1978 and 1979 to discuss it. The 1979 memorandum that resulted from the East-West dialogue on the *filioque* clause
concluded that all churches should revert to the original form of the creed
without *filioque*, and that further ecumenical attention should be given to
the problem the Western church tried to solve by adding the *filioque* in the
first place: the relation between the Son and Spirit (Vischer 1981b: vi). In
other words, more work was needed to better understand the person and
work of the Holy Spirit, "as the one who in his fullness both rests upon
Jesus Christ and is the gift of Christ to the Church" (Memorandum 1979:
18). As Heron points out, this effort was not to detract from christology,
but was for the sake of a properly christological understanding: pneumatology is needed in order for christology to be truly *christ*ology, the doctrine
of Jesus as the Christ, meaning the one anointed with the Spirit. One-sided
emphasis on Pentecost in the theology of the Spirit needs to be balanced by
attention to Jesus' baptism (1983: 126–27). So the memorandum emphasized that the relation between the Spirit and Jesus Christ "is not described
solely in a linear or one-directional fashion" of the Son sending the Spirit,
but that it is one of "mutuality and reciprocity" (see Memorandum 1979:
17, 18).

To appreciate the Orthodox mission theology of the Holy Spirit better,
we will first look at some Orthodox perspectives on mission, as presented
in English by various individuals and groups. In keeping with their theology of unity, on many ecumenical occasions the Orthodox churches have
spoken with one voice; these statements will be given priority, but use of
the collective voice is not intended to suggest uniformity or lack of diversity in the East. The limitations on sources will inevitably introduce some
distortion by emphasizing points at which East and West differ. Next, we

will look at the trinitarian theology of mission articulated in the *missio Dei* paradigm, which met with a large measure of ecumenical agreement, and then at the reasons for Orthodox objections to the dominant theology of the Spirit in creation at the Canberra Assembly (1991). Finally, we will consider how the mission theology of the Spirit articulated by Western systematic theologian Jürgen Moltmann at the time of Canberra is influenced by Orthodox thinking.

The Mission of the Holy Spirit: Life, Eucharist, Witness

In the course of the *filioque* discussions, the Orthodox stressed that their main interest was not inner-trinitarian relations, but the doctrine of the Spirit's "going out" into the world to sanctify it, draw it together in Christ, and present it back to the Father (see, for example, Staniloae 1981: 178–80). Orthodox reflection on the relationship of the Holy Spirit and mission does not begin with the activity of the church and proceed to the Spirit of mission, as modern Western missiology has tended to do. Rather, its starting point is the triune God as confessed in the Nicene-Constantinopolitan Creed. Aram Keshishian, Catholicos (Head) of the Armenian Orthodox Church, introduces the Holy Spirit in his book on Orthodox perspectives on mission by making two general points: first, that because God is not an abstract concept but "a revealed reality," Orthodox theology is concerned with "the fundamental reality of Christian faith," not with speculation. Second, God is revealed to the world as Trinity and acts in the world as Trinity. The work of the Holy Spirit is only one dimension of God's activity, and it is impossible to talk of the Spirit without also discussing the other two persons (1992: 39–40): what happens "in the Spirit" is also "from the Father" and "through the Son" (: 41). In the words of Keshishian, "the Holy Spirit receives his existence from the Father and his mission from the Son." The Holy Spirit is not subordinate or secondary in any sense, because the Spirit is of the same substance as the Father; the two persons are regarded equally, and share all the same divine attributes (: 40).

Keshishian continues that as "co-creator," the Holy Spirit is involved with the Father in all aspects of creation, and "the creation is full of his energies." However, there is a functional order to the Trinity—Father, Son and Spirit—which is reflected in the ancient creeds. Creation is described as "beginning from the Father, advancing through the Son, and completed in the Holy Spirit" (Keshishian 1992: 42). In most Western sources, the Nicene-Constantinopolitan Creed shows four parts, each beginning "We believe in . . ." However, the Greek text (which is determinative for Orthodox theology) divides the creed into only three parts, corresponding to the three persons: Father, Son and Holy Spirit. So the section from "We believe in the Holy Spirit" to the end is one whole:

> We believe in the Holy Spirit,
>   the Lord, the giver of life,
>   who proceeds from the Father.
> Who, with the Father and the Son, is worshipped and
>   glorified,
>   who has spoken through the Prophets.
> We believe in one holy catholic and apostolic Church.
> We (acknowledge) confess one baptism for the forgiveness
>   of sins.
> We look for the resurrection of the dead,
>   and the life of the (world) age to come.
>   (WCC 1991a: 12, cf. 11)

Orthodox pneumatology may be seen as an exposition of this text, in which the Spirit is characterized as the giver of life (cf. Gen 1:1; 2:7). For the Orthodox, therefore, the mission of the Spirit is life-giving, or the renewing of creation.

The creed has the whole universe in view, and all of time, so Orthodox thinking about mission and the Holy Spirit begins in cosmic terms. The life of the Spirit is not only widespread in creation but also eternal, being described in the creed as "the life of the age (or world) to come" and connected with "the resurrection of the dead." Orthodox theology of creation is an emphatic rejection of pantheism, which is the view—common in the East—that the world is an emanation of God or is God. As Greek Orthodox theologian Nikos Matsoukas explains, the world is created by God from non-being and must be distinguished from God, who is uncreated and who creates. However, the creation participates in the uncreated energies of God the Holy Spirit; therefore it exists and is capable of being perfected. Nothing exists between creation and God because God and creation—heaven and earth—are organically united. This unity is manifested in Orthodox theology, sacraments, art, icons and liturgy, which are a spiritual expression—and also an anticipation in the Spirit—of the world to come (1989: 399–400; Ware 1993: 240).

In Orthodox theology, the life of creation and re-creation is one; creation is not one act but an ongoing, dynamic activity of the triune God (Keshishian 1992: 42, 46; Matsoukas 1989: 403–404). The specific role of the Spirit in creation is the perfection, or sanctification, of humanity and the whole created world: "the Father ordains, the Son accomplishes, the Spirit sanctifies"; hence the Spirit is "Holy" (Keshishian 1992: 44–45). Sanctification begins when the energies of the Spirit purify the human soul by baptism—a personal Pentecost—and this outpouring extends to the whole creation, which is cleansed by it. Through the descent of the Spirit, the original relationship between God, humanity and creation is restored—a process known as *theosis*, or "deification," or "divinization." This does not imply that humans ever share in the divine essence, but that we partake of the divine life (: 45, 47). All creation is good, but it runs the risk of being perverted or annihilated, unless it is constantly perfected by the energies of God (Matsoukas 1989: 403). Sanctification also liberates from death and the dominance of Satan, so the freedom of human beings and creation are bound up together (Rom 8:22) (Keshishian 1992: 44, 47). In Orthodox understanding, therefore, mission is a participation in the Spirit with the energies of God—a synergy or working together (cf. 2 Cor 4:7)—and it is also the process of our salvation. Being reconciled with God and nature, human beings become co-workers with the Spirit toward the reconciliation of the whole creation (Matsoukas 1989: 403–404; Bria 1986: 7).

Keshishian and other Orthodox theologians strongly emphasize that the Spirit is inseparable from the Son in God's redemptive work. The purpose of the incarnation was also to bring about *theosis:* God became man, so that man might become God (2 Cor 8:9; Jn 18:22–23; 1:51) (Keshishian 1992: 41–42, 44–47). Both Son and Spirit are sent into the world, where they act differently—but not independently—in a "double economy." The "double economy" of Son and Spirit is rooted in the Father: the Son reveals the intention of the Father and the Spirit accomplishes it. Jesus' ministry and sacrifice is "in the Spirit," and so is the life of the church. "The Holy Spirit actualizes and establishes the reality of the presence of Christ as the incarnate word of God," and the Spirit leads to the Son, and through the Son to the Father. So Keshishian describes the Holy Spirit as "the icon of the Son" (: 43–44). Likewise, since the body of Christ and the Spirit of Christ are inseparable (Clapsis 1989: 340; cf. Eph 4:4–5), there is no sense in Orthodox theology that the Spirit works in creation independently of the church of Jesus Christ. So Keshishian concludes his chapter on the theology of the Holy Spirit by linking the Spirit and the church, as the creed also does. The church is "in the Spirit"; it is "the permanent *epiklesis*" or "coming down" of the Holy Spirit; it is the continuation of Pentecost (1992: 47–49). So it is through the church, the body of Christ, that the Spirit gives life to the whole creation. It is axiomatic for Orthodoxy that the life of the Holy Spirit is experienced through the sacraments and spiritual gifts in the life of the church, and even the mystics of Orthodox worship have been accommodated within the church (Burgess 1989: 3–5).

In his classic introduction to the Orthodox church, Timothy Ware (Kallistos Ware) points out that the word "orthodoxy" means both "right doctrine" and also "right glory" (or "right worship"), and that these meanings are inseparable. So, Orthodox theology is primarily expressed in the worship of the church, which is giving glory to God. Worship is principally expressed through the liturgy ("work of the people") of the eucharist, which has been the strength of the faithful through times of oppression. Ware further characterizes Orthodox worship as "heaven on earth." The liturgy performed on earth is one with the liturgy of heaven, and represents a coming together of the two worlds, or states of being. In the celebration of the eucharist, God is present among humans and the earth is represented in heaven (1993: 264–67). Therefore, the church is trinitarian, christological and pneumatological: "the Church as a whole is an icon of God the Trinity, reproducing on earth the mystery of unity in diversity" (: 240); the church is also the body of Christ, uniting the spiritual and material, the mystical and the earthly; and the church is the fullness of the Spirit, a continued Pentecost. Ware quotes Irenaeus: "where the Church is, there is the Spirit, and where the Spirit is, there is the Church" (: 239–43).

"The liturgy after the liturgy" was the phrase Romanian Orthodox theologian Ion Bria used in his presentation of the mission typology that emerged from Orthodox deliberations on their own understanding of mission, which took place in the 1970s and '80s (1996: 1). The phrase "the liturgy after the liturgy" reflects the view that the dynamics of the liturgy "go beyond the boundaries of the eucharistic assembly to serve the community at large" (: 20). That is, there is an intimate connection between eucharist and mission (see Vassiliadis 1998). The word "eucharist" originally meant "thanksgiving," and has come to mean "offering" or "sacrifice." So the eucharist may be seen as a missionary event, the worship or sacrifice of lives (Rom 12:1). This relationship may be expressed pneumatologically in two dimensions or movements. First, there are the gathering of the people and the offering of the (elements of) creation in the Holy Spirit. It is the Spirit who purifies what is lifted up, and makes it acceptable to God. And second, there is the invoking of the Holy Spirit in the church for the transformation of the world. The eucharist can only be effective by invoking the power of the Holy Spirit through prayer (the *epiklesis*), which is made for the community, and not just for the elements (Bria 1996: 6). Therefore, through the *epiklesis*—"the supreme moment in the Orthodox liturgy"—the Holy Spirit descends on the church, renewing the congregation and through the church the whole creation (Keshishian 1992: 48–49). In this way Orthodoxy is able to hold together theology, mission and spirituality.

In the liturgy, the history of salvation is remembered by pointing back to the incarnation, and forward to the second coming (Bria 1996: 9). Through the Holy Spirit's action, the memorial becomes a living reality (1986: 28). The creed confesses that the Holy Spirit has spoken through the prophets; in other words, the Spirit in the church today is the same Spirit that inspired the Hebrew prophets and the prophets of the early church, as recorded in the Scriptures. However, the role of the Spirit in inspiration is not much discussed in Orthodox missiology, perhaps because of a wish to move ecumenical discussion away from mission as proclamation. In keeping with this theology of the Spirit as creator and sustainer, the direction of Orthodox mission history has been more toward collaborative working than prophetic challenge. Bria emphasizes that the Spirit descended at Pentecost as a divine person, not an impersonal force (1996: 86). The living Spirit of God creates relationship and fellowship, and the eucharist creates, nurtures and sustains this. So the eucharistic community is known as the fellowship or *koinonia* of the Holy Spirit (2 Cor 13:13), and to be part of the church is to be "in the Spirit." The Spirit sends gifts, which are gifts of service (*diakonia*) for the enrichment of the church's life and witness (1 Cor 12:4–7; Keshishian 1992: 48). In the fellowship of the Spirit, Christians are guided by the Spirit in their lives (Gal 5:25), and grow in understanding of "all truth," that is, what Jesus did for salvation. Though it is believed that the Spirit helps believers to discover their own personality within communion with God, Orthodox spirituality does not encourage individualistic approaches or privatized religion. True fellowship is needed to regulate personal spirituality (Bria 1996: 7–9; cf. Bria 1986: 7).

In Orthodox thought, "the 'sending' of mission is essentially the sending of the Spirit (Jn 14:26), who manifests precisely the life of God as communion (2 Cor 13:13)." In light of this, "mission does not aim primarily at the propagation or transmission of intellectual convictions, doctrines, moral commands, etc., but at the transmission of the life of communion that exists in God" (Bria 1986: 3). Orthodox theologians have preferred to use the concept of *martyria*, or witness, to describe this concept, rather than the word "mission," which may be associated in Orthodox minds with Western political programs of expansion, often at the expense of Orthodox lands (Bria 1980: 3; Anastasios of Androussa 1989: 63). As mentioned earlier, the Orthodox world expanded eastward in the first millennium. Some Orthodox churches have also spread the gospel far from their homelands, for example in the sending of Cyril and Methodius to the Slavs in the ninth century and the Russian missions to Japan in the nineteenth century (for details, see Stamoolis 1986). However, bitter experience has led Orthodox church leaders to condemn proselytizing movements. As a response to Orthodox feeling, in 1956 a World Council of Churches special commission condemned proselytism as a "corruption of Christian witness" in which "cajolery, bribery, undue pressure, or intimidation is used—subtly or openly —to bring about seeming conversion" (World Council of Churches 1956: 48, 52). The historical experience of the churches of the East has led them to place more emphasis on maintaining the local witness of self-governing national churches than on creating a universal church "at a geographical level"; on manifesting the kingdom rather than annexing new territory (cf. Jn 1:39); and on the missionary as saint rather than preacher (cf. 1 Thess 1:8). Local churches have been deeply inculturated in the life of the common people, and identified with ethnic and national concerns. In order to bear faithful local witness in unfavorable historical conditions, the Orthodox churches have focused on liturgical ritual, the unity of the church, personal renewal and sharing suffering (Bria 1980: 4–8). On the whole, theirs is an "unhurried mission, without fanaticism and without proselytism at the expense of other religions and among ourselves" (Parthenios 1991: 28–37, 35). Orthodox understanding of the mission of the Spirit tends to be reconciliatory rather than confrontational.

There is strong biblical ground for understanding mission as "witness." According to Luke, the Spirit was sent as "power from on high" that made the disciples witnesses (Lk 24:29; Acts 1:8), and witness becomes the main way of describing mission in the book of Acts. So in the interpretation of mission as witness, the Spirit is the primary witness. Summarizing Orthodox perspectives, Bria writes that in Orthodox theology:

> The Spirit plays such an important role in Christian witness that he too can be said to be the witness of Christ in the world: "The Spirit of truth himself who comes from the Father will bear witness to me" (Jn 15:26). For it is in the Spirit that God raises Christ (Rom 8:11); it is in the Spirit that he glorifies him (Jn 16:14–15); it is the Spirit who convicts the world in the trial which brings it into contradiction with Jesus (Jn 16:8). The Spirit bears this witness by means of the church. He makes the church the body (1 Cor 12:13) and thus the manifestation of Christ in this world. The Spirit is communion (2 Cor 13:13) so he unites us to Christ; and in the same movement, brings about communion among men and women.
>
> The Spirit comes upon the faithful and makes them also witnesses of Christ (Acts 1:8). In him the word and action of Christians becomes "a demonstration of spirit and power" (1 Cor 2:4). We must encounter Christ to be his witnesses, to be able to say what we know about him (cf. 1 Jn 1:3–4; 4:14). It is the Holy Spirit who enables the faithful to meet Christ, to experience him. Believers are led to witness to their faith before humankind, because the Spirit witnesses to Jesus in their hearts (Jn 15:16–17; Rom 8:16; Gal 4:6). In the debate between Jesus and the world, he takes the part of Jesus in strengthening believers in their faith (Jn 16:8; cf. 1 Jn 5:6), but he also deepens the faith of believers by leading them to the whole truth (Jn 16:13). He is thus the master of Christian witness enabling us to say "Jesus is Lord" (1 Cor 12:3), he is the inspiration and teacher of the church (Jn 16:13) (Bria 1986: 96–97).

Orthodox interest in the mission of the Spirit challenged Western mission pneumatology, which tended to focus on the role of the Spirit in the church's mission (the Spirit of mission). It stimulated Western pneumatology to develop beyond the "Spirit-in-the-church-and-in-the-heart" model, toward an interest in the Spirit's presence and activity in the world—a mission pneumatology (cf. Bria 1986: 6). During the *filioque* discussions, Dumitru Staniloae observed the lack of interest in Western theology "in the sending of the Spirit into the world, as uncreated energy." He related this to a difference in doctrines of redemption between East and West: in Catholic theology, he remarked, the Spirit produces a created grace in human beings while remaining on a transcendent level, whereas in Orthodox theology the Spirit, "by his (uncreated) energies . . . , himself as a Person come(s) down into the level of human existence, raising man to the divine level, making him Spirit-bearing and deifying him" (1981: 178–79). Thus the Eastern doctrine of *theosis*, of God's involvement with creation through the Spirit, is seen to be a crucial difference between East and West. The affirmation of creation implied in *theosis* was the main Orthodox contribution to Canberra, as expressed in the theme, "Come, Holy Spirit, renew the whole creation" (Orthodox reflections 1990: 88).

However, Staniloae hastens to add, "The Spirit does not go beyond the Son." It is only the recognition of the interpenetration of the missions of Son and Spirit that, in Staniloae's words, "safeguards us from a theological rationalism on the one side and a purely sentimental enthusiasm on the other" (Staniloae 1981: 178–82). Furthermore, though "God has not left himself without a witness" anywhere (Acts 14:17), this interpenetration of the missions of Son and Spirit is chiefly expressed in the church. Reflecting on the Canberra theme, Orthodox leaders declared: "Without limiting the Spirit to the institutional church, we have always to remember that the destiny of the whole creation somehow passes through the church, where the world finds its true meaning and salvation" (Orthodox reflections 1990: 88–89). In other words, in Orthodox missiology, the life of the church is the primary witness of the Spirit to the world, and is crucial for the whole creation.

In the Creed, the church, which witnesses to Jesus Christ, is described as "one, holy, catholic, and apostolic." Each of these characteristics is related, in Orthodox thought, to the work of the Spirit. We have already discussed the Spirit's role in bringing about holiness, or sanctification. The church is also a unity in Christ, by the Spirit. The fellowship of the Spirit that characterizes the local church fulfills the prayer of Christ "that they may be one, even as we are one" (Jn 17:11) (Bria 1986: 69–70). In ecumenical discussions the Orthodox have repeatedly reminded the churches that "the division of Christians is a scandal and an impediment to the united witness of the church." In other words, it hinders the Spirit's work of transformation in the world (: 70–71). So the Orthodox churches have pressed for unity, not for pragmatic reasons, but to pursue the goal: "the communion of the Holy Spirit, heaven on earth" (: 17). It is unthinkable in terms of Orthodox theology that unity in Christ should not be expressed in a tangible way on earth, or that this unity means anything other than incorporation into the tradition of Christ and the apostles, of which the Orthodox believe themselves to be the heirs (: 70–71). Christian unity began at Pentecost, is celebrated in the eucharist, and "is to be consummated and manifested when Christ appears in glory." Furthermore, it is only achievable "in Christ, by the Spirit, with the triune God" (: 69–70). The model for Christian unity is the Trinity (cf. Jn 17:11); that is, diversity in unity or unity in diversity. This is what is described as the catholicity of the church, which is inspired by the Spirit. Catholicity, writes Bria, "is not to be confused with geographical expansion and universality" (: 12), but is expressed in fullness of the Spirit in each local church, as evidenced by the use of different languages (Acts 2:1–9), the admission of all races (Acts 10:34–35), and positive regard for local cultures (1 Cor 9:20–23) (: 15–16.). The church's apostolicity is also due to the Spirit, who empowers the church to proclaim the kingdom of God to the world, and guarantees the coming kingdom (: 10). Thus, as a result of the gift of the Spirit, the church is not merely the instrument of mission, but mission belongs to the very nature of the church, in all its aspects. The church's apostolocity is inseparable from its unity, holiness and catholicity (: 11–12). In all these respects the church witnesses, in the power of the Spirit, to one God, who is Father, Son, and Holy Spirit. God is glorified through the healing and liberation of creation, beginning in the church, and so, as stated in the creed, the Spirit is worshipped and glorified with the Son and the Father.

Trinitarian Theology of Mission: *Missio Dei*

Western rediscovery of the teaching of the Church Fathers, particularly in the theology of Karl Barth, led to a convergence of thinking between East and West on mission in the mid-twentieth century. This resulted in the classic expression of what came to be known as the *missio Dei* (God's mission) paradigm, drafted at the meeting of the International Missionary Council at Willingen, Germany in 1952. *Missio Dei*, which emerged largely from deliberations of German, Dutch and American groups in the post-war, post-colonial period, has since found widespread acceptance in East and West among most churches and international networks (see Bosch 1991: 390–91). Unlike earlier International Missionary Council statements, this one was explicitly trinitarian in tone. (In keeping with the times it also unashamedly used masculine language for God, in all three persons.) Though it was entitled "A statement of the missionary calling of the Church," it declared that "the missionary movement of which we are a part has its source in the Triune God Himself" (International Missionary Council 1953a: 189).

The sending of the Son by the Father was described as for the purpose of reconciliation, "that we and all men might, through the Spirit, be made one in Him with the Father" (International Missionary Council 1953a: 189). The same conference also produced a statement on the dual calling of the church to "mission and unity" (International Missionary Council 1953b). Though not clearly articulated at Willingen, the missionary nature of the church was implied by the *missio Dei*—because if God is a missionary God,

God's people are missionary people—and it became a central plank of the doctrine (see Bosch 1991: 372). Again, in keeping with Orthodox perception, the "missionary obligation of the church" was summarized as "to be His witness to all men everywhere" (International Missionary Council 1953a: 189). Indeed "the Church's words and works, its whole life of mission, are to be witness to what God has done, is doing, and will do in Christ" (: 191). The trinitarian foundation is again evident when the mission of God is recognized in two parts, the sending of the Son and the sending of the Spirit (: 189). The mission of the Spirit is described in the following way:

> On the foundation of this accomplished work God has sent forth His Spirit, the Spirit of Jesus, to gather us in one Body in Him, to guide us into all truth, to enable us to worship the Father in spirit and in truth, to empower us for the continuance of His mission as His witnesses and ambassadors, the first fruits and earnest of its completion (: 189).

This section strongly asserts the agency of the Spirit in all aspects of mission within a "post-Pentecost" pneumatology ("on the foundation of this accomplished work"). The Spirit was further recognized as that which empowered the missionary movement and gave it "sure confidence for the final victory of His love" (: 190). The Spirit is described in terms of love, not life, and the statement does not have in view the energies of the Spirit in renewing the whole creation. However, there is a further section that affirms the church's "solidarity with the world." By this, the statement recognizes that the word "witness" cannot possibly mean that "the Church stands over against the world," but that the church, in compassion, identifies with the world (: 191–92). Mission was also described as a process of "discerning the signs of the times" and bearing witness to "the mighty works of the Spirit" in the "great events of our day," which included enlargement of human knowledge and power, political and social movements, and personal experiences (: 192). The *missio Dei* may thus be said to be the movement of the Spirit in the world.

God's action in the world outside the church was discussed at Willingen, but no reference to this was included in the statement, which was emphatically ecclesiocentric (Bosch 1991: 391). Nevertheless, the idea that the Spirit was at work in a way that was independent of the church or independent of the Christ was to surface repeatedly in World Council of Churches deliberations in the years to come. In the secularizing movements of the 1960s led by J. C. Hoekendijk; in the theology of dialogue as it was developed by Stanley Samartha in the 1970s (see chapter 5); and in the eco-theology of the 1980s and '90s, of which Chung Hyun Kyung is a prime example, the Spirit tended to become disconnected from the Son. To some extent, Lossky's work encouraged this interpretation of the Trinity when, in stressing the way that Orthodox theology distinguished all three persons, he treated the Son and the Spirit as having two separate economies rather than sharing one "double economy" (see Lossky 1957: 135–55, 156–73). The suggestion by Lossky and others of a certain "hypostatic independence" implied to some Protestant and Catholic theologians a way of using pneumatology to distinguish the universal work of God in the world from its particularly Christian aspects, thus marginalizing the institutional church or explicit Christian confession in theology, if these proved awkward. Such a distinction was certainly not the intention of Lossky, who called the church "the centre of the universe" (: 178), and it would certainly be contrary to Orthodox tradition to suggest that the Spirit's mission is in any way subversive of the church or Christian community. As mentioned above, the Greek version of the creed does not separate the statements about the Spirit from those about the church that follow from them. And, like the Roman Catholic Church, the Orthodox Church also has a doctrine of *extra Ecclesiam nulla salus*, because "salvation is the Church" (Ware 1993: 247).

John Zizioulas, perhaps the most influential Orthodox theologian today, criticizes Lossky and does not regard setting a distinct "economy of the Holy Spirit" alongside that of the Son as a legitimate interpretation of the tradition. He also disputes the priority given to pneumatology over christology by Lossky and others (including Boris Bobrinskoy). Zizioulas is concerned that Orthodoxy has not yet achieved a proper synthesis between christology and pneumatology. On examination of the biblical and early church tradition, he finds that there is no agreement on which is prior, and concludes that as long as the unity of the two is upheld, the question of priority is not important (1985: 124–29). On the question of the distinctive content of pneumatology and christology, Zizioulas again takes issue with Lossky, who related them to the subjective and the objective, the internal and the external, the personal and the organic aspects of faith respectively (Lossky 1957: 174–95; Zizioulas 1985: 125). Zizioulas outlines the distinctive content of pneumatology: First, only the Son is incarnate—enters history—so the Spirit liberates from history; in other words, christology has an historical character whereas pneumatology is eschatological. Second, pneumatology introduces the corporate dimension to the personality of Christ, and so is associated with communion (*koinonia*), reconciling the one and the many, the local and the global. Finally, pneumatology is concerned with inspiration and sanctification (1985: 129–32).

Applying his synthesis of Son and Spirit to the church, Zizioulas concludes that Christ institutes the church and the Holy Spirit constitutes it (1985: 140). The church does not exist before or without the Spirit. Only if pneumatology is integral to christology can the church be a communion that respects the one and the many, the local and the global, rather than a pyramidal institution. Equally, pneumatology is required for the church to rise above historicism and be opened up to an eschatological perspective.

Tradition, he argues, is not enough to justify any permanent ecclesial institution, which must reflect the kingdom and point beyond history (: 132–40).
In Zizioulas' synthesis, it is the Spirit who brings the cosmic and corporate
dimensions to our understanding of Christ. In other words, the significance
of Christ for all time and space, and the nature of the church as Christ's
body, both depend on pneumatology. It is the Spirit who makes churches
"iconic," offering a foretaste of what is to come, being heaven on earth.
"Pneumatology," he concludes, must "condition the very being of Christ
and the Church," otherwise the Orthodox churches will face the same problems of "clericalism, anti-institutionalism, Pentecostalism, etc." that he sees
afflicting the Western churches (: 139–40). In other words, the people will
discover the Spirit outside the institution. Similarly, Keshishian reminds the
institutional church that it is "only a means, a channel of charismatic life.
Therefore, it is itself exposed to the judgment of the Holy Spirit" (Keshishian
1992: 49).

"Come, Holy Spirit, Renew the Whole Creation": Orthodox Reaction to Canberra

"*Epiklesis* challenges the self-sufficiency of the church and makes it totally
dependent on the grace of God," writes Keshishian (1992: 49). However,
for all their emphasis on the sovereign Spirit, the Orthodox churches do not
give the impression of dependence on the grace of God. Their tendency to
equate the (Orthodox) church with the kingdom of God does not seem to
leave room for expectation and surprise at the Spirit's movement, or for cultural diversity. Their emphasis on holiness means that the energies of the
Spirit seem to be limited in their activity to the narrow channels of the
liturgy of the Orthodox churches and the male priesthood. Furthermore,
their awareness of centuries of tradition lends an air of rigidity to church
organization, which stifles new expressions of spiritual life and heightens
desires to protect geographical territory (however understandable this is in
the light of persecution of Orthodox churches). Orthodox involvement in
the World Council of Churches has not been easy, but the commitment to
unity in the Spirit has been paramount. Parthenios, Patriarch of Alexandria
and All Africa, who was invited to address the opening plenary of the
Canberra Assembly in 1991 on the theme of the Holy Spirit, was prevented
from attending by pastoral duties relating to the Gulf War. This backdrop
of conflict added depth to the reminder in his paper, which was read to the
assembly in his absence, that "This working together for unity on the part
of us all, ancient, more recent and younger churches, takes much love . . ."
especially as "each member has its own history, some going back many centuries, some only just of yesterday" (Parthenios 1991: 35). Parthenios
affirmed that all churches live in the Holy Spirit (: 28), and reminded them

that "we have no right, nor is it an act of love, to restrict [the Holy Spirit's] movement and his breathing" (: 36).

The theme "Come, Holy Spirit, renew the whole creation" for the Canberra Assembly was welcomed warmly by Parthenios and other Orthodox leaders, as it was the first time a World Council of Churches assembly had taken a pneumatological approach (cf. Parthenios 1991: 28). However, it is evident from papers presented before the conference that Orthodox leaders were worried that the agenda of the program on "Justice, Peace, and the Integrity of Creation" would eclipse the work on "Faith and Order," and that the agenda of eco-theology would bypass the church. Before Canberra, Orthodox writers emphasized "the intimate relationship between the church, the body of Christ, and the Spirit of God" (Clapsis 1989: 340; Orthodox reflections 1990: 89). Orthodox theologians reflecting at Crete in 1989 warned against identifying the Holy Spirit with human movements "in an absolute manner." They stressed that there is one aim of the Father, pursued through the Son and in the Spirit working together, expressed in the church, which is to unite the world in Christ (Orthodox reflections 1990: 92).

Chung Hyun Kyung's presentation (see Introduction) and Parthenios' paper were radically different. Emmanuel Clapsis, a Greek Orthodox, summarizes the divergence between the two:

> Patriarch Parthenios began his presentation with doxologies and theological statements on who the Holy Spirit is in relation to the Father and the Son. He then studied the constitutive work of the Holy Spirit in the church and the ecumenical movement and concluded with some ethical exhortations of what the Holy Spirit expects from the people of God. Quite the contrary, Prof. Chung began her presentation by emphasizing what the Holy Spirit does in God's creation, without referring to who the Holy Spirit is in relation to the Father and the Son. There was no explicit trinitarian affirmation in her presentation, and she referred to Christ only once, as "our brother" (Clapsis 1991: 328–29).

This use of the language of pneumatology without reference to "Jesus Christ as the world's Savior" was one of the main issues that antagonized the Eastern and Oriental Orthodox delegates at Canberra, prompting them to issue their "reflections" on the Assembly and to list a number of concerns about the direction the Council was taking (Clapsis 1991: 329). They stated that, for them, the main aim of the World Council of Churches must be the restoration of the unity of the church, not the unity of humanity and creation, although they believed it would contribute to this. In their view, church unity would only be achieved through solving issues of faith and order. They complained of a departure from the Christian basis of the World

Council of Churches, which they saw reflected in the failure to affirm Jesus Christ as the world's Savior in Council documents, and in the neglect of the Christian understandings of "the Trinitarian God"; salvation; the "good news" of the gospel itself; human beings as created in the image and likeness of God; and the church. They expressed disquiet at certain steps in dialogue with people of other faiths that seemed to "change" the biblical faith in God, and called for study to agree on the theological criteria that should define the limits of diversity. More specifically, they reported their "alarm" at some presentations which tended "to affirm with very great ease the presence of the Holy Spirit in many movements and developments without discernment" and to "substitute a 'private' spirit, the spirit of the world, or other spirits for the Holy Spirit." In particular, they found it "impossible to invoke the spirits of 'earth, air, water and sea creatures.'" They also said that they felt misunderstood with regard to their insistence that communion could only be celebrated together when unity on matters of faith and order (such as the ordination of women) had been reached, and asked for a change in the decision-making systems of the Council to allow their voice to be heard; otherwise, they warned, they might have to "review their relations with the World Council of Churches" (Reflections of Orthodox participants 1991).

Reflecting on Canberra, and asking "What does the Spirit say to the churches?," Emmanuel Clapsis tried to hear the "melody" above the "cacophonies" of the assembly (1991: 328), and suggested that it pointed to a way of knowing that "conceives everything as relational subjects whose particularity needs to be discovered and be affirmed in a communion of love" (: 333); only on these grounds could Parthenios and Chung meet and learn from one another (: 329). As a result of the controversy at Canberra, the contentious subject of the Holy Spirit was barely mentioned at the next World Council of Churches assembly at Harare (1998), which was concerned above all to preserve ecumenical unity under the theme "Turn to God—rejoice in hope!" (see Kessler 1999). The extra plenary called at Canberra to address issues raised by Chung's presentation was on "gospel and cultures," and post-Canberra missiological reflections also developed around this issue (see Brown 1991: 302–303; Fitzgerald 1991: 319–20; Clapsis 1991: 332), which became the theme for the next World Council of Churches mission conference at Salvador, Brazil in 1996 (see Duraisingh 1998). The Salvador meeting (1996) did refer to some aspects of the Canberra theme under the heading of "gospel and cultures." Section IA of the Salvador report made the connection with Canberra by "discerning the Spirit at work in all cultures" (World Council of Churches 1998a: 30–34), and the preparatory Bible studies, entitled *Spirit, Gospel and Cultures*, acknowledged that "The Spirit affirms identity, creates community" (World Council of Churches 1995: 10–14). But it was not until the mission conference at Athens in 2005 that the World Council of Churches again invoked

the Holy Spirit in a conference title, and this time the organizing committee played it safe by choosing to focus on healing and reconciliation (see
Epilogue).

The Spirit of Life: A Universal Affirmation?

The German Reformed theologian Jürgen Moltmann was the initiator of
the East-West discussions on the *filioque* in the 1970s, to which he
acknowledged his theological debt (1981a: xv). Furthermore, Moltmann's
is a mission theology, because it "does not merely want to interpret the
world differently. It wants to change it" (Moltmann 1992: 110; see also
Moltmann 2000: 19). It arises from his awareness of the complicity of
German Christianity with Nazism, and from a desire to renew the church
as a messianic movement for others. It is not only influenced by post-war
German experience, biblical reflection, and East-West dialogue, but also,
particularly from 1978 onwards, by interaction with theologians of liberation (Hennecke 2003). Conversely, Moltmann's characteristic emphasis on the penultimate future, "the end in history," rather than on
metaphysical speculation, was an inspiration to theologians in diverse contexts to give hope in contemporary society. As we move from a largely
European discussion, thus far, to theologies of the Spirit in India and
Korea, this is an appropriate point to examine Moltmann's theology of
the Spirit in the world.

Moltmann's first trilogy—*Theology of Hope* (1964), *The Crucified God*
(1974 [1972]) and *The Church in the Power of the Spirit* (1975)—was
strongly christological in approach, but it is a christology that points to the
future. Though his doctrine of God in *Theology of Hope* is not explicitly
trinitarian, "Moltmann's theology cannot do without a doctrine of the
Trinity, since the eschatology which controls it is founded on the cross and
resurrection of Christ and is in process through the work of the Spirit"
(Bauckham 1987: 92). This is revealed in the third volume, where he opens
a dialogue with Orthodox theology, and with new movements of a
Pentecostal variety. Moltmann attempts a creative synthesis of Reformed or
christological theology with Orthodox or pneumatological theology, at least
as far as the church is concerned. He appreciates insights of Orthodoxy on
the doctrine of the Holy Spirit, but is concerned that emphasis on the
breadth and fullness of the Spirit may lead to "pneumatomonism." He
draws parallels, in broad terms, between the emphasis on the kingdom of
God in the synoptic Gospels and the Johannine eschatology of the Spirit,
between the salvation-historical interpretation of "the history of Christ"
and "the history of the Spirit" in the last times (1977: 33–37). In
Moltmann's theology, the messianic history of Christ, which is the work of
the Spirit, cannot bypass the cross. He criticizes Berkhof for neglecting the

"changeover point" of the cross, "when from being the bearer of the Spirit [Jesus] becomes its sender," and praises the papal encyclical *Dominum et vivificantem* (1986) for stressing that before Jesus could send the Spirit he "gave up his spirit" (Jn 19:30). This changeover point is the point at which pneumatology "brings christology and eschatology together" (Moltmann 1992: 69–70). So Moltmann goes on to expound the presence of the Spirit in the church in word and sacrament, and the power of Spirit in ministry to the outside (1977: 198–99). He emphasizes that the Spirit is not to be conceived as within the sacraments and ministries, but rather that these should be understood to lie within the movement of the Spirit toward the future, in which the church participates only as—by the grace of Jesus Christ—it exists in the Spirit (: 289; cf. Bauckham 1987: 118).

From the *filioque* discussions, Moltmann concluded that the phrase "and the Son" was "superfluous" to the Nicene-Constantinopolitan Creed, but at the same time he became aware of the need for further enquiry into the doctrine of the Trinity, and in particular, the need to clarify relations between the Spirit and the Son (1981b: 164–65; 1992: 306), which he himself took up in his next book, *The Trinity and the Kingdom of God* (1981a). Here he is particularly indebted to Orthodox recognition of the history of the Spirit; that is, the Spirit's role as a full person and subject in the Trinity, the breadth and abundance of the Spirit's gifts, and the Spirit's role in glorifying the Father and the Son (cf. Moltmann 1977: 36). However, he resisted the Orthodox emphasis on the Father as sole cause within the Trinity, because he found it militated against differentiating the distinct roles of each person and the different relationships of the Son and Spirit to the Father (1981b: 172). Moltmann develops the particular character of the Spirit, and reorders the Trinity at decisive points in the history of the kingdom to show which of the three persons is the primary actor on each occasion (1981a: passim.). He explains the reciprocity between pneumatological christology and christological pneumatology, brought belatedly to Western theology's attention through the *filioque* discussions, but wishes to focus attention not on the twofold relationship of Christ and the Spirit, but on the threefold relationship of the Trinity (see his comments on the papal encyclical *Dominum et vivificantem*: Moltmann 1992: 59–60, 69–73). He insists that "The unity of God rests in the triunity of the Father and the Son and the Holy Spirit" (1981b: 173).

Unlike Orthodox thought, Moltmann's pneumatology remains wedded to history and eschatology, which were the predominant concerns of his mid-twentieth-century European post-Enlightenment context (cf. Moltmann 1977: 197–98). In connecting the Holy Spirit with progress and the end times, he is deeply influenced by the twelfth-century Italian mystical theologian Joachim of Fiore (also known as Joachim of Flores). He argues that Joachim's theology of the third age of the Spirit has had a profound influence on European theology and the Enlightenment. However, he complains,

Protestantism reduced Joachim's three kingdoms—Father, Son and Spirit—
to two, the kingdom of nature and the kingdom of grace, which in the
Enlightenment became the kingdoms of necessity and of freedom.
Moltmann wishes to restore the eschatological dimension of the kingdom
of the Spirit in Joachim's original schema, which is consummated as the
kingdom of glory. Like Joachim, Moltmann sees world history in terms of
three successive eras but, unlike him, Moltmann argues that in each, God
acts as Trinity. However, Moltmann recognizes Joachim's contribution when
he describes how in each era the persons of the Trinity act together in a different way and in a different order (1981a: 202–209). In *The Trinity and
the Kingdom of God*, he shows how the kingdom of the Father "consists of
the creation of a world open to the future," because the Father who reigns
is the Father of Jesus Christ, and men and women are created in the image
of God in order that one day they may become God's children. The kingdom of the Son "consists of the liberating lordship of the crucified one," in
which people are redeemed from death through his surrender, and brought
into open fellowship with him and with one another in love. The kingdom
of the Spirit "is experienced in the gift conferred on the people liberated by
the Son—the gift of the Holy Spirit's energies," in which the direct presence
of the Holy Spirit indwells the soul, and is experienced in the new community. The kingdom of the Spirit is historical, but it is also the dawn of the
kingdom of glory, to which all three kingdoms are directed, but which is yet
to be consummated (1981a: 209–212). So Moltmann shows that the Spirit
is not limited to applying the work of Christ, as Protestant theology has
tended to suggest. The Spirit is a full person of the Trinity with a particular
contribution to unify and glorify the Father and the Son, and gathers the
whole creation into this trinitarian glorification (: 122–26; cf. Bauckham
1987: 98–99, 118).

The breadth of Moltmann's theology of the Spirit becomes clear in *The
Spirit of Life*, published in German in 1991, the year of the Canberra
Assembly. Its title indicates his indebtedness to Eastern thought, but the
book also interacts with theologies of liberation and with Pentecostal-charismatic perspectives. He begins by dispensing with the antithesis introduced
by Barth and other dialectical theologians between "theology from above"
and "theology from below," which led in the West to the association of the
Spirit with either divine revelation or with personal experience, but not both.
He argues (against Berkhof and Heron) that this is not the main problem
for pneumatology; in fact it is a false alternative, because the Spirit of God
is not revealed unless experienced and the divine Spirit is not experienced
unless revealed (1992: x, 5–8). Furthermore, the tendency in Western theology to view the Holy Spirit solely as the Spirit of redemption, and the
restriction of the fellowship of the Holy Spirit to the church, which he
blames on the influence of Plato and the *filioque*, logically "makes it impossible for the church to communicate its experience of the Spirit to the

world." "This redemptive Spirit," he complains, "is cut off both from bodily life and from the life of nature," and does not offer renewal of creation. He calls Western theology to recognize the continuity between Yahweh's *rūach* and the Spirit of Christ, discovering the "cosmic breadth of the Divine Spirit" (: 8–10). Moltmann broadens the theology of the Spirit by associating the Spirit with life—"not life against the body," but "life that brings the body's liberation and transfiguration"—and by considering the Spirit's role in all dimensions of salvation: liberation, justification, rebirth, sanctification, charismatic power, mystical experience and fellowship (: 98, 81–82). In relating these to the political as well as the personal, the material as well as the spiritual, he attempts to show the "holistic" nature of pneumatology—a point which is captured in the original German subtitle but not in the English, "a universal affirmation" (1992: xiii; see Kärkkäinen 2002: 126). He also demonstrates the ecumenical nature of his pneumatology by his interaction with Latin American liberation theology, the Reformed tradition, pietism, holiness movements, Pentecostalism and mysticism (chapters 5–10 respectively), and his emphasis on the fellowship of the Spirit (chap 11).

Moltmann believes that by the "*epiklesis*, continual invocation of the Spirit, and unconditional openness for the experiences of the Spirit," the church opens itself for the wider operation of the Spirit in the world (1992: 230–31). He defends the thrust of Latin American liberation theology as an example of the joining of historical liberation and eschatological redemption, which he sees as evidence of the Spirit's work (: 109–114, 120–22). He affirms Pentecostal-charismatic experience (: 180–97), and challenges Pentecostals to "personal and political discipleship of Jesus Christ" (: 121). He insists that Reformed and Orthodox ecclesiologies must be reconciled, "for where the Word is, there the Spirit is too—otherwise the Word is not the Word of God; and where the Spirit is, the Spirit shines from the Word and illumines the understanding of faith—otherwise it is not God's Spirit" (: 231). Moltmann summarizes his book in a series of metaphors for the experiences of the Spirit, drawn from biblical reflection and grouped systematically: personal metaphors—lord, mother and judge; formative metaphors—energy, living space and configuration of life or formation; movement metaphors—tempest, fire and love; and mystical metaphors—light, water and fertility (: 269–85). These lead him to define the personhood of God the Holy Spirit as "the loving, self-communicating, out-fanning and outpouring presence of the eternal divine life of the triune God" (: 289).

In *The Spirit of Life*, Moltmann's agenda is to widen the fellowship of the Spirit beyond the historic churches to other denominations and the wider society; the focus is on the world as humanity. In his earlier work, *God in Creation* (1985), he relates the Spirit to the natural world, as the power and life of the whole creation. "Everything that is," writes Moltmann, "exists and lives in the unceasing inflow of the energies and potentialities of the cosmic Spirit and is interrelated to everything else" (: 9, 11). He rejects the narrow Augustinian identification of spirit with consciousness, and instead uses ecological concepts of spirit to interpret Christian doctrine of the Spirit as that which connects God, human beings and nature. He does not see creation as contrary to evolution, or integration as opposed to self-transcendence (: 17–19), so his creation theology considers both space and time, calling for a combination of ecological wisdom with historical awareness (Deane-Drummond 1997: 180). In his dialogue with feminist theologians, Moltmann is prepared to use the feminine pronoun for the Spirit. He describes her as "Mother of life" on the grounds that believers are "born" again from the Holy Spirit (Jn 3: 3–7); the Spirit also "comforts" as a mother comforts (Jn 14:26; Isa 66:13). He even briefly entertains the idea of the Trinity as the "heavenly family" that is found in some ancient depictions (1992: 157–60). However, feminist theologians complain that this willingness to use feminine language does not impact on the rest of Moltmann's theology, because "Moltmann's God suffered as son not as daughter" (Choi 2005: 103–104; cf. Johnson 1992: 234).

A desire to bring Christianity down to earth is evident in Moltmann's thought, throughout which he stresses the bodily nature of the cross and resurrection, the concrete application to society, and the need to overcome the divide between Barthian theology of revelation and natural theology. But the application of pneumatology to the natural environment was new to many Protestants, particularly Reformed theologians, because Protestant theology since the Enlightenment has largely focused on the category of "history" rather than "nature" (Deane-Drummond 1997: 2). Moltmann has many interlocutors, including process theology, ecology, and feminist theology, but the key doctrines he uses are Hebrew and Jewish theology of the shĕkīnâ, or glory of God, and Christian theology of the Trinity, both of which he believes express the tension of God being both separate from and also involved in the world, being transcendent and immanent (1985: 13–16). This book—variously subtitled "Ecological Doctrine of Creation" or "New Theology of Creation and the Spirit of God" (1985; 1993)—made a major contribution to the discussion at the Canberra Assembly, and Moltmann entered into the debate directly through an essay published in a preparatory volume. In "The Scope of Renewal in the Spirit" (1990), which focuses on the ecological crisis, Moltmann claims that the West has to be helped to "rediscover the immanence of the Creator in the creation," and its divine mystery (: 33). He suggests reflection on creation both through the Word of God, which "specifies and differentiates," and through the Spirit of God, which "unites and creates harmony." He points out that Word and Spirit combined are the Wisdom of God (: 34). He claims that "Limiting the church merely to the world of human beings was a dangerous modern constriction," because essentially the church is "cosmically oriented" (: 35). So when creation suffers, the church also suffers, and since it is the Spirit's presence in creation that sustains it, God suffers with creation in the ecological disasters due to human expansion and exploitation (: 35–37). The renewal of creation begins with Christ's resurrection by the Spirit, which is the renewed creation of light (2 Cor 4:6), and anticipates the rebirth of the whole cosmos (: 37–39.). And he concurs with Orthodox belief that it is "in and through this body of Christ, the church, that the Spirit sustains creation," though for the Orthodox this is a function of their worship rather than the direct action which Moltmann urges (: 35; Orthodox reflections 1990: 91).

By adopting an understanding of the Trinity from Orthodox theology that prefers triunity over oneness, Moltmann was able to discuss the Holy Spirit in the whole creation within a theological framework in which the cross and resurrection of Jesus Christ remained central. As a result, Moltmann developed a theology of the Spirit in creation that is holistic and ecumenical, without losing the sense of movement toward the future—the eschatological urgency—that characterized his earlier work. Moltmann's theology is inadequate, from an ecological point of view, in its scientific grounding and vision for earth's reconstruction, but it is helpful in challenging ingrained attitudes to the natural world (Deane-Drummond 1997: 272–76). There is also a contradiction in his approach. While his use of symbols from paganism and other ancient religions, and his ascription of feminine gender to the Spirit, are helpful in making connections with New Age movements and indigenous spiritualities, the description of the Holy Spirit as the personified life-force, or Earth Mother, is not the kind of "cosmic Spirit" that he wishes to portray. He simultaneously distances himself "from all 'spiritualist' and animist notions," because his starting point is "the revelation and experience of 'Holy Spirit' in the church of Christ." What he is describing is not pantheism, or even the more differentiated "panentheism," but Trinity, in which God is seen as both immanent and transcendent (Moltmann 1985: 98–103). If this is the case, then he might do better to stress the difference between the Creator Spirit and the Earth Mother, rather than confuse radically different systems of thought (cf. Deane-Drummond 1997: 276). Despite his reference to the Gaia hypothesis and contemporary cosmology, Moltmann views the universe as an open system, in which "the Spirit preserves and leads living things and their communities beyond themselves" to God, and to "his future" (1985: 103).

Despite his apparent openness to other worldviews, what emerges when his vision is spelled out in political terms is that, rather than accommodate other visions, Moltmann wishes to co-opt individuals into his particular mission of the Spirit, which focuses on the salvation of an earth threatened with destruction, and involves arms limitation, measures to stem destruction of natural resources, population control, and investment in the future (Moltmann 2000: 19–34). Though promoted as "universal" (1992: subtitle), Moltmann's eco-theology is heavily loaded towards European interests, and seeks to ally the church with a European environmental movement.

Geiko Müller-Fahrenholz's book of "applied pneumatology," which follows up the "Justice, Peace, and the Integrity of Creation" program and the Canberra Assembly, and is endorsed by Moltmann, illustrates this point. Written from the perspective of middle-class Germany, though claiming Costa Rican influence, Müller-Fahrenholz suggests "an ethic for the earth" that includes "respectable poverty" (for the rest of the world) and population control (elsewhere) in order to solve global crises (Müller-Fahrenholz 1995: 152–55). Clearly there is a need for cooperative global action to solve environmental problems, but third-world theologians recognize the political implications of such "global master-plans" (cf. Van Butselaar 1992: 363–73). Back in 1973, Nigerian theologian Bolaji Idowu, speaking on "the Spirit of God in the natural world," drew attention to colonial attitudes in which "the natural world" meant "the remainder of the world, when Europe and America have been subtracted from it," and suggested that the newly emerging Western theologies of the Spirit and creation may not be free from colonial motives (Idowu 1974: 9–19). It was apparent at the Canberra Assembly, particularly in the debate on the Gulf War, that there are many interpretations of what constitutes life, not all of which were compatible, and that difficult decisions need to be made as to which life is to be saved.

Though neither he nor other Orthodox writers dwelt on it, Parthenios gently reminded the Canberra Assembly of "another mystery" that is "alive and present everywhere," the reality "of evil, of the devil, Satan, the 'spiritual hosts of wickedness in the heavenly places' (Eph 6:12)" (1991: 33; cf. Clapsis 1989: 344). Chung, on the other hand, focused attention on the struggle between the "culture of life" and the "culture of death," in terms of the oppression of *han*-ridden spirits by spiritual powers and authorities. The biblical material (e.g. 1 Sam 16:14; Ps 51:11) implies that there are areas of the created world from which the Spirit is absent, or at least not present in fullness, or where there are other spirits involved. The chief complaint made by Pentecostal and charismatic theologians about Moltmann's *The Spirit of Life* centered on what they saw as a lack of awareness that there are many spirits, and of the need for discernment of spirits (Stibbe 1994: 13; Kuzmic 1994: 22; Macchia 1994: 27; Chan 1994: 36,40). This is true, for example, of his contribution to the Canberra Assembly, in which Moltmann projected one cosmic Spirit sustaining and renewing the creation from death, but did not use the language of many spirits. His theology of the Spirit is about affirmation rather than discernment. In fact, Moltmann divided the Spirit and the Word, associating the Holy Spirit with creating unity and harmony, and the Word with the more critical work of specifying and differentiating (1990: 31–39). In other words, whereas Pentecostals focus on the "particular" and "transcendent" dimensions of the Spirit, Moltmann emphasizes the "universal" and "immanent" (Lord 2003: 271–87).

In his more recent work, Moltmann interacts to a greater extent than before with people of other faiths, and also returns to a more eschatological focus (Moltmann 2000). In discussing "the holistic mission of the life-giving Spirit," he identifies the life-giving energies of the Holy Spirit with "the powers of the age to come" (Heb 6:5) (: 20). However, this does not mean that mission should be determined by apocalyptic expectation, as he regrets it was in the imperial and clerical missions of previous centuries. Threat of God's final judgment is also seen in the eschatology of the more recent style of evangelistic campaign, which calls for personal conversion to the lordship of Christ. He argues that such globalizing movements that seek aggressively to seize the whole world are not Christian, because they do not recognize that the last judgment is not the end—it is penultimate. Christian faith looks beyond judgment toward the recreation, which is God's last word (Rev 21:4) (: 24–28). Returning to the language—but not the strict dispensationalism—of Joachim, Moltmann believes that mission in the twenty-first century should be "mission in the name of the Holy Spirit," through whose energies life on earth is renewed (: 29). To avoid the dispute about whether these energies are "uncreated"—as in the Orthodox tradition—or "created"—as in Western medieval theology—he prefers to talk about "the creative energies of the Spirit, which link what is uncreated with what is created, renewing human life from its roots, and making it immortal, in eternal fellowship with God" (: 32). From this standpoint, Moltmann is able to review the question of interfaith dialogue, which he prefers to locate under pneumatology because it is a question of life. For him, in the mission of the Spirit, everything that affirms life is good, and whatever destroys it is bad, so that people of different religions can work together for what Christians understand as the kingdom of God, and "everything a person is, and everything which has put its impress on him culturally and religiously" becomes "his charisma" (: 32–34). This is a constructive approach that seeks to avoid the extremes of exclusivist rejection of other religions on the one hand and relativistic indifference on the other, but its individualism would not seem to be transferable to a situation where religions are bound up with particular communities and cultures.

As he himself recognizes, Moltmann's is a European theology, though written in dialogue with theologians elsewhere. He sees it as a contribution to theology from Europe, but not Euro-centric, nor reflecting the ideas of the dominating nations (Moltmann 1981a: xi). Moltmann rightly emphasizes that theology must be developed in ecumenical fellowship (: xiv). Much of what he writes reflects openness to other voices, and a measure of ecumenical consensus. Nevertheless, in contradistinction to some Southern voices (see chapters 5 and 6), and even though he recognizes that John's portrayal of the Spirit as Paraclete dispenses with salvation-historical language, Moltmann insists it is necessary to highlight the *history* of the Spirit, within which the church lives. He argues that because the Spirit is the Spirit of Christ, there is necessarily a historical perspective (1977: 33–37). But Moltmann's historical perspective is a European one. This restricts the contribution of emerging theologies from parts of the world with a different history and where Christian history began only recently; it also means that his work appears to support a European political and ecclesial agenda. Like the Orthodox, European theologians also tend to a particular vision of the end that is the result of local theological formation, worldview and interests, and this means that, however broad and holistic, their interpretation of the mission of the Spirit will not be universally affirmed.

After the Canberra Assembly, ecumenical veteran Philip Potter reflected on how he had long agonized over how to share the life of the Spirit in a broken world. He testified that "It is when our sharing the world's pain and expectation overwhelms us that the Spirit continues Christ's work of reconciliation, of exchange with us, standing in our place and interceding for us with sighs too deep for words, according to God's will" (Rom 8:24–27). Potter concludes that the basis of mission is God's reconciliation of the world through Christ crucified and risen, and participating in God's personal and cosmic ministry of reconciliation. This is not so much a matter of achieving a particular goal, but of living "in the Spirit that empowers us by sharing our weakness and that of creation." Potter was not suggesting any retreat from challenging evil or pursuing justice, which remain key issues for him as a Caribbean, but rather less European dogmatism about what constitutes "God's design" (1991: 312–13). In the next two chapters we shall see how Christians in India and in Korea have understood what it means to experience the Holy Spirit in a complex world.

CHAPTER 5

Mission in the Spirit:
Dialogue, Inculturation, Liberation

Indian Christian Theologies of the Holy Spirit

Indian Christian theology has a history of nearly two hundred years (for an overview, see K. Kim 2004a; see also Boyd 1975 [1969]; Baago 1969; M. M. Thomas 1970; Samartha 1974a). Looking back over its development in his classic *Introduction to Indian Christian Theology* (1975 [1969]), Robin Boyd predicted that "the doctrine of the Holy Spirit may become the cornerstone of Indian Christian theology." He found that Indian Christian theologians tend to see all God's dealings with the world primarily in terms of the Spirit and, furthermore, that they particularly appreciate the way this is expressed in John's Gospel (: 241–42). The Catholic theologian Felix Wilfred explains that, in keeping with Eastern religions in general, Asian Christian theologies recognize particularly "the inexhaustible aspect of the divine mystery which St. John expresses laconically: 'God is spirit' (Jn 4:24)." In practice this means that the language of Indian theology is one of signs, images and symbols, rather than the propositions and doctrines of Western theological discourse (Wilfred 1998). The point that both Boyd and Wilfred are making is that, as we might expect, Indian Christian theology reflects the dominant Hindu religious understanding that God is Spirit; this leads to a relatively more developed pneumatology, and also produces a special affinity with John's Gospel. Indeed, the literary style of that gospel has so much in common with Hindu scriptures that it has sometimes been referred to as "the Johannine Upanishad."

In this chapter we will examine Indian Christian reflection on the Holy Spirit by studying the work of three twentieth-century theologians who have a particularly developed pneumatology. We will try to understand the cultural concepts of "spirit" that lie behind their interpretations; the questions from their contemporary situation that they put to the biblical text and Christian tradition; and the discussions they have with one another that arise because of their different theological starting points. This will lead us to highlight some contributions that Indian Christian pneumatology may make to the wider conversation about the Spirit in the world (for further detail see K. Kim 2003a).

In order to understand the context from which this reflection emerges, it is necessary to note several salient features of the Indian situation. India is a continent in itself, composed of many different ethnic groups with great cultural variation according to region, and eighteen nationally recognized languages. Though it is no longer officially sanctioned, many Indians recognize their place in the ancient system of castes and outcastes, which regulates social norms. Despite significant Muslim and Christian minorities and the presence of outcaste and tribal groups, what we now know as the Hindu religion or way of life has been a unifying factor on the subcontinent for several thousand years (for a readable introduction to Hinduism, see Lipner 1994). Its holy language of Sanskrit is the root of many Indian tongues and of the national language of Hindi. Christians make up between two and three percent of the population of the present Indian nation; the majority of them come from outcaste or tribal groups. Many accepted the Christian faith during the Western colonial period, which began with the Portuguese, who introduced the Roman Catholic faith. During British rule, Protestant missionary work saw mass movements to Christ, as well as individual conversions. However, there are also the St. Thomas Christians, who claim to originate from a visit to India by that disciple of Jesus, and some of whom still follow a Syrian Orthodox tradition dating back to the second century (for details, see Neill 1970). Particularly in the run-up to independence, the formation of the constitution and post-independence nation-building, Indian Christians had an influence out of all proportion to their numbers (see S. Kim 2003). Most Christian denominations are represented in India, and there are also two united churches, the Church of South India and Church of North India, which were founded in the post-independence era as unions of denominations formed by colonial missions (Abraham and Thomas 2004: 502–505). There are Pentecostal churches and also indigenous forms of Christian faith, many of which express a revival or Pentecostal-charismatic type of spirituality (several examples are given in Hrangkhuma 1998).

One of the greatest Indian Christian theologians to date was M. M. Thomas, who was at one time the moderator of the World Council of Churches, and who identified three strands of Indian Christian theology. The first emerged as a response to the renascent Hinduism of British India, and aims to inculturate the gospel in the religious and philosophical terms that Hindu scholars and leaders can appreciate. The pioneer of this approach was Brahmabandap Upadhyaya, a nineteenth-century convert to Christian faith and a Brahmin (a member of the upper, priestly caste) from Bengal, who described himself as a Hindu-Catholic: that is, Hindu by culture and Catholic by religion (Lipner 1999). The second arose out of Christian involvement in the nationalist movement for independence and in campaigns for social justice for the outcastes of India. Thomas himself is most appreciated for this view. Its concern is for liberation of the oppressed, whether at a global or local level. The third strand is one that recognizes the religious plurality of Indian society and seeks to promote interfaith dialogue in the interests of harmonious living between all the communities of India. India is known as a "laboratory" for initiative in dialogue (Knitter 1995: 157), and has produced leaders in the field such as Stanley Samartha (see below) and Raimundo Panikkar (Thomas 1997). Looking at it another way, contemporary Indian Christian theologians face three main challenges in their attempts to express the Christian gospel in India: the dominant Hindu culture, the reality of poverty and oppression faced by at least one-third of the population, and the multi-religious nature of Indian society. The three theological strands of inculturation, liberation and dialogue—also recognized by Catholic theologians of the Indian Theological Association (1991)—are attempts to address these problems respectively. We shall see that pneumatological reflection is found in each strand.

Indian Reflection on the Spirit

Three different Hindi or Sanskrit words are used to translate the word "spirit" among Indian Christians; they are *atman, antaryamin* and *shakti*. Boyd pointed out that each reflects a different spiritual tradition and carries different connotations (1975 [1969]: 241). *Atman*, also translated "soul" or "self," and its cognates—including *Paramatman* (Supreme Spirit) and *antaratman* (inner spirit)—derive from the classical tradition of advaitic Hinduism, particularly the Vedantic philosophy of Sankara from the eighth century. *Advaita* means "oneness," or more literally "not two-ness" or "non-duality." Upadhyaya sought to reconcile Christianity and Hinduism by expressing Christian faith in Hindu philosophical terms and as the fulfillment of Hindu ideals. Advaitic philosophy centers around the pursuit—by various paths—of self-realization, which means becoming conscious that the *atman* within is one with *Brahman*, God, who is the Universal Spirit. Describing the Spirit as *atman* draws attention to the interior dimension, the spirit within, and its union with the universal Spirit, *Brahman*. The twentieth-century Catholic ascetic Abhishiktananda, a French monk who immersed himself in Hinduism and adopted the lifestyle of a *sannyasi* or holy man, described the Holy Spirit as "the *advaita* of God, the mystery of the non-duality of the Father and the Son" (1984: 184). Critics of this approach generally regard it as elitist in appealing to the highest caste of Hindu society, and even as capitulating to a Hindu worldview by trying to find a place for Christianity within it. Its supporters argue that the philosophy of *advaita* represents the highest of Hindu culture, and therefore the most worthy vehicle for the gospel.

In view of its popular appeal, some have preferred to express Christian faith in terms of *bhakti,* in which faith is expressed in terms of love for a personal deity. Because the popular form of *bhakti* devotion does not entail the discipline of the classical path that leads to the knowledge of non-duality, it may be regarded as a lower form of religion by advaitins (see, for example, Vandana 1991a: 13). *Antaryamin* or "Indwelling One" is particularly associated with *bhakti* tradition because the notion of God's indwelling is found in the most popular Hindu religious text, the Bhagavad-Gita, the classic story of the battle between good and evil. In one sense, the closeness of the *bhakti* love-relationship with the Divine needs no mediation, and therefore no developed doctrine of the Holy Spirit. This is the argument of Vengal Chakkarai, a member of a group of radical Indian theologians in the 1930s known as the Madras "Rethinking Group." He regarded the Holy Spirit as the continuing presence of the resurrected Jesus, the permanent *Avatar* or appearance of God, and concluded that "the Holy Spirit is Jesus himself taking his abode within us" (Chakkarai 1981 [1932]: 116–31). However, in the 1920s and '30s, A. J. Appasamy, Bishop of the Anglican Church and later of the Church of South India, made extensive use of *antaryamin* to interpret the doctrine of the Holy Spirit in terms of the "abiding" in John's Gospel, understanding this to refer to the inner life of the believer, particularly in its moral dimensions. Appasamy likened *antaryamin,* and therefore the Spirit, to the love between the Father and the Son in which the believers share (Appasamy 1928: 10–16, 22–27, 57, 130, 226–28). Believing also that the Bible affirmed the presence of God in creation from the beginning, Appasamy identified the meeting place of the communities of India as a spiritual one, and this paved the way for the dialogue with religion and society initiated in post-independence India by P. D. Devanandan.

The third Sanskrit word translated "spirit" is *shakti.* Though *Shakti* is recognized in classical Hinduism as the consort of the god Brahma, this goddess predates the rise of the Brahmins and the Hindu caste structure. In pre-Aryan religion, *Shakti* was a fertility goddess and thus represented the feminine power of the creation, primal energy, an overpowering and at times uncontrollable force. Consequently this term is attractive to those who reject the hegemony of Vedic Hinduism and seek to subvert it. Pandipeddi Chenchiah, the radical leader of the "Rethinking Group," developed the interpretation of the Spirit as *Shakti* in the pre-Aryan sense, by using the evolutionary (Hindu) philosophy of Aurobindo to interpret the Spirit in terms of cosmic power to bring about social and scientific change (see Chenchiah in Thangasamy 1966: 123–33). Chenchiah reversed the traditional norms by exchanging the ideal of withdrawal from the material world and embrace of *advaita* mysticism for the affirmation of creation and activity, on the grounds that the universal Spirit or *Brahman* is manifested in the power of *Shakti,* or the Spirit, which empowers a process of evolution of creation toward a better humanity (see Boyd 1975 [1969]: 145–47). In

Appasamy's view, the Christian experience of the Holy Spirit was an inten-
sification of the general presence of the Spirit that preceded it (Francis 1992:
70–81), but Chenchiah emphasized the "new cosmic energy" of the Holy
Spirit released in "an outburst or inrush into history" by the resurrection
of Jesus Christ, as if it had not been present before. He believed "the raw
fact of Christ" would lead to the establishment of a new universe by a
process of unconscious change, in which the Spirit—like a gas—was infused
into history (Chenchiah 1938: 49–56, 61). Rejecting Appasamy's *bhakti*
path because he saw it as a way of retreat, as opposed to a dynamic way
forward (Boyd 1975 [1969]: 157), Chenchiah insisted that the uniqueness
of Christianity could not depend on its institutions or doctrines, but only
on its transcendence over other faiths as the religion of new birth by the
Holy Spirit. In order to interpret the gospel for modern, secular India, M.
M. Thomas followed Chenchiah in making the new creation wrought in
Christ the starting point for theology. Thomas saw that the language of non-
brahminic *shakti* contains within it a "spirituality for combat," and therefore lays a pneumatological foundation for theologies of liberation (Thomas
1990). The feminine nature of *shakti* is particularly attractive to feminist
theologians, who have used the *shakti* tradition, especially its close association between the female and nature, to motivate eco-feminist commitment
to the liberation of both women and creation (Gnanadason 1993: 95–105).

   To sharpen our understanding of the Holy Spirit in Indian Christian theology, we shall concentrate on the work of three Indian theologians whose
writing (available in English) is explicitly pneumatological: Stanley
Samartha, Vandana, and Samuel Rayan. These three theologians of the
Spirit represent the three strands of Indian Christian theology identified
above: dialogue, inculturation, and liberation, respectively. They are all con-
temporaries, born in the early 1920s. Samartha died in 2001, but the other
two are still living at the time of this writing. They come from different parts
of the country: Samartha from the state of Karnataka, Vandana from the
Parsi (Zoroastrian) community in Mumbai (formerly Bombay), and Rayan
from the state of Kerala. Samartha was an internationally known ecumenist
from a Protestant background; Vandana converted to the Roman Catholic
Church and became the leader of a religious order for women; and Rayan
is also a Catholic—a Jesuit priest and theological educator. Samartha's main
interest was in interreligious relations; Vandana's is in mystical knowledge
of God; and Rayan's in the struggle of India's poor for liberation.

The Holy Spirit and the Theology of Dialogue of Stanley J. Samartha

Stanley J. Samartha, an ordained minister of the Church of South India, has
told the story of his life journey "from Mangalore to Bangalore" (Samartha
1996). Mangalore is a provincial town, where the harmonious day-to-day

relationships between different faiths later provided a model for his vision
for interfaith dialogue. Born in 1920 into a Christian home, he was nur-
tured in the Basel Evangelical Mission Church, where he was grounded in
the Evangelical and neo-conservative Reformed theology of Karl Barth and
Hendrik Kraemer. Later, under the influence of Chenchiah, he was to criti-
cize this theology for its negative view of other religions. In 1947 Samartha
left Mangalore for graduate study in the United States, where he studied
under Paul Tillich. Ironically, it was in the United States that he first came
to appreciate Hindu philosophy, which was part of his doctoral research.
Returning to India, he took a professorship in the more liberal setting of the
United Theological College, Bangalore, where he ventured into interreligious
dialogue. He later moved on to the World Council of Churches in Geneva,
where he set up the World Council of Churches' first unit for dialogue with
people of other faiths and, as director, laid down their *Guidelines for
Dialogue* (Samartha 1979), before retiring to Bangalore, where he continued to write until his death in 2001. Throughout his life, Samartha was
active in ministry and preaching.[1]

Samartha's doctoral thesis was eventually published as *The Hindu
Response to the Unbound Christ* (1974a)—an analysis of varied responses
to the Christian gospel by Hindus. The title indicated the thesis that though
"Christianity belongs to Christ, Christ does not belong to Christianity"
(: 10), and the book emphasized the right of Hindus to understand and
appropriate the biblical revelation as they saw fit. He regarded Hindus who
responded to Christ without joining the Christian community as constitut-
ing a wider "unbaptized *koinonia*" (: 119). Samartha set himself against
what he called the "exclusive claims" of conservative Christians to have a
monopoly on truth, and advocated greater understanding by Christians of
the Hindu tradition. He became increasingly critical of the institutional
church's lack of "courage for dialogue," and was embarrassed by what he
saw as its "smell of foreignness" in India (Samartha 1981a: 131–32, 56–58).
He suggested that the best way forward to develop Christian theology that
was relevant in India, and sympathetic to her rich religious heritage, was to
use the advaitic tradition, which he saw as the unifying force in India
(1974a: v). However, he was quite cautious at first about doing so, lest he
be accused of syncretism.

Samartha's first experience in interfaith dialogue was with P. D.
Devanandan at the Centre for Religion and Society (CISRS) in Bangalore.
This work led him to have deep respect for Hindus and people of other
faiths, while continuing to hold to his own. He rejected the terminology of
"non-Christians," preferring to talk positively about "our neighbors of other
faiths" (1981a: 1, 12, 45). When he moved to Geneva, he broke with the

---

[1] The following discussion is based on a more thorough study of all Samartha's published work to be found in K. Kim 2003a: 14–77.

confrontational style and bilateral mode of interreligious relations, and developed a round-table model. He tried to establish dialogue as an alternative to mission (: 98–99). However, Samartha faced considerable opposition in this from Evangelicals, on the one hand, who wished to emphasize the importance of proclamation, and from secularizers, on the other, who were impatient with interreligious discussions in the face of the urgent needs of society. Evangelicals accused Samartha of syncretizing Christianity and other religions, and relativizing what they saw as absolute. *Courage for Dialogue* (1981a) brings together many of his arguments against those whom he believed promoted a culture of fear of other faiths, and who worried unnecessarily that dialogue meant a watering down of Christian conviction. Debate came to a head at the Nairobi Assembly of the World Council of Churches in 1975, but four years later Samartha's *Guidelines for Dialogue* were eventually accepted as representing the policy of the Council toward people of other faiths. He described dialogue as an "encounter of commitments"; that is, on openness to the other's view, together with commitment to one's own, which begins with respect for another's right to hold different beliefs, and a desire for mutual understanding (1981a: 1, 32). The initiative for dialogue arises from the need for the different communities of the global village to find a way of living together in peace (: 100), which will only be possible when there is also considerable "traffic across the borders" to create a community of communities (: 75).

Samartha also sought to establish theological foundations for dialogue, and included in these a pneumatological foundation based on John 16:13, "the Spirit will lead into all truth" (1981a: 10–14). He understood "all truth" to include the truth of other religions, on the basis that truth is one. This interpretation was strongly disputed by Lesslie Newbigin, missionary theologian and Bishop of the Church of South India, who argued that, since all truth is found in Jesus Christ, "the Holy Spirit does not lead past, or beyond, or away from Jesus" (Newbigin 1982: 216–17). Samartha adopted the Vedic view that "since truth is one and God is truth, there obviously cannot be a Hindu truth and a Christian truth" (1991a: 107–111; 1981a: 142–57). Since he understood the Spirit to be the unifying principle of the Godhead and of the universe itself, he regarded dialogue as entering into this Spirit. Therefore dialogue was not so much a method or technique, but "a mood, a spirit, an attitude of love and respect" for "our neighbors of other faiths." That is, dialogue takes place in the "milieu" of the Spirit (1981a: 100, 75). Samartha's pneumatological reflections were further stimulated by his encounter with Eastern Orthodox theology of the Holy Spirit, which associated the Spirit with universal concepts of life, truth and creativity. In particular, under influence of Georges Khodr (and indirectly Vladimir Lossky), Samartha took Irenaeus' teaching, that the Son and the Spirit could be regarded as "two hands of the Father," to allow for a cer-

tain "hypostatic independence." On this basis, he argued that the Spirit may
be at work beyond the boundaries of Christianity, in people of other faiths.
He published this idea in a seminal paper, "The Holy Spirit and People of
Various Faiths, Cultures and Ideologies," in which he strongly criticized
Barth for limiting the Spirit to his own brand of Western Christianity, and
stressed instead the boundlessness of the Spirit's activity. He suggested looking for existential evidence of the Spirit's work wherever there is life with
creativity, order with truth, and community with sharing (1974c). Samartha
rebelled against exclusiveness because it is too stifling and does not take into
account the freedom of the Spirit to blow at will (Jn 3:8): "[Exclusiveness]
does not recognize the need to leave some doors unlatched in order that the
gentle breeze of the Holy Spirit may enter the Christian home, sometimes
from unexpected quarters" (1981a: 96).

In his book, *One Christ—Many Religions*, Samartha attempted to develop
a framework for interreligious dialogue that was "biblically sound, spiritu-
ally satisfying, theologically credible, and pastorally helpful" (1991a: ix). It
was motivated by the practical concerns of ministry in the Indian context,
rather than by metaphysical questions. Samartha claims his is "a theology
from below," a "bullock-cart theology," in contradistinction to that of a
"theological helicopter that can help us to rise above all religions and to
look down upon the terrain below in lofty condescension" (: 115–6). The
tone of *One Christ—Many Religions* is that of a liberation theology on
behalf of religions oppressed by colonialism and its missionary activity. He
seeks to free them by emphasizing that Christianity is one among many religions. He sees this as necessary because of the growing problem of communalism, and the emergence of Hindu as well as Christian fundamentalism,
which threaten social cohesion and the future of the nation. Samartha rejects
the Greek philosophical framework in which the Chalcedonian Creed
expresses the incarnation, believing that the statements there about Christ's
nature as human and divine lie behind the exclusive claims made by
Christians about Jesus Christ, which he regards as so divisive in the multi-
religious context of India (: 154–55, 159–60, 163–65). He also rejects the
Catholic mystical approaches of "anonymous Christians" or "hidden
Christ," because he sees such inclusivism as "exclusivism's patronizing
cousin" (: 86, 3). On the other hand, Samartha does not wish to see multi-
religious societies becoming "a sea of relativity in which different boats
flounder aimlessly without rudders," so he puts forward what he regards as
a "middle way" of "commitment and openness" (: 7).

Leaving behind Greek and Western philosophy, which he regarded as
dualistic and therefore encouraging of dichotomizing approaches to other
traditions (1991a: 85, 103–11), Samartha set about constructing a theology
of religions using the concept of *advaita* (non-duality or oneness). He
believed that the pervasive influence of Sankara's advaitic philosophy in the
Indian consciousness provided a "unitive vision," holding all Indian com-

munities together and encouraging the dialogical relationship they have enjoyed for centuries, and argues that there are certain key elements of *advaita* conducive to harmonious relationships in the context of religious plurality (: 110–11). The first element is "a mood of awe . . . before the Mystery of Truth or God or Ultimate Reality." Samartha's studies in Hinduism had convinced him that it is "Mystery" that "provides the onto-logical basis for tolerance" (: 82). As long as it is recognized that no faith or way totally comprehends the Ultimate Reality, but that this remains mys-terious, he argues, there is room for different religions to coexist. The sec-ond element is "an unwillingness to claim finality to particular responses to Truth," which allows for openness to different visions of truth. Samartha adopted the term "Mystery" or "Ultimate Reality" in place of "God," as terms to which he hopes people of all religions will be able to relate. The third element is "a suspicion of all rationalistic formulations of truth." Samartha repeatedly stresses that cognitive knowledge must be subordinate to intuition or experience. The fourth is "a non-triumphalistic attitude toward other religions," which recognizes that dialogue is necessary because truth is relational not propositional, being apprehended in community. Fifth is "the emphasis on inwardness, meditation, contemplation and discipline in religious life," because this form of religion is not aggressive but seeks peace. And sixth is "the importance given to signs, symbols, and images, and so to the aesthetic dimensions of life." Samartha wished to express the-ology not in dogmatic assertions but in art, poetry and music that would connect Christians with other religious communities, rather than set them apart.

Alongside Samartha's advocacy of *advaita* there runs a reconstruction of Christian doctrine. He argues for the priority of God, not Christ, in the Bible, and points out that Jesus Christ himself was theocentric. He criticizes fixation on Jesus Christ in the form of "Jesusology" or "christomonism," and argues for a recovery in Western theology of the doctrine of the Trinity without the *filioque* clause, because he believes this will provide "theologi-cal space" for Christians to express the mystery of God and recognize the work of the Spirit in the lives of those of other faiths (1991a: 82–89, 95–96, 115). Vinoth Ramachandra suggests that Samartha's book would perhaps be better named "One Mystery—Many Religions," because he sees it as dis-placing christology and substituting a Hindu world-view for a Christian one (1996: 10). Indeed, Samartha's view does have much in common with John Hick and Paul Knitter's pluralistic theology of religions, about which Ramachandra makes the same criticism, and he contributed a chapter to their book, *The Myth of Christian Uniqueness* (Hick and Knitter 1987: 69–88). Samartha's outright rejection of the Chalcedonian model of the incarnation, as inappropriate in the Indian context, certainly gave the impression that he was abandoning distinctively Christian belief altogether. However, he was adamant that he was proposing only that Christians adopt the "unitive vision" of *advaita*, not the Hindu religion itself. Paul Knitter later suggested that what Samartha was actually trying to do was to formulate a Spirit christology in place of the Logos christology of the creed, and a pneumatocentric theology of religions. Though it seemed to come as a surprise to him, Samartha welcomed this insight into his work, which does indeed make better sense of it, though he emphasized that he did not wish to separate the Holy Spirit from "the love of God and the fellowship of the Lord Jesus Christ" (Knitter 1991; Samartha 1991b). There are parallels between *advaita* in Hindu thought and the concept of the Spirit in Christian theology, as has already been pointed out. This is true of John's Gospel, particularly, where the Spirit is portrayed as the one who brings about the unity of Father and Son and the oneness of believers in Christ.

The title *One Christ—Many Religions* is not intended to imply that Christ unifies all religions, but to set Jesus Christ in a pluralistic context. What is not expressed in the title is the very significant role Samartha gives to the Spirit in theology of religions. During his theological development, it seems he transferred the attribute "unbound" from "the unbound Christ" —the recognition that Indians of all religions have been influenced by and responded to the gospel of Jesus Christ—to the unbound Spirit. The Spirit blows where it wills to bring a refreshing breeze into interreligious relations, by encouraging the crossing of religious boundaries in a spirit of respect and openness. As this Spirit of love of neighbor characterized Jesus Christ, so Samartha believes the same Spirit is also characteristic of Hinduism. In fact, he described the Spirit as the *advaita*, the Spirit of oneness (1991a: 83). In this way, Samartha attempted to establish dialogue on a pneumatological foundation both for Hindus and for Christians. He urged Christians to have a spirit of dialogue as an integral part of their Christian faith (1974b: vii–xvii):

> To be open to God cannot mean prejudging the mind of God and erecting our own neat lines of demarcation as if we knew just where the Spirit of God is and is not at work. He is not bound by our prejudging. Nor is it to abandon commitment to Truth as this has become known to us. It is rather, gratefully to acknowledge that the fullness of Truth is always wider and deeper than our present apprehensions of it and that the Spirit is at work, in ways such that we do not know where He comes from nor where He is going, to guide us into all Truth (1974b: xvii).

For Samartha, the Spirit, or *advaita*, is the Spirit of dialogue, which creates the willingness to cross over to the shore of another's experience that is necessary for interfaith understanding. Wherever this attitude is to be found, he suggested, the Spirit is at work.

While trying to establish dialogue, Samartha generally avoided the term "mission," which he felt had anti-dialogical connotations and had been mixed up in India with "military conquest, political domination, and economic exploitation"—and "with racial arrogance as well" (1991a: 101–102, 148–49). When he came later to relate dialogue and mission, his emphasis on having the right attitude to others meant that he understood dialogue as the spirituality for mission. For him, dialogue is a prerequisite for genuinely missionary activity. Only in a situation where there is the mutual trust and openness created by dialogue can the mission of God truly take place, leading to the conversion of all parties. On the fiftieth anniversary of the meeting of the International Missionary Council at Tambaram, India, Samartha refuted Kraemer's understanding of mission as "the Christian message in a non-Christian world," which dominated mission thinking in those days (: 142–54). For Samartha, mission is not the proclamation of a message about Jesus Christ, but a continuation of the work of Jesus of Nazareth by the leading of the Spirit. Nor is the world necessarily hostile to the message, but only to the imperialistic spirit in which it is proclaimed. Samartha believes that what the people of India find attractive about Christianity is not its doctrines but its life—exemplified in Jesus Christ—and that the spirit that inspired Jesus Christ is the spirit of dialogue. What Samartha calls for in the face of religious pluralism is not so much a new theology as a new spirit: dialogue. Dialogue is mission, in the sense of being involved with the Spirit in the lives—both the struggles and the spirituality—of our neighbors. Samartha therefore defines mission as "God's continuing activity through the Spirit to mend the brokenness of creation, to overcome the fragmentation of humanity, and to heal the rift between humanity, nature, and God," in which Christians, together with their neighbors of other faiths, are called to participate (: 149). He generally prefers to call this "witness."

Samartha believed dialogue should lead to a "critical engagement" of the religions, in which mutual challenge could take place, as well as mutual learning (1981: 84–86). In other words, for Christians, it is an activity of discerning the Spirit. This is elaborated in a second paper on "The Holy Spirit and People of Other Faiths," published in preparation for the Canberra Assembly, twenty years after the first one (1990). The question in Samartha's mind was not *whether* the Spirit was at work among people of other faiths, but *where* and *how*, and he looked for the work of the Spirit in any or all of the partners in any dialogue (1990: 59). He recognized that there might be evil spirits involved as well, but warned Christians against assuming that the false spirit was that of another religion: "[T]he struggle between the Holy Spirit and the spirits of this world, between God and idols, between truth and distortions of truth, is going on *within* every religious community in history. Christians should avoid the temptation of transforming it into a struggle *between* Christianity and other religions in the world" (: 60). Similarly, he cautioned Christians against assuming that they could always claim to have the Spirit of God, insisting that such a claim is not for us to make, but for our neighbors to recognize (1981b: 670). Christians, therefore, encounter their neighbors of other faiths with humility, not knowing how the Spirit will blow, but in anticipation that the Spirit will work to lead the participants further into "all truth." Discernment is intended to recognize the activities of the Spirit, not to control them, and therefore, he argued, the evidence of the fruit of the Spirit must be given greater weight than prior doctrines of the Spirit (: 61). Samartha suggests four biblical marks of the Spirit for use in discernment: freedom, "boundlessness," the power to bring about new relationships, and power to create new communities of people. He recognizes that new relationships cannot be brought about without breaking down oppression. The Spirit is both the fire to do this and also the Life-giver (: 58). Where liberation and new life are experienced in other faiths, he asks, "are there serious theological reasons to *deny* the presence of the Spirit among them?" (: 59).

Samartha did not wish to limit himself to ethical questions in discerning the Spirit. Reflecting on the Spirit as *Antaryamin*, the Indwelling God, he pointed out that one of the marks of the Spirit is inwardness. Not activism, but peace through abiding in Christ is the sign of the Spirit's presence, and in all religions, he believed, inwardness is recognized as a sign of authentic spiritual life (1991b: 33–34). In later work, Samartha was also prepared to consider the gender of the Spirit and suggested that in India, where the Spirit is regarded as *Shakti*, the feminine power of God, the feminine pronoun is most appropriate and he had no objection to considering the Spirit a mother figure (1994: 45). Ultimately, Samartha says, it does not matter how the Spirit is described in human theology, because the Spirit is "unbound" by gender or any other category. What does matter is that the Spirit is experienced, because the Spirit "is associated with life," particularly community life (1990: 50).

A weakness of Samartha's conception of the Spirit is his tendency to disconnect the Spirit from human reason. By linking the Spirit strongly to inner life and communal harmony, he puts the category of "being" before "doing," and subsumes "thinking" into "being," in what he sees as a characteristically "Asian" fashion. But this limits the effectiveness of his pneumatology to encounter rational thought, and to deal with secularism, science and modernity in the Indian context. Instead of using his understanding of the Spirit—which leads us into *all* truth—to bring Western and Asian thought together, he argues for the priority of an Asian worldview for the purposes of "freeing" the Spirit from dogmatic theology. However, this resistance to rational understanding is also a limitation on the Spirit. His dichotomizing of the thought of East and West is difficult to sustain and justify in history. In particular, he affirms contemporary Eastern Orthodox theology for its trinitarian stance and yet rejects the Chalcedonian (Greek) formulations of christology as "Western." Furthermore, he defends the Trinity, but denies the doctrines about Jesus' divinity that necessitated trinitarian thinking in the first place.

Despite his criticism of dogmatism, Samartha's approach has its own exclusivity. There is also a universal claim. While taking great pains to meet those of other faiths in dialogue, he is impatient with many of his co-religionists, whose popular religion he fails to appreciate. As Ramachandra points out, "It is a pity that Samartha does not extend the same respect that he urges *vis-à-vis* our non-Christian neighbors to those Christians with whom he disagrees" (1996: 13). Underlying Samartha's attempt at a pneumatocentric christology is the assumption that the "spirit of dialogue" is a universal category, universally regarded, whereas one of the main features of contemporary India is the rise of undialogical forms of faith (both Christian and Hindu fundamentalism). He also assumes that India is a microcosm of the world, and tends to idealize interreligious relations there. Nevertheless, the limitation that Samartha's pneumatology (as any theology) reflects his local background and experience is also its greatest strength, as he is able to offer a perspective on the Spirit from his own experience of interreligious dialogue.

Samartha's work is significant because of the questions he raises about the Holy Spirit in a world of many faiths—questions that were, as he himself pointed out, "important enough to be noted" in ecumenical discussion, but also "difficult enough to be avoided," raising as they do fears of syncretism and relativism (Samartha 1990: 52). Samartha's main concern was to promote dialogue, not to work out a systematic theology of religions, but the pneumatological foundation for dialogue that he sketched out is of continuing importance. In the long term, it has become accepted as the ecumenical approach. The report of the World Council of Churches Conference on World Mission and Evangelism at Salvador, Brazil in 1996, for example, clearly affirmed in a number of places the presence of the Holy Spirit in other religions and cultures, and encouraged Christians to look out for marks of the Spirit in their encounters with other peoples (World Council of Churches 1998a: 33; 1998b: 57, 62). Samartha's attempt to affirm Jesus Christ within the spirit of *advaita*, and his reflection on the Spirit in the Indian context, lead to some seminal thinking that challenges traditional Western mission pneumatology. The advaitic perspective, in which everything takes place within the milieu of the Spirit, draws attention to mission spirituality, that is, to the primary importance of motives and attitudes in mission, which is an important contribution to post-colonial missiology. His sense of the Spirit as *atman* and *antaryamin* stresses the devotional and meditative resources from which mission involvement springs. But most importantly of all, his insistence that the Spirit shares the characteristics of Mystery—unpredictable and unknowable, not amenable to rational description, yet all-pervasive—encourages a willingness to listen to, learn from, and appreciate people of other faiths and their worldviews. Samartha's development of a theology of discernment is an important counterpart to this, which saves his approach from naiveté, and grounds his pneumatology in his particular commitment to Jesus Christ.

The Ashramic Spirit-uality of Vandana

Vandana, also known as *Mataji* (Mother), was born Gool Dhalla to a Parsi family in Bombay in 1924.[2] The Parsis are of Persian descent and Zoroastrian religion. She received a Catholic education at Sophia College in Bombay under the tutelage of the sisters of the Society of the Sacred Heart of Jesus. When she was of age she made a profession of Christian faith and decided to join the order. Her conversion caused controversy at the time, because it appeared the College was abusing its trust and proselytizing the students. However, Vandana denies that her conversion was anything but her own decision, as a result of admiration for the sisters, and her awareness that "the Mother of Jesus was there" in the College (1991a: x–xi). She later likened her experience to "falling in love" with Jesus, an irresistible pull of the heart not prompted by any political or even religious motive (1997: 29; 1998: 27). Vandana went on to become a lecturer in social science at Sophia College, and the provincial supervisor of the Society of the Sacred Heart of Jesus in India, but later underwent a deep encounter with Hinduism, and became a leader of the Catholic ashram movement in India.

Vandana's involvement with ashrams—Hindu religious communities—was inspired by Abhishiktananda, who made her realize that "our church was not Indian, it was foreign," and challenged her to live her religious life "in an Indian setting" (Vandana 1993b). She adopted the Sanskrit name Vandana, meaning "prayer," to express her new intention, and began to study Hindu music as a way of appreciating her Indian heritage. Once she retired as provincial, she obtained (with difficulty) permission from the Catholic Church to reopen a former Anglican Christian community known as the Christa Prema Seva Ashram in Pune, leading several of her religious sisters in an ecumenical venture with Anglican sisters, of living together and trying to express their faith in traditionally Hindu religious forms (Noreen 1994).

Following this experience, Vandana spent several years living in various Hindu ashrams and recording her reflections on their religious life (Vandana 1988 [1978]). She describes an ashram as "an open community of *guru*(s) and *shishya*(s) [disciples] engaged primarily in contemplative pursuit of *Brahmavidya* (knowledge of God)" (1995c: 237). An ashram is not founded as a community, as she had previously thought, but arises from the life of a guru who draws disciples, and is therefore centered around him or her

---

[2] The following discussion is based on a more thorough study of all Vandana's published work to be found in K. Kim 2003a: 78–137.

(1988: 19, 37, 19–41, 32–35). She expresses particular admiration for Swami Chidananda of Shivanandashram (Divine Life Society), whose gentle and kindly spirituality she sees as Christlike (see the dedications of Vandana 1987; 1989; 1991a). As a sign of her surrender to the contemplative life in Hindu tradition, she adopted the saffron robes of the *sannyasi* and went on to found her own ashram, Christ-centered but open to Hindus, which she called *jeevan-dhara* or "living streams." Her practice of Christianity in a Hindu style drew criticism from some Hindu nationalist leaders, who accused ashramites of dissembling, and questioned whether any Hindu had initiated her into the faith, as she claimed (S. Kim 2003: 117–21). Vandana dismissed these allegations (Vandana 1988: xxiii), without perhaps really appreciating the significance of the fact that not everyone shares her view that all religions are witnessing to the same universal experience.

Jeevan-dhara, which was first located by the River Ganges and later in the Himalayas, was open to both Christians and Hindus. Vandana insisted that the primary presence of Christ in the ashram was in the form of the Spirit, and not the eucharist, as Abhishiktananda and others argued (1991b: 81–82). Therefore, she believed activities should center on meditation, in which Hindus and Christians could participate together, rather than Christian ritual. In the ashram she practiced and developed what she called "ashramic Spirit-uality." The spelling is intended to show that "spirituality" is "life lived according to the Spirit." She described this spirituality as "flowing like water, flexible like bamboo, fiery like love, feminine like Mary" (1993d: 103). Daily life at the ashram is based on the practice of yoga. Vandana understands that yoga literally means "yoking" or "one-ing," and therefore is a way of experiencing the union with the Divine to which both Hindus and Christians aspire (: 103). She emphasizes the importance of each of the paths of yoga: *jnana* (knowledge), *bhakti* (devotion) and *karma* (deeds) (e.g. 199b: 79), and she rejoices in the bodily nature of yogic practice, which she sees as representing a holistic approach to life, lacking in traditional Christianity (1993d: 105).

This apparent preoccupation with the mystical pursuits of the upper castes provoked strong criticism of Vandana's movement by liberation theologians, who were concerned for the rights of the poor and outcastes (Soares-Prabhu 1991: 55–99). According to the founder of her religious order, "the inwardness is for the outgoing," not for its own sake, so Vandana countered that Hindu meditative techniques can enhance the religious life of Christians, and therefore lead to more effective service in society (Vandana 1993c). However, it is clear that, for Vandana, the mission of the ashram is one of peacemaking, rather than changing society; of inculturation of the gospel in Hindu tradition, rather than agitating for liberation. The method she advocates is "going out while remaining within" (1993d: 99–102); that is, she claims the missiological priority of silence (a feminine word in Sanskrit) over sound (masculine), or of Spirit over Word (1992a). She demonstrated this in her response to the crisis at Ayodhya, which led to Hindu militants destroying a mosque in 1992. Vandana led a multi-faith group to the city, not to remonstrate or preach, but to sit there in a silent witness of peace (Vandana 1992b).

Vandana also advocates ashramic theologizing. The open ashram, where members of different faiths live together, is, she argues, a more appropriate place to do theology than the academy (1993c: 84). She adopts Sankara's *advaita* as her framework for theologizing, because she believes it represents "the soul of Hinduism," which is fundamentally different from Western philosophy in being essentially concerned with experience, rather than logical thought. Theology for Vandana is a form of *jnana* yoga in which God is known "from the experiential meditative viewpoint" (Vandana 1981). Critics may regard this approach as a Gnostic heresy (*gnosis* and *jnana* derive from the same root). Vandana does indeed suggest that "most Christians," who follow *bhakti* yoga, are on a lower level of spirituality (Vandana 1991a: 13). However, she is not a cult leader; her approach is inclusive, and she sees herself as an educator working to extend the horizons of all people (: 43–44, 56). An important legacy of Upadhyaya's classical Indian Christian theology is a hymn to the Trinity in terms of a Hindu trinitarian formulation, *sat-chit-ananda* (*saccidandanada*)—being, consciousness, bliss—which he compared to Father, Son, and Holy Spirit. Referring to this, Vandana describes the Holy Spirit as "*ananda*," "joy"— a characteristic she finds lacking in Western Christianity but sees everywhere apparent among India's people, who celebrate so often and so liberally (1993d: 223). By connecting *sat-chit-ananda* with another Hindu trinity, *satyam-sivam-sunderam* (truth, goodness, beauty), Vandana links joy with beauty, creativity, art and music. She comments, "In general in Christianity I find that we have dwelt on Him almost exclusively as Truth (in our theologies), and as Goodness (in our 'good works'), but too inadequately on God as Beauty" (1992: 108–10).

In the context of the ashram, Vandana began theologizing by adopting a Hindu method of reading scripture, the *dhavani* method, which involves meditating on the text so that its meaning moves from the mind to the heart. She justifies this approach on the basis that the Bible is "an Asian book," and therefore Asian methods are the most appropriate to understand its message (1989: 105). She finds John's Gospel particularly suited to the Hindu psyche, due to its emphasis on the interior life, its use of symbolism, its concern with the meaning of historical events rather than historical fact, and its emphasis on joy (1992a: 223). The result of her application of the *dhavani* method to John's Gospel is the commentary *Waters of Fire* (1989 [1981]), which is also a theology of the Spirit. It was hailed as an original and genuinely Indian commentary, which "throbs with the very heart of India and thereby in incarnated identification with its reality" (D. S.

Amalorpavadass, back cover). Vandana does not comment systematically on each verse, but identifies water as a key theme for John. She also notes the centrality of water in Indian as well as Palestinian life, the important role of water in the Vedic tradition, and the fact that India's greatest river, the Ganges, is known as "the mother of life" (: 78–80, 190–202, 203–16, 217–22). She then examines ten passages in the gospel where water appears. "Living streams" is the key chapter of the book, which treats the story of Jesus' conversation with the Samaritan woman at the well (Jn 4:1–30). The main point is shown in an illustration by Indian Christian artist Jyoti Sahi of Jesus seated cross-legged with palms together, in the typical posture of a meditating guru, or religious teacher. He is seated above the well, and the living water from the well of spiritual tradition is pouring out of his heart, and into the cupped hands of the outcaste woman, transforming her body into a stream of water (1989: 77; see 19–20, 90–91). Similarly, in "Water to drink" (Jn 7:37–39), where Jesus invites anyone who thirsts to come to him, the source of living water, Vandana describes Jesus as the *Param* (Supreme) *Guru*, whose heart, or self, or spirit is the source of life for all (1989: 123–39). The abundance of that offer is shown at Cana in Galilee in "God's extravaganza," when Jesus changed water into wine (Jn 2:1–11) (1989: 39–51).

A guru is someone who has attained self-realization, that is, who has reached the awareness that *Brahman*, the ultimate and only reality, is one with *atman*, one's self or soul. When Vandana reads the account of Jesus' baptism by John in the Jordan River (Jn 1:29–34) through Hindu eyes, she comes to the conclusion that these were the "waters of awakening" of Jesus to consciousness of his oneness with the Father. In other words, at his baptism Jesus experienced essentially the same spiritual experience to which Hindus aspire: Jesus' baptism was his awakening to "His Self—the *Atman*, the Spirit" (1989: 25–38; see 36). In Vandana's approach (which is here particularly indebted to Abhishiktananda), the baptism seems to take over from the cross as the central event of Jesus' life, so that the cross becomes a further example of the pattern of dying and rising, passing from death to life, that first took place in the waters of the Jordan. While the parallel between the two events is justified from a biblical point of view (see, for example, Rom 6:4; Col 2:12), there is undoubtedly far more weight given in the gospels to Jesus' passion.

In his discussion with Nicodemus about the "waters of rebirth" (Jn 3:1–15), Vandana sees Jesus the guru explaining to his disciples "the Christian *advaita*"; that is, the rebirth by which we become united with Christ, and through him with the Father (1989: 53–75, 32, 188). The "healing waters" of the pool at Bethesda (Jn 5:1–15) reveal the power of Jesus the guru to heal not just the exterior, but also the interior; Vandana stresses the recovery of self-respect, or self-awakening, of the sick man, as the real gift of God (1989: 93–107). Vandana regards the account of Jesus walking on the waters (Jn 6:16–21) as evidence of the power of his inner resources, which can be developed by all through the disciplines of meditation, using both Christian and Hindu techniques (1989: 108–22). But whereas the typical Hindu disciple expects to wash the feet of his guru in a ceremony called *guru pad-puja*, this custom is transformed by Guru Jesus (Jn 13:1–20), whose enlightened consciousness of his inner life led him to selflessly wash his disciples' feet (1989: 140–59). Vandana regards the "principle of love" that Jesus taught and demonstrated as what sets Jesus apart from other gurus, and draws people to him (1987: xiii–xiv, 10–12). That was most clearly revealed on the cross when, according to John's Gospel, blood and water flowed from his side (Jn 19:31–37). Inspired by her own Sacred Heart tradition of Catholic mysticism, as well as by reflection on the Hindu scriptures, Vandana sees these as the "waters of salvation," streaming from the depths of the guru's inmost self and drawing all within (1989: 160–79). In the final chapter, the Sea of Tiberias, by which Jesus appeared to his disciples after his death, becomes the "waters of awakening," as they realized "he was the Lord" (Jn 21:1–23) (1989: 180–89).

Waters of Fire represents a confluence of the worldviews of Christianity and Hinduism, in which Jesus Christ is presented to Hindus in a form that they can understand. Without endorsing all she writes, it can be said that Vandana certainly does reveal striking parallels between Hindu and Christian mystical thought, and casts new and intriguing light on familiar passages in John's Gospel. While suggesting that the two religions have a common goal of union with the divine, she also expresses her belief that Jesus offers the best (but not the only) way to self-realization, the way of selfless love. In a small booklet, *Jesus the Christ* (1987), written for Hindu enquirers, Vandana develops her vision of Jesus as *Param* (Supreme) or *Sat* (True) *Guru*, the one "who is so without self that he can communicate the Self" (1989: 106). In her view, it is by his spiritual teaching that he showed the path of self-realization, leading beyond Hinduism and Christianity. It is noticeable that Vandana rarely refers to Jesus' deeds; these are less significant in a country where there are many miracle-workers. What she regards as important is not the signs themselves but their "depth-meaning," which is revealed in Jesus' discourse. She argues that Jesus taught the way of the Spirit, which is the way of love, exemplified by the love between Father and Son. She does not mention claims about Jesus' humanity and divinity; she does not regard them as necessary, since all gurus are regarded as partaking of the divine nature in any case. Her emphasis is not on Jesus' divine origins, but on his ascent to heaven through self-realization, so that others can follow. She does not advance arguments for his uniqueness or universal lordship either; in common with many Indian theologians, she finds this debate counterproductive in India, where there are many rival truth claims. What is exceptional about Jesus Christ, she argues, is the strength of his connection to the Source, that is, his Heart or Spirit. So the call is not to conversion from one religion to another, but for Hindus and Christians to combine the spiritual techniques of Hinduism with the principles of Christianity, to share the same Spirit. In this vein Vandana presents ashramic spirituality as a holistic approach to life, leading to and flowing from a realization of oneness with the One Spirit, and hence a connectedness with the universe and with "spiritual" people regardless of gender, caste and religion (1993a).

Vandana's theology of religions is expressed in an extraordinary book, *Shabda Shakti Sangam* (1995a). This is an anthology of writings on various aspects of Christianity and Hinduism, to which eighty scholars and mystics of both Christian and Hindu traditions have been persuaded to contribute, including such internationally known Christian theologians as Raimundo Panikkar, Paulos Mar Gregorios, Klaus Klostermaier, Lucien Legrand, and Stanley Samartha. The book is divided into two halves— Hindu and Christian—which begin at opposite ends of the volume and meet in the middle. Thus it illustrates what it is trying to prove: that Hindu and Christian thought flow naturally together; *sangam* means "confluence." The two parts are joined by a painting by Jyoti Sahi, which combines a crucifix and a dancing Shiva by means of streams of water. In a further provocative move, the section on Hinduism is headed *Shabda* ("Word"), and has the symbol of *Om*; that on Christianity is titled *Shakti* ("Spirit") with the symbol of the dove, which is drawn to resemble the *Om*. Both sections follow the same outline, of eight parts subdivided to parallel each other, so that Christianity and Hinduism are portrayed as mirror images, meeting at the looking glass of a common spiritual experience. Each section is written by a mixture of Hindu and Christian authors. Vandana has contributed articles to both sections and supplied introductions throughout. The implication is that the seeker can start from either side of the mirror, but the aim is the confluence point, the heart of each, which is also the point at which they merge into one. *Shabda Shakti Sangam* is intended to illustrate Vandana's view that religions, like the distributaries of the Ganges delta, flow (backward) together toward the one source of them all. The religions are living streams of water that come from the one stream, *Shakti*, the Spirit:

> . . . the deepest religious experience of all humankind is one of peace, harmony, love, joy, freedom, unity. The Spirit or *Shakti* is seen to be the same Spirit of "Oneing," a unity underlying all diversities of race or religion, creed or caste. At the highest depth or deepest height of our spiritual experiences we become one, all religious differences and doctrines fall off (1995a: Hinduism section 190).

Vandana seeks, through shared meditative practice, to penetrate beyond the boundaries of particular religions, and break out of the restrictions of dogma and ritual, to reach the common experience of the Spirit, who is beyond any religion and, she believes, shared by all.

Behind much of Vandana's thought lies the conviction that the Spirit, like *Shakti*, is feminine, and in her Catholic tradition the feminine is supremely exemplified by Mary, the mother of Jesus. She regards the institutional Catholic religion—from which she is on the whole excluded—as masculine, but believes that "all spirituality, especially Indian, is feminine"; that is, it is peaceful, contemplative, and silent (1993d: 103). She is a great admirer of the Hindu guru Ramana Maharishi, famous for communicating without words, and argues that the Spirit, who is "silence-in-Love," has a "gentler, quieter witness" than the more forceful "masculine" proclamation of the Word (1998: 90–92, 28; cf. 37–38). In *And the Mother of Jesus Was There* (1991a), a book dedicated to the sisters of Sophia College, she pictures Mary as the epitome of compassion and tenderness, combined with vigor and courage. She sees Mary as the archetypal Mother, as Sophia (wisdom) and the creative life-force, as Mother Earth (1991a: passim). Vandana's reflections along these lines are enhanced by meditation on Saraswati, consort of *Brahma*, who represents the absorption of *shakti*, the life principle, into advaitic Hinduism (1995e). In many respects Vandana gives priority to the feminine, and recognizes the primacy of motherhood in much Indian thought. It was, she writes, the Holy Spirit "who formed the Heart of Jesus in the womb of Mary" (1991b: 1; cf. 23, 57–60). This suggests that Vandana is advancing an alternative to the institutional Catholic Church, one in which women are the leaders and spirituality has priority over theology. This is not explicit, but she certainly puts forward ashrams as an alternative to the Western model of church (e.g. 1991b).

In her commentary on the story of the wedding at Cana (Jn 2:1–11) (1989: 76–92), Vandana parallels Mary with water: both are instrumental in bringing fullness of life, in the form of new wine, to the wedding party. She concludes that the Holy Spirit, Third Person of the Blessed Trinity, is the "Motherhood" in God. However, in practice, Vandana's concept of the Godhead rarely comes across as truly trinitarian, but seems to oscillate between binity and monism, because of the ambiguity of motherhood and the feminine in her understanding of the Spirit. On the one hand, when the submissive nature of the Spirit is emphasized, the Father and Son appear primary, and the role of the Spirit is reduced to that which keeps them together. So when she describes the Spirit as the mother figure, who is the "Love-Energy . . . standing between the Father and the Son" (1995f: 52–53), the reader cannot help remembering that Vandana stresses the submissive, self-effacing, and background nature of motherhood. Sometimes the personhood of the Spirit is further reduced by descriptions such as: the Spirit is "the Speech," "the Love," the "kiss" between Father and Son. On the other hand, when the power of the feminine comes to the fore, the Spirit appears as the universal life principle, in which case the Spirit is strong and primary, and the Father and Son serve in her reflections merely to illustrate the Spirit's work. In common with Hindus, Christians can say, "God is

Spirit" (Jn 4:24), so Vandana claims that the Spirit is the *atman* within, the "soul" or "self" that is one with *Brahman*, the very "ground of being" (1975: 35). In this description the First and Third Persons appear one and the same, and there does not seem to be any room for Jesus Christ in the Godhead. For this reason Vandana may sometimes be accused of pantheism or "Spirit-monism." The focus of her meditation is on Jesus Christ, but sometimes it seems that Jesus Christ leads to the Spirit, and not the other way round.

Vandana's theology is not systematic, and often lacks clarity, but it comes from her heart, from the depths of her experience. In her readiness to embrace Indian spiritual traditions, Vandana sometimes fails to discern the distinctiveness of each one, and seems not to consider the possibility that spirits other than the Holy Spirit are at work in the world. However, her achievement in leading the Catholic ashram movement, and her courage in challenging religious institutions, especially as a woman, are greatly to be admired. Her biblical interpretation is very original, and she shows how the images and nuances of "spirit" in Scripture are much wider and richer than a simple word study can reveal. Vandana looks for the Spirit that is the breath within the tradition, rather than the wind that blows from outside. She seeks to affirm the mystical heritage of India, and to work with it and through it to overcome conflict between religions. She therefore develops a missiology of the Spirit that emphasizes the Spirit's unifying presence, and plays down the action of the Spirit in judgment and purging. When she describes the Spirit as "waters of *fire*," it is not the "refiner's" fire of the Baptist's preaching (Lk 3:16–17) to which she refers, but to the tongues of fire at Pentecost, and also to the Vedic tradition that fire is born of water (1989: 27).

Vandana's perspective, as an Indian Catholic woman, allows her to take a bold and refreshing look at many aspects of Christian scripture and tradition, resulting in a mission pneumatology derived from her ashramic experience. What her theology lacks in polish is made up for in innovation and breadth, and she presents her case persuasively. Vandana's aim is the inculturation of the gospel of Jesus Christ in the mystical traditions of India. Her work is a challenge to a deeper interaction with Indian categories of thought; this encounter reveals pneumatology as of primary importance.

Breath and Bread:
The Liberation Pneumatology of Samuel Rayan

The third Indian theologian of the Spirit for us to consider is Samuel Rayan, a Jesuit priest who has been teaching at Vidyajyoti College of Theology, Delhi for more than thirty years.[3] He has achieved considerable distinction as a liberation theologian, and is acclaimed in his festschrift by such well-known international figures as Gustavo Gutiérrez, Jon Sobrino, James Cone and Kosuke Koyama (John 1991). He has had a long involvement with the ecumenical movement, serving as the Director of the Ecumenical Centre in Bangalore, and on the World Council of Churches' Commission on Faith and Order. He is also a founding member and spokesperson of the Ecumenical Association of Third-World Theologians (EATWOT).

Rayan was born in 1920 to a Catholic family, and spent much of his early ministry in his native Kerala, working with highly politicized students and young people who were strongly influenced by Marxist thought. He became involved in campaigning for the human rights of outcastes or *dalits*. His dialogue with Marxism and secular humanism led him to seek a theological link between the gospel and "human well-being on earth." This involved criticism of caste Hindus for their failure to denounce caste discrimination, and even more strident condemnation of the institutional church, for failing to live up to the good news—which Rayan saw proclaimed in the eucharist—of the sharing of God's gifts with all (Rayan 1972). Rayan embraced the reforms of Vatican II, which he believed led to a new view of the mission of the church, as "listening to the Spirit," and involving itself in the most appropriate way in the circumstances (1970: 426). Drawing further on the Vatican II documents, and in particular the reflection on the Spirit's role in creation, in the document *Gaudium et spes* (paragraphs 43, 26), he sought to justify Christian involvement in development work by developing "a theology of earthly things" (1971). He saw the Spirit of God as uniting the human and divine, grace and nature, sacred and secular. These were truly reconciled, he writes, in "the man Jesus," who is "the ultimate basis of the connection between . . . bread for breakfast and for the Eucharist," because he is completely human and yet "wholly graced with the Spirit of God" (: 43, 45). So he argues that sacred and profane history are one, and that the church's religious mission and its human mission to meet people's material needs are united "[b]eneath the hovering Spirit" (: 45; the quotation is from the nineteenth-century Jesuit poet Gerard Manley Hopkins' poem, "God's grandeur"). Through his efforts to link evangelization and development in the category of mission (see also Rayan 1975), Rayan sketched the mission pneumatology and Spirit christology that he was to continue to formulate over the next quarter of a century.

Though informed by social studies and current theology, most—perhaps all—of Rayan's theological insights are the fruit of a creative reading of the Bible, particularly the synoptic gospels. He seeks to understand these within the socioeconomic and political environment of first-century Palestine, and to relate them to contemporary "Indian realities" (see, for example, Rayan

---

[3] The following discussion is based on a more thorough study of all Rayan's published work to be found in K. Kim 2003a: 138–94.

1978). His conviction, derived from the synoptic gospels, of the writers' concern for the material and historical, leads him to reinterpret John's Gospel for the Indian setting, demonstrating that the mystical vision of the fourth gospel is equally grounded in Jesus' concern for human need. He recognizes the Indian appreciation of John's Gospel for "its atmosphere of mysticism and its contemplative horizon," but tries to show that "[i]ts contemplation fixes on . . . Jesus' love for and service of the people" (: 213). He does this by drawing attention to evidence of historical structure and context, pointing to stories of liberation in common with the synoptics, and highlighting the themes of the "bread-less" (Jn 6) and "wine-less" (Jn 2). He sees the raising of Lazarus (Jn 11:1–44), who is known as a poor man in the synoptics (Lk 16:19–31), as representative of the resurrection life Jesus gives to all the wretched of the earth, and shows how this episode, in which Jesus sided with the poor, leads directly to the killing of Jesus (Jn 11:45–53), which becomes his "glorification" in John's account. Rayan concludes that for John, the glory of God "is not some marvelous light shining on the mountain tops; it is the revelation of his love in concrete services to meet concrete needs" (1978: 219).

In the early 1970s, in debate with other third-world theologians, Rayan questioned the inculturation approach to contextualization, on the grounds that it did not take into account the sociopolitical context: "Inculturation fails to see that every church is in fact inculturated. The real question is, in what class?" (1982b: 116). He found that the chief impact of the Christian gospel for Indians had not been primarily in the area of spiritual life, but "in the social sphere and in the area of human values," as seen in the work of the Hindu reformers, and pre-eminently of Mahatma Gandhi (1972). He urged the church to "break out of narrow ecclesiastic concerns, and cease building its own little world, in order to collaborate with men for universally human causes" connected with the material welfare of humanity (1974a: 288). So Rayan was one of the first to appreciate the importance of the theology of liberation emerging in Latin America, especially the work of Gustavo Gutiérrez, and to develop an Asian theology of liberation.

Though his focus was liberation, he also recognized that, for liberation theology to be relevant in Asia, it would have to take into account culture, religion and spirituality for liberation, and not be restricted to the language of socioeconomic analysis or to the Judeo-Christian tradition. In order to include all the people of India in God's liberation, he began his theology from the creation, not the exodus (1989b: 453). Furthermore, as Gutiérrez later pointed out, in liberation theology's key text, Luke 4:18, Rayan recognized early a link between "good news to the poor" and "the Spirit of the Lord is upon me" (Gutiérrez 1991: 4). So, beginning with the brooding of the Spirit over the waters at creation, he redefined history as the movement of the Spirit to bring liberation. In this way he aimed to bring human history into one, and overcome the difficulties of Asians with salvation history, which appears to privilege those nations who have been part of the Christian movement longest. This "history of the Spirit" moves across religious boundaries, and is recognized by the liberation of the downtrodden into life (Rayan 1980). Rayan identified the Spirit at work in historical revolutions that liberate the poor, whatever the cultural or religious milieus in which they take place (1979: 2–9). He debunked the idea that Asian peasants are passive, and drew attention to repeated revolts over the centuries, as examples of movements of the Spirit for liberation (1992: 15; 1999d: section 8). With his colleague Sebastian Kappen, he advocated spiritual struggle—following the example of Jesus—to overcome the forces of violence and oppression in society, and to bring about justice (1985b: 104–116).

While appreciating Stanley Samartha's concern for dialogue, Rayan differs in his choice of dialogue partners. Rayan rejects dialogue in which "the religion/faith-practice of partners [is] presumed to be socio-politically pure," and states categorically that "action for justice and liberation is the [proper] basis for dialogue." Therefore he declines dialogue with the Brahminic leaders of Hindu society, as long as they support caste oppression. He opts to talk with those whom he terms "the people" or "the poor," and to talk about the "concrete situation," not "abstruse, etherial, esoteric matters" (1989a: 68–73). He finds that their spirituality is of the *bhakti* type, and judges that the Bhagavad-Gita and other epics have wider influence in India than the Vedas of classical Hinduism (1974b). Similarly, he declines to use what he sees as the elitist traditions of philosophical Hinduism (such as Sankara's *advaita*), and prefers the "little traditions" of the poor—drama, dance, poetry and song—to express his gospel. The use of artistic, rather than scientific, forms and of "the language of the people" is part of Rayan's "decolonization" of theology to reflect the concerns of Asia, not Europe (1999a). He is particularly keen on poetry, which he also writes himself, and describes the Spirit as a poet, in that the Spirit sees beneath the surface level, reveals hidden meaning and can inspire subversive resistance (1979: 109–110). Rayan's interest in depth-meaning in this regard is reminiscent of Vandana, since both share—through their respective religious orders—the theology of the Sacred Heart, and relate this to *atman*. However, for Rayan this interiority is experienced not as peace, but as wrestling with God, which leads to greater involvement in the liberation struggle (1989b).

Rayan published his reflections on the Holy Spirit, developed while leading retreats, in *The Holy Spirit—Heart of the Christian Gospel* (1979 [1978]), a book whose title shows that Rayan founded his liberation theology on the mission of the Spirit. He begins by defining the Christian gospel as the message "that our life and our world stand bathed in the Holy Spirit, the Spirit of God and of Jesus Christ." This he regards as "the central point of God's redemptive activity," "the basic experience of salvation," "the heart of the Gospel and of Christian hope" (: 2). Drawing primarily on Luke's Gospel, he characterizes the Spirit as the "Breath of Fire," who comes "to enable us to re-create our earth, not to put us to sleep," and is present "not in ethereal euphoria, but in committed historical action" (: vii). For Rayan, fire evokes judgment and revolution, and is fearful and uncontrollable, unlike the flame in the heart and in ritual devotion on which Vandana reflects. He sees the Creator Spirit as also the Liberator, "the Initiator of fresh developments and the Leader of new movements," who brings about fullness of life for all. It is also the Spirit who gives dreams of new society, and empowers people to bring about their own liberation (: 3–9).

Rayan begins his reflections by calling attention to a "fact not always noted": namely, that due to the events of Pentecost, "uppermost in the consciousness of the early church was the reality of the Holy Spirit" (1979: 1–2). He calls for the reformation of the institutional church, so that love becomes its distinguishing mark (Jn 13:35) (1979: 25–26). This will only be possible, he believes, when the church severs its links with the status quo, and rediscovers the gifts of the Spirit, which encourage a "socialistic" lifestyle (Acts 2:44–45), in which the church is led by the people (1979: 60–61, 63–64). He sees this transformation already happening in the "base communities" of liberation theology, as lay people support one another in action to change society, on the basis of their re-reading of the Bible (: 77–94). As a member of the Faith and Order Commission of the World Council of Churches, Rayan pioneered a reinterpretation of the eucharist, the central act of the church's life, as a redistribution of the world's wealth inspired by the Spirit's mission of liberation: "Our task is . . . to communicate the One Spirit who impels us to fulfill justice and liberate the downtrodden and to invite men and women to come to taste the One Bread or Rice-Bowl of life which all of us are called to become and break with one another" (1985a: 186).

Rayan pioneered an Indian "Spirit-uality" of liberation, in which he regards spiritual life as "the whole of human life inspired and led by the Spirit," arguing that "[p]eople are spiritual in their struggles for daily rice, in their devotion to their children, in their love for one another, in their simple prayers, their trust in God, and the responsibility they assume for new generations of people" (1999c: section 15, i). He described "Spirit-uality" as revealed in history, both as the aspiration for freedom and as the energy behind "every struggle . . . for liberation and life" (1992: 17). In dialogue with Samartha, Rayan considers the different strands of Hindu spirituality—*advaita, bhakti* and *shakti*—and prefers *shakti*, which he regards as "far less prestigious than *advaita*, less known than *bhakti*, but somehow implicit in most Indian experiences" (1977: 189). Reflection on *shakti*—the source of life, energy and creativity—lies behind his pneumatology, and is one of the reasons for his use of the feminine pronoun to describe the Spirit. He has in mind not only the life-principle, but also the pre-Aryan goddess who, as the invincible Durga, destroys evil and, as the ferocious Kali, frees from demonic forces. As in the philosophy of Aurobindo, Rayan envisages

Shakti as leading a forward movement, which ruthlessly overthrows all hindrances and energizes new life (see 1999c: section 15, xviii–xix). Rayan
eschews mystical spirituality for its own sake; for him the aim of "Spirituality" is not personal enlightenment, but social liberation, as he writes in
one of his poems:

> the invitation is to . . .
> bring the whole wealth
> of this aesthetic-mystic experience
> to our work for life and people,
> and to our co-work with God
> for the realization of His rainbow-dreams
> for our earth (1994b: 73).

In his writings, Rayan also sought to develop a pneumatology of religions
appropriate to the Indian search for the Universal Spirit. He saw in the documents of Vatican II, particularly *Lumen gentium* (16) and *Ad gentes* (3, 4,
9, 11, 15), an understanding of the Universal Spirit, which gives implicit
knowledge of God. The evidence for this, he believed, lay in the belief inherent in "all faith traditions" that the Divine is on the side of "goodness, justice, freedom, love and life," and against "evil, oppression, deprivation and
domination" (1989a: 65–66). While recognizing other religions as sacraments
of salvation, he continued to hold a special place for Jesus Christ, in whom
he sees the work of the Spirit focused. However, for Rayan, the basis for
Christian claims to uniqueness, and claims about the universality of
Christianity, cannot be matters of doctrine, but only liberative action. They
rest on the extent to which Christians "live and act from the Spirit of Christ,"
without which tangible expression of Christian truth Hindus and others cannot be expected to hear the gospel of Jesus Christ (1982a: 131–34).

Rayan does not see religions as discrete systems, but as interrelated, and
in an article comparing the book of Job, the Bhagavad-Gita and the poems
of Gitanjali, a Muslim girl, he aims to demonstrate "the overlapping of so
many stresses, the coincidence of the spirit they breathe, and the convergence of their ultimate thrust" (1989b: 450). When Indian theologians were
criticized by Vatican authorities for suggesting that "the mystery of God is
[not] exhausted in Jesus Christ" (Tomko 1990b: 240), Rayan pointed out
the lack of pneumatology in the Vatican's reasoning, and justified his own
stance by reference to the Creator God and the diverse and unpredictable
work of the Spirit. He affirmed religious plurality, seeing religions as "joint
creations of the Spirit and the Spirit-experience of human groups," because
mystery is expressible "only in a thousand mediations." "The real question," as Rayan sees it, "is whether the religions can now muster their
resources to act together with the oppressed, to struggle for the liberation
of all, and for a new-creative pro-existence" (1990: 136–39).

From the start, Rayan was motivated to lay a theological basis for Christian commitment to human development and liberation, and he found pneumatology to be the best starting point for this effort. Later, as he explored the systematic consequences of this starting point, he came to the conclusion that, in the Indian context, Spirit christology—not the traditional Logos christology—was the most appropriate way of explaining the significance of Jesus Christ (1999b). For Rayan, the movement of the Spirit always takes concrete historical form, and nowhere more so than in the life and work of Jesus Christ. He regards the annunciation to Mary as "the second creation of the Spirit" in the conception of the Messiah, whose baptism in the Jordan confirmed his Spirit-filled nature. Rayan described Jesus' bodily resurrection from the dead to new and liberated life as "*the* work of the Holy Spirit," and as "the one meaningful and meaning-giving center of historical existence." Jesus Christ then sent that Spirit, now stamped with his own personality, on the disciples at Pentecost, an event that revealed the significance of Jesus for human history (1979: 3–9). Rayan describes Jesus as "the symbol of the Holy Spirit," and argues that he, and not the church, is properly termed the "universal sacrament of salvation" (1970: 424). Hence he does not find it necessary to argue that all liberating acts of the Spirit are historically connected through a particular salvation history; they can occur in any time and place, but he measures them alongside the liberating ministry of Jesus Christ. In Hindu terms, Rayan argues that Jesus Christ should be understood in the popular language of *bhakti* devotion as *Avatar*, one who descends from heaven at different moments in history to save the people. But in Jesus Christ's case, he believes the descent is also decisive and complete, so that Jesus is "the final and perfect living Image of God," "the flaming Focus of history" (1970: 422).

Rayan's interest in creation extends beyond humanity to the earth, which promotes and sustains life. Reflecting on parallels in the Lord's Prayer (Luke 11:1–13; Rayan 1970: 420), he describes the earth as our "bread" (e.g. 1994a: 133–34). His theology of the environment was also informed by the image of *Shakti*, understood as the Breath that makes the earth live. He sought to develop a "pneumatological cosmism," in which the Spirit infuses the whole creation, bringing about its evolution and even revolution toward the kingdom of God (1999b). "Bread and breath," the converse of a phrase from Hopkins' poem "The wreck of the Deutschland," was used as the title of his festschrift, because it is "suggestive of the two main poles around which Samuel's own theological reflections turn: the question of Bread for all, with the justice this demands at all levels of our national and international society, and the role of the Spirit, the inspiration which faith and God's action provide for a commitment to those who go hungry" (John 1991: xii). However, the two words are more integrated in Rayan's vocabulary than this suggests. "Bread and breath" is a richly poetic way of combining the two natures of Christ, the secular and the sacred, the immanence and transcendence of God, and the liberative and evangelistic dimensions of mission. It is a way of bringing earth and heaven together. The Spirit is the "breath" or yeast of new life that invigorates the "bread," which is the earth, and brings about a redistribution of its resources to the benefit of all. Rayan uses his sacramental theology of bread and breath to motivate mystics to seek human well-being, and encounter the Spirit in their neighbors. Conversely, "bread and breath" expresses to activists and historians the importance of spirituality. The phrase is also a symbol of the eucharist, which is seldom far from Rayan's thoughts, and in which the bread of life is broken and shared with all, under the inspiration of the breath of God. His understanding of the earth as a theological and a liturgical reality has made Rayan a leading voice in eco-theology in international circles; he laid a pneumatological framework for ecumenical creation theology (Rayan 1994a).

Rayan's emphasis on the universality of the Spirit and the Spirit's unifying role is sometimes criticized as too all-embracing, and even overwhelming. It is possible for *shakti* to be as totalizing as Rayan complains *advaita* is, if both posit a spirit that it universally present. Furthermore, he rarely discusses the Trinity, except as a model of unity. Thus there seems little room in Rayan's theology for genuine diversity within unity. His idea of a latent spirituality in all people could be described as paternalistic, and his work for church unity has been seen as "suffocating" minority church traditions (see Athappilly 1984). His socialist political agenda, too, suggests totalitarian tendencies. In this sense, despite his support of the downtrodden, and his willingness to recognize the work of the Spirit in diverse contexts, Rayan's theology remains "from above." On the other hand, in refusing to set the work of the Spirit within a linear historical framework, Rayan breaks decisively with traditional theologies, and affirms the experience of the marginalized. For the theologian this raises questions not only of hermeneutics, but also of ecclesiology, given that the Holy Spirit was poured out on the church. Unlike Samartha, for whom the "unbaptized *koinonia*" was the result of historical encounter with the Christian gospel, Rayan has a mystical understanding of the pervasive influence of the Spirit. For the historian, this discontinuous view of history is unsatisfactory, because liberating events in history are viewed in isolation from one another, and then juxtaposed, without an appreciation of historical development and context. Rayan sees the causes of these events as due to contemporary social factors and to the in-breaking of the Spirit, rather than to historical antecedents. This also applies to some extent to the event of Jesus Christ. The lack of attention to historical narrative tends to give the impression that the events are mythical, rather than set in a particular time and place.

Rayan appears to be formed by multiple contexts, life experiences and influences—Christian, Indian and Marxist—and the theme of the Spirit would seem to emerge from all or any of these contexts. However, it is the Spirit's mission of liberation that most interests him. For Rayan, mission starts with the Spirit, grows by the Spirit's witnessing in human hearts and culminates in the life of the Spirit, so that the church's mission should become "listening to the Spirit speaking in the Gospel and in the hearts of men" (Rayan 1979: 105–106). In light of the Spirit's role in creation, and the Spirit-filled mission of Jesus Christ, he insists that the aim of mission is fullness of life for all, beginning with the poor. Furthermore, he regards authentic spirituality as mission spirituality, which is recognized by action on behalf of the downtrodden. What he advocates is "mission in the Spirit," because "mission is the sphere of the Spirit," "the work of the Spirit" and "the extension in space and time of the Incarnation of God's Word"; and "[t]hose who engage in it are co-workers of the Spirit. . . . to the extent that they live in the Spirit" (1999c: sections 11, 16). Rayan has developed a theology of "mission in the Spirit" that is also a comprehensive approach to the whole of life, in which contemplation serves to motivate historical action.

The Holy Spirit in Dialogue, Inculturation, and Liberation in India

Though they represent different strands of Indian Christian theology, the shared cultural background of Samartha, Vandana and Rayan contributes to commonalities in their general approach to theologizing in India, which they each justify by their reflections on the Spirit. They all insist that theology is not a dry, academic exercise, but should be creative and mystical. They characterize it as art rather than science, expressing a preference for signs, images and symbols, rather than propositions and doctrines. Samartha explains, and the others would agree, that in theology experience is more important than logic, and that what is heard takes precedence over what is written (1991a: 5, 61, 82–83, 105). So they all claim that their theology is from below, by which they mean that it does not begin with a rigid framework, but is lived and relational. None of them attempts to be systematic, and they are willing to live with mystery. They are more concerned with the general tenor of scripture, rather than with biblical and historical criticism of the text. They read the Bible to interpret and apply it, rather than to analyze and dissect it.

The prominence of the theme of the Holy Spirit in the fourth gospel escapes the attention of none of our theologians. Samartha focuses chiefly on the Spirit leading into all truth (Jn 16:13), Vandana emphasizes the Spirit of peace (Jn 20:21–22), and Rayan stresses that the truth will make you free (Jn 8:32), primarily in the sociopolitical sense. In Rayan's interpretation, John tells a story of revolutionary social change brought about by the Spirit, in which "the working class is now enabled and challenged to liberate themselves from the oppression of contempt and marginalization" and "from the prisons of narrow religious traditions" (1978: 220). Vandana, by contrast, in her commentary on John, uses the gospel to relate Christian experience to the contemplative traditions of India, through the language of the Spirit and the practice of spirituality. Both Vandana's and Rayan's studies of John's Gospel are selective, Rayan favoring those acts of Jesus that reveal a deeper meaning of the Spirit, and Vandana preferring to dwell on the symbolic meanings expressed in the discourses, and their parallels with Hindu thought. Neither of them chooses to comment on John 14:6, "No one comes to the Father but by me," which Samartha immediately recognizes as an "exclusive claim," and therefore a stumbling block to dialogue. He counters this by emphasizing the unifying activity of the Spirit in John, together with the Spirit's association with peace and all truth.

Each of these theologies of the Spirit aims to address issues raised by Indian realities. For Samartha the key issue is communalism (in the sense of sectarianism); for Vandana it is ignorance; and for Rayan, poverty and oppression. So Samartha discerns the Spirit in "renascent movements" that help to bind Indian society and culture; Vandana looks to the ashram movement as an Indian spiritual means of promoting knowledge of God (*brahmavidya*); and Rayan sees the marks of the Spirit in "movements for liberation" that empower the oppressed. From these starting points they develop their distinctive theologies of dialogue, inculturation and liberation. It is noticeable that Samartha and Vandana prefer to talk about the *presence* of Spirit, who is already there in Indian religiocultural tradition, waiting—as it were—to be discovered, whereas Rayan prefers to talk about the *activity* of Spirit, who takes the initiative and challenges the settled state, the status quo. Rayan is interested in the Spirit's work in history to bring about social transformation; Samartha sees the Spirit as leading beyond the particular histories of different communities, to where he believes truth is located; and Vandana focuses on the experience of the Spirit that is timeless and regardless of history, but which may be fed back to improve human society.

All three theologians relate the Spirit to the different concepts of spirit in Indian thought: *atman*, *antaryamin* and *shakti*. None of them uses any one of these terms exclusively, but Vandana shows a marked preference for *atman*, the self, and Rayan for *shakti*, the energy of creation. Samartha refers to each, but spends most time discussing the Spirit as the *advaita*, the unity of *Brahman* and *atman*, the Father and the Son. Using mainly Johannine language, Vandana and Samartha focus on the presence of the Spirit within human hearts (Vandana) and communities (Samartha). Rayan draws particularly on Luke's Gospel, and conveys a greater sense of the Spirit's intervention from outside of human experience, of the Spirit's "sentness" and in-breaking into society. Rayan tends to emphasize the sudden and powerful experience of the Spirit, as at Pentecost, whereas Samartha and Vandana are more influenced by the fourth gospel's description of Jesus proclaiming peace, and breathing his Spirit into the disciples. Samartha concentrates on the Spirit in human relationships, Vandana in mystical experience, and Rayan in liberating events and in creation. The difference in choice of language between Vandana and Samartha on the one hand, and Rayan on the other, reflects the conflict in Indian Christian theology between emphasis on the inculturation of the gospel in Vedic terms, and concern for a theology of liberation for the poor. Caste Hindus, educated in their philosophical traditions, may appreciate the former, whereas the poor prefer the folk tradition, and see caste tradition as a major cause of their poverty. The use of *atman* and *antaryamin* tends to lead to theologies of the Spirit of peace, who promotes cooperation and mutual respect, and who brings personal and religious harmony; this contrasts in India with theologies of non-Brahminic *shakti*, the Spirit of fire, who refines and humanizes society. In Rayan's work, the Spirit flares up like a fire from below, whereas in Vandana's reflections the Spirit appears as bestowed or poured out from above.

When it comes to the relationship of the Spirit of Christ with Indian religions, all three theologians agree that Jesus Christ "does not exhaust the mystery of God," and find that a pneumatological theology of religions leaves room to encounter truth (Samartha), peace (Vandana) and justice (Rayan) in the people, practices and movements (respectively) of other faiths. They all agree on the need for interreligious dialogue, but differ as to whether this should be a dialogue of inculturation or of liberation. Samartha finds the Spirit at work in the very willingness to dialogue itself; Vandana finds the entry point for dialogue in the mystical traditions; and Rayan wishes to join with the Spirit in movements among the outcastes for freedom. They all stress the unpredictability of the Spirit, and the need for openness to the Spirit's work beyond the boundaries of religious communities (Samartha) and institutions (Vandana and Rayan). In each case, their theology of dialogue—which is positive toward the other—is challenged by the rise of fundamentalism in both Christianity and Hinduism.

The call for conversion signified by baptism is central to Hindu objections to Christianity, because the change from one community to another is a political as well as a religious act, especially in view of the church's ties with the colonial era. In this context, Samartha, Vandana and Rayan all define the church pneumatologically as "a community led by the Spirit," and use pneumatology to reform the church—or even (especially in Vandana's case) to circumvent it. Samartha seeks to relate to the "unbaptized *koinonia*" of those who have responded to the gospel, and been united with Christ in the Spirit, but remained within the Hindu community. Vandana and Rayan advocate the formation of new types of Christian community—open ashrams (Vandana) and base communities (Rayan)—as authentic expressions of Indian Spirit-uality. All regard the Trinity *ad intra* as a symbol of unity, and the Spirit as the chief agent of that unity, though none is particularly interested in metaphysical speculation about the Trinity. This is because they are more concerned to use existing Hindu frameworks in their theologizing. In their desire to relate to *advaita*, which is monistic, Samartha and Vandana sometimes seem to make trinity a penultimate, rather than final, description of God, even for Christians. Raimundo Panikkar questions whether this need be the case, even in the Indian context, when he argues—on the grounds that human religious experience is necessarily in terms of belief in an absolute, worship of a personal God, and experience of divinity—that belief in God as Trinity, at least *ad extra*, is universal (Panikkar 1973). His suggestion is one that warrants further investigation.

In relating the Holy Spirit to Indian plurality, all three theologians—at least in their later work—find it helpful to discuss spiritualities rather than religions, and they distinguish Christian spirituality by its centeredness on Jesus Christ. Samartha works for a harmony between Indian spiritualities that will result in peaceful coexistence. Vandana looks for convergence of spiritualities into a common stream that is both Indian and Christian, whereas Rayan is more likely to see different spiritual traditions as challenging one another; in particular, the spirituality of the poor challenges esoteric and academic theologizing, and the Spirit of Jesus Christ challenges the church and all authorities with the prophetic message of good news for the poor. None of the three is doing theology as a member of an outcaste group (*dalit*), though Rayan is an active campaigner for their cause, and works to overcome the caste system. For many who are specifically developing *dalit* theology as theology done by *dalits* as *dalits*, any dialogue with Hindu philosophy is anathema, unless it also rejects the caste system (e.g. Razu 2001). So, two Indian theologies are evident: classical Indian Christian theology and *dalit* theology (Devasahayam 1998). A. P. Nirmal began *dalit* theology in the 1980s when he sought to affirm *dalit* identity forged in the pathos of servitude by describing Jesus not as a friend of *dalits*, but as a *dalit* himself. As Son of Man, Nirmal observed, Jesus was rejected, mocked and despised by those of the dominant religion, and he suffered brokenness ("broken" is the root meaning of *dalit*) when he died on the cross (Nirmal 1994 [1988]). As originally proposed by Nirmal, *dalit* theology has a trinitarian outline, but as yet its theology of the Holy Spirit has not been developed, though Sathianathan Clarke has made some interesting suggestions as to the form it might take, given the spiritual traditions of *dalit* peoples (Clarke 1999: 43–48). Raj Sekhar Basu observes that *dalit* Christians of the Paraiyar caste—particularly the women—retain popular belief in demonic possession, and therefore believe in many spirits (Basu 2000).

This leads to a final point: all three theologians appear to be working with a cosmology that conceives of one Universal Spirit, wherever this Spirit is to be found. Neither Samartha nor Rayan gives much consideration—and

Vandana gives none—to a scenario in which there are other spirits at work. None of them inhabits a spirit-world, and they tend more to pantheism than dualism. Even though Rayan appreciates the "little traditions" of the poor, which in many cases would include belief in a spirit-world, he uses their cultural symbols, rather than the belief systems themselves, to express his theology. It is significant also that none of the three theologians directly discusses the fast-growing Pentecostal movement in India, which emphasizes the gifts and power of the Spirit, and applies the biblical language of spirits and other powers literally. Though it has worldwide links, this is an indigenous movement with at least phenomenological connections to popular Hinduism (Bergunder 2001). Pentecostal groups pose a threat to the established churches, which may also, more positively, be a motivation to spiritual renewal, but the Pentecostal groups are generally not seen as dialogue partners (see, for example, Kavunkal 1998). Samartha tends to dismiss popular movements in Christianity because of their "exclusive claims," which prejudice dialogue. In the twenty-first century, the need for intra-Christian discussion of the Holy Spirit that includes Pentecostal-charismatic perspectives is very pressing.

The Indian Mission of the Spirit

Interaction between Indian theologians on the theme of the Holy Spirit sheds new light on the biblical testimony to the Holy Spirit, and enhances understanding of the nature and work of the Spirit. Indian reflection on the Holy Spirit draws attention to the mission of the Spirit in the world, and particularly to the Spirit's presence and activity outside or beyond the Christian heart, the church or the Christian community. This is because Christians are a small minority in India, and if they are to engage constructively with the wider society, they need a theology that enables them to cross religious boundaries. It is also due to the richness of pneumatological reflection in Hindu traditions, and the wealth of spiritual experience in India. Indian pneumatology also addresses many of the questions raised in international debate, such as how the Spirit is discerned, the relationship of Christ and the Spirit, and the role of the Spirit in mission.

The fact of the varied nuances of the Spirit as *atman, antaryamin* and *shakti* indicates the breadth of the concept, and at the same time highlights the difficulty of discerning the Spirit. This multiplicity of meanings raises the question of whether the one Spirit appealed to by religious leaders (both Hindu and Christian) is always legitimately identified with the Spirit of God, and reveals the way in which spiritual backgrounds and mission interests shape discernment. The diversity of interpretation calls into question categorical claims that a particular tradition, or spirituality, or movement represents the work of the Spirit to the exclusion of others.

The three theologians we have studied discern the Spirit according to different criteria. Samartha looks for the Spirit of dialogue, who creates openness to others, and enables "traffic across the boundaries" of one religion and another. In order to bring communities together for the task of nation-building, he discerns the Spirit where there is cooperation and mutual respect. Vandana seeks to build bridges between Christians and Hindus by inculturating the gospel in terms of Hindu traditions of spirituality. She sees the Spirit in the common spiritual experience which, she believes, lies at the heart of both Hinduism and Christianity: the experience of the oneness of the inner self with the Divine Self, or of the unity of the Son with the Father. She therefore looks for the Spirit of the waters of life, who brings personal peace and religious harmony. Rayan discerns the Spirit at work in movements for the liberation of the poor and oppressed. The "Breath of Fire" is an uncontrollable wind that consumes the unjust structures oppressing the poor, and frees them to experience the good news of the kingdom, where there is "bread for the breadless" and "wine for the wineless." As we noted above the use of *atman* and *antaryamin*, preferred by Samartha and Vandana, leads to theologies of the Spirit of peace, who promotes cooperation and mutual respect, and brings personal and religious harmony. These contrast in India with theologies, like Rayan's, of non-Brahminic *Shakti*, the Spirit of fire who refines and humanizes society. The divorce between these approaches reflects caste divisions within Hinduism, which will continue to affect Indian Christian theology, as well as tensions in Christian faith. They should be kept together, as two aspects of the work of the one Spirit, because the Spirit of mission is a way of peace with justice, in the knowledge that the Spirit of Jesus Christ both inspires whatever is good and true, and empowers challenge and change.

Samartha's Spirit of truth, Vandana's Spirit of abiding in God, and Rayan's transforming Spirit of fire are all recognizably biblical models of the Spirit. Samartha and Vandana draw mainly on John's Gospel, and Rayan primarily on Luke. None of them alone is a full interpretation of the biblical witness to the Spirit, and this suggests that all three aspects of the Spirit's work need to be taken together. The Spirit is associated with contemplation *and* devotion *and* acts of liberation, rather than exclusively with one kind of religious expression over against another. Sebastian Painadath suggests that, in Hindu terms, the Spirit is found in the combination of the three paths: *jnana* (knowledge), *bhakti* (devotion) and *karma* (deeds). That these are practiced together may be the true evidence of the Spirit's work (Painadath 1993: 12–14).

The minority status of Christians in India, and these theologians' respect for the long traditions of the country, lead our Indian theologians to an openness to people of other faiths, and a willingness to affirm what is good and true (as they define these terms) in other religious traditions. Indian Catholic theologians were criticized by Vatican authorities for this approach, because it seemed to imply that "the mystery of God" is also revealed through other religions, and therefore to downplay the importance of proclamation (Tomko 1990b: 240). Rayan responded that it was significant that the critics singularly failed to mention the Holy Spirit, without whom there can be "no mission, no Church, no Lord Jesus," and that "[t]he suggestion that God provides for peoples' salvation only with the life and death of Jesus of Nazareth is unfair to God, too narrow for biblical perspectives, and too inept for a Spirit-led [human] history of over two million years" (1990: 136). This led Rayan and others to stress the presence and activity of God's Spirit from and in creation, and to see the particular ministry and mission of Jesus Christ as set within this wider sweep of God's work. They therefore regard the mission of the Spirit as preceding—as well as continuing beyond—the incarnation, a view that is known as "Spirit christology." Indian Catholic theologians and others with Indian experience, particularly the Belgian Jesuit Jacques Dupuis, have largely succeeded in establishing the legitimacy of Spirit christology, as long as it is understood that it is complementary to traditional christology, not an alternative (see chapter 7) (Dupuis 1997). In a Spirit-christological approach, the contentious phrase "all truth" in John 16:13 would be understood to be as broad as the Spirit's work in the whole creation, and also focused in Christ. The Spirit is both the Spirit of God and also the Spirit of Jesus Christ.

India not only has an awareness of God as Spirit, it is also a land of many spiritualities, of which *advaitic* Hinduism, *bhakti* devotion and *shaktism* are three major types. "Spirituality" is a very difficult term to define, but it is used here to distinguish religious approaches or attitudes from religions themselves, and thus it crosses the boundaries of religious communities. So Samartha identified and utilized a spirituality of dialogue, which he found in some members of all religious traditions. The awareness of God as Spirit explains why Indian theology ascribes much more importance than does Western theology to the categories of interiority, experience and mystery. In other words, there is a close relationship between theology and spirituality, and between the mode of theologizing and the religiocultural traditions of the society in which it takes place—in this case, India (Wilfred 1998). This enables Vandana to define spirituality as "life lived according to the Spirit" (1993d: 103).

M. M. Thomas recounts how the Hindu reformers, who sought to relate their faith to the modern world, struggled with the classical Hindu concept of the world as the unfolding of the Universal Spirit, which encouraged withdrawal from the world and passivity in society. They sought to transform the classical concept into a purposive one in which the Spirit is "the dynamic of cosmic evolution" (1990: 216). Though they largely succeeded in so doing, as evidenced by Hindu social involvement today, in Thomas's view they still tended to lack a "realistic appreciation of the depth of evil which the Spirit of God has to contend with," as described in the New Testament by the language of Satan and evil spirits (: 218). Thomas argues that this "spirituality for combat" lays a pneumatological foundation for theologies of liberation in Christianity, and that the recovery of the language of pre-brahminic *shakti* may do the same for Hinduism (: 221). In this case, the term "spirituality" need not apply only to "passive self-interiority or transcendentalism"—though it is most often used in this way—but also to active response to the world, issuing from a relationship with the Divine (Selvanayagam 1998). Rayan's awareness of the Spirit's activity in the world as Liberator, and presence as Creator, brings together action for human welfare with aesthetic and mystical concerns. Indian theologians, and Rayan in particular, have developed a spirituality of liberation, a mission spirituality in which spiritual resources empower action, and involvement with the world renews spirituality. Their work points to the Johannine version of the "Great Commission," in which Jesus sent the disciples as he breathed on them the Holy Spirit (Jn 20:21–23). In this perspective, mission should be understood, not primarily as a task, but as a spirit or spirituality. It is a way of being in Christ that orients us to share the gospel in order to transform lives.

The Indian spiritual tradition brings a distinctive contribution to the understanding of mission: the sense that mission, however it is done, should be "in the Spirit," and therefore, there is a need to consider mission spirituality, to ensure that the means of mission are consistent with its end. "Mission in the Spirit" calls into question some traditional models of mission, and opens up the way to missionary activity that is sensitive and appreciative of the cultural and spiritual heritage of others. Awareness that the Spirit of peace is also the Spirit of fire should serve as a reminder of the need for both presence and prophecy, for affirmation as well as discernment in mission. The Spirit that is within, and also comes from outside to inspire, is the medium in which true mission takes place.

CHAPTER 6

Mission among the Spirits:
Release, Blessing, Harmony

Korean Christian Theologies of the Holy Spirit

Christianity is only the latest in a succession of religious influences in Korea's long history, which is traced back to the legendary foundation of the nation in 2333 BCE by Tan'gun. While it is possible that Nestorian Christianity existed briefly in Korea in the tenth century (see Moffett 1998: 461–62), Korea did not have an established Christian community before modern times. Yet estimates of the proportion of Christians in South Korea today range from twenty-six percent of the population, according to the United States Central Intelligence Agency, to forty-one percent in the *World Christian Encyclopedia* (CIA 2005; Barrett, Kurian and Johnson 2001: 682). The latter figure is almost certainly over-optimistic; however, even in the lower case, this is the largest Christian percentage of any country in Asia apart from Georgia and the Philippines. In this chapter we shall briefly consider the history, and the religiocultural understanding of Spirit and spirits, that form the background to Korean Christianity, and follow the spiritual experience of Korean Christians, which includes the excitement of revival movements and spectacular church growth on the one hand, and persecution, division and struggle on the other. We shall then identify some key figures and strands of theological thinking, and see some different ways in which Korean theologians have treated the theme of the Holy Spirit. This will put a new perspective on the nature and mission of the Holy Spirit, and give a more complete picture of what Korean theology has to offer in debate about the Spirit in the world, than was presented by Chung Hyun Kyung at Canberra (as described in the Introduction). Though some background is necessary, this chapter is not intended to be a general introduction to Korean Christian theology, but a discussion of distinctively Korean theologies of the Holy Spirit.

Korean Spiritual Traditions

The Korean people are believed to have migrated in prehistoric times from North and Central Asia into the Korean peninsula, which is very mountainous. The tribes had a primal religious belief in a supreme or heavenly Spirit, the Lord of Heaven or Mountain God, who was worshipped as *Hanŭnim*.[1] A body of heavenly spirits was believed to carry out the will of God; these included spirits of the household, the land, the village, the ancestors, rocks, mountains, trees and streams. Certain unusual persons—shamans—were recognized as able to communicate with the realm of the spirits. These beliefs, which arose in hunter-gatherer society, became combined with the concerns for fertility of an agricultural society. At the two main Korean festivals of harvest and the lunar new year, local leaders would take on a shamanic role as "great spirits" and intercede for the people; the king was also regarded as a shaman. Besides these great rites, each clan maintained shrines and conducted rites for their ancestors. Korean traditional religion has changed over the centuries; it has lost its official status and become a folk religion, whose most dominant characteristic is shamanism (Grayson 2002: 216). Shamanism is mainly practiced by women and confined to the private side of life. The shaman may use forms of divination to tell fortunes and discern the spirits, give practical or medical advice, and make offerings to the spirits. If matters are serious, she may communicate with angry or playful spirits in a trance-like state, and exorcise or placate them through ecstatic dancing to the beat of drums, in what is known as *kut* (classic studies of Korean shamanism are Janelli and Janelli 1982; Kendall 1985; see also C. Kim 2003). Most commentators agree that shamanism continues to be deep-rooted in Korean life, but paradoxically, as a religious practice in Korea it is almost universally despised by women as well as men. This state of affairs may not be unconnected with gender issues, but a deeper reason for this may lie in the nature of shamanistic understanding. Shamanism is not dignified with the name "religion," partly because it is not regular or institutionalized, but also because it is the "waste disposal" of the religious world, a way of dealing with the unmentionable, the abnormal, the irrational aspects of life that are not countenanced in the ordered world of public life. Through the shaman, the spirits tell "stories never to be told," as the hidden, often sordid or tragic underside of life is

---

[1] Korean words are transliterated using the McCune-Reischauer system, unless another transliteration is in common use. In the latter case, the well-known form is preferred and the McCune-Reischauer equivalent is given in parentheses in the first instance of words that are used more than once. The exception to this is Korean names used in English-language publications, in which cases no other form is given. Where Korean texts are referred to, the translations are my own.

momentarily revealed, before being laid to rest; therefore it is not correct to describe shamanism as a popular religion (C. Kim 2003: 82–100, 189–91). Through the centuries shamanism has been regarded as "superstition" and "women's religion" by the (male) leaders of organized religions.

From the fourth and fifth century of the common era, the people of the Korean peninsula increasingly came under the influence of the two great emerging religiocultural forces of Asia, China and India, the latter mainly mediated through China. By the end of the sixth century Buddhism (of the Mahayana type) had become dominant in each of the three kingdoms of Korea, and was to hold sway in cultural and political circles for nearly a millennium (Grayson 1985: 16–62; Korean Buddhist Research Institute 1993). Korean Buddhism spawned many philosophical schools, stimulated by direct contact with India in the earlier period, as well as with China. Some of these emphasized the teaching and study of the scriptures (kyo), whereas others preferred various forms of meditation, developed in Korea as Sŏn Buddhism (known in Japan as Zen) in monasteries in the mountains. In its movement from India to Korea, popular Buddhism was influenced by Taoism in China and by shamanism in Korea. These influences are visible in the widespread presence of esoteric practices, in the emphasis on intercession for the people's prosperity and happiness, and in the recognition of various gods and spirits. The rulers of Koryŏ (918–1392CE) adopted Buddhism as a national ideology, believing its practice would protect the nation and cure the land, but the popular form of Buddhism in Korea over the centuries has been Pure Land Buddhism, which focused on a Pure Land in the west where the Amitabha Buddha, who is petitioned by means of devotional rituals, provides a respite from the hindrances of the world and from karmic rebirth, and helps devotees reach nirvana.

The teachings of Confucius have also influenced Korea for most of the last two millennia, particularly through the medium of Chinese education and letters, which were adopted as prerequisites for public service. Confucianism is a philosophy for social harmony, based on certain ancient texts. It is a way of life that emphasizes right behavior according to the law of Heaven, especially loyalty by a son to his father. The main religious rituals of Confucianism are the ancestral rites, performed only by the men of the family, and the social order is built around male genealogies. There are also four other important aspects of the Confucian social order: obedience to rulers, subservience of wife to husband, respect for elders, and loyalty in friendship (Berthrong and Berthrong 2000; Keum 2000). The neo-Confucians, who followed the school of the Chinese philosopher Zhu Xi (Chu Hsi,[2] 1130–1200), believed that the basis for moral living was conformity with the Ultimate Reality, and thus introduced a metaphysical

---

[2] Chinese terms are given primarily in the pinyin system, and secondarily in Wade-Giles.

dimension into what had until then been largely an ethical and practical philosophy in Korea; this provoked a clash with Buddhism (Grayson 2002: 100–104). In the fifteenth century, neo-Confucians achieved political power on the Korean peninsula and established the kingdom of Chosŏn. The new rulers exiled the Buddhists from the cities and centers of power, accusing them of corruption. In Chosŏn the scholar represented the cultural ideal, and was revered not only for his learning and political influence, but also because, in Chu Hsi's philosophy, education was the way to a higher moral state of harmony with the Ultimate Reality, leading to moral purity, honesty and simplicity of lifestyle. For the next five hundred years, Korea followed the Confucian social order more closely than did any other state.

Though Confucianism in Korea promoted a remarkable social stability, the severely hierarchical and patriarchal social structures it upheld were not flexible enough to cope with modernity. Furthermore, Confucianism's emphasis on the maintenance of tradition meant that the kingdom of Chosŏn failed to initiate technological development or to modernize. Lying between China, Japan and the Siberian territories of Russia, the Korean peninsula occupies a highly strategic position and has repeatedly been a battleground for competing powers. In this period Korea looked to China as an "elder brother," the source of Korea's classical language and culture; in keeping with Confucian filial piety, the aristocratic leaders of Chosŏn maintained allegiance to China even when the latter's power was waning toward the end of the nineteenth century. Korean reformers, however, seeing the rise of Japan, looked to form alliances with that nation and with the Western powers, in order to modernize the country. The Japanese, who had invaded Korea in the past, pursued designs on the country, until eventually, in 1876, they forced Korea into an unfavorable treaty. Taking advantage of the weakness of China, the imperial powers of Europe and America also interfered in Korean affairs, and engaged in "gunboat diplomacy" to persuade Korea to open her borders. The collapse of independent Korea was rapid. Japan defeated China in 1895 and Russia in 1905, and in 1910, with the acceptance of the Western powers, annexed the peninsula. The domination of Korea by its "younger brother" was the ultimate insult to the Confucian order, and a national humiliation. It was not until the Liberation in 1945 that Korea was recognized again as an independent nation.

In the late nineteenth century, Korea, which claimed an independent history stretching back five thousand years, faced national ruin. Internal tensions had weakened the monarchy and administration, and the country was threatened from outside by foreign powers. At this juncture, the traditional religions were not able to inspire the people. Confucianism appeared old-fashioned and was associated with China, which was weak; Buddhism was still suspected of being corrupt; and Korean primal religion appeared primitive in the face of modernity. Into this religious vacuum came three new religious movements: Roman Catholicism, *Tonghak*, and Protestantism.

Though Catholic missionaries had been trying since the sixteenth century to gain a foothold on the peninsula, Roman Catholicism was finally introduced to Korea when, in the late eighteenth century, a Korean student in China became a Catholic and brought back the gospel message to fellow scholars. The "western learning" spread, particularly among certain disaffected branches of the upper classes (for details, see Yu 1996). However, the spread of Catholicism was strongly resisted by successive governments because they wished to limit Western influence, and particularly because the Roman Catholic Church of that era condemned the ancestor-veneration practices that were the foundation of Confucian social structure. There were several persecutions of what became an underground movement of the dispossessed; the last and most severe was in 1866–67, when eight thousand people, a quarter of the Catholic population, were martyred. Whereas from the mid-1880s Protestant missionary activity was welcomed, the Catholic Church continued to be regarded with suspicion. It grew less spectacularly than Protestantism, and did not wield political power until the 1970s (Grayson 2002: 171; Yu 2004: 7–37), but it now represents about forty percent of Korean Christians (Barrett, Kurian and Johnson 2001: 682).

The second new religious movement was *Tonghak*, or "Eastern Learning." This was a religious movement begun by Ch'oe Che-u (1824–64), a synthesis of Asian religions, with a shamanistic character and a Christian appreciation of liberty. Though Ch'oe saw Roman Catholicism, which was known as *Sŏhak* or "Western Learning," as a threat to Asia, its influence is shown in the name of his movement. While suffering from a mysterious illness, Ch'oe claimed he was called by "a Great Spirit" (*Hanŭnim*), the Supreme Being (*Ch'iki*), Ruler of Heaven (*Ch'ŏnchu*). The Spirit gave him a talisman to cure disease, and taught him that human beings can identify with the Spirit by worship and repetition of a sacred phrase. This led to an egalitarian message and the hope of building a perfect world in this time and place (Grayson 2002: 198–202). Ch'oe's thought was deeply pneumatological, being concerned with the identification of the Supreme Being—the Spirit without—and "that-which-nurtures-God" (*shich'ŏnchu*)—the Spirit within. This was a pneumatology with profound implications for the material world, which was to be highly significant in liberation movements in Korean history and Christian theology (Sang Jin Ahn 2001: 49–71). In the late nineteenth century, under deteriorating socioeconomic conditions and partly inspired by Ch'oe's philosophy, peasants demanded land redistribution, tax reduction, democracy and human rights, in what became known as the *Tonghak* Revolution of 1894. Nowadays *Tonghak* is called *Ch'ŏndo-gyo*, or "Teachings of the Heavenly Way."

The third religious movement to influence Korea in the critical period at the end of the nineteenth century was Protestantism. In the century or so that followed the *Tonghak* Revolution, Christianity—often mediated through Western culture and the process of modernization—became the dominant religious influence on the nation (Grayson 2002: 2). It was Protestant Christianity, and in particular a revivalist spirituality, that caught the imagination of the people at this point, and led to the unparalleled growth of the church. From 1832 onwards a succession of Protestant missionaries had attempted to enter Korea with the Christian message. They were largely unsuccessful, but portions of the New Testament were translated and disseminated by Korean believers. As the message spread, Korean leaders pressed for the entry of foreign missionaries; so it was that in the establishment of Christianity in Korea, "the efforts of the missionaries to spread the Gospel were matched by the efforts of Koreans to import Christianity" (Yi 2004: 40).

The first Protestant missionaries to be officially received arrived in 1894–95 from the United States, which was also the first Western nation to sign a treaty with Korea. They were Protestants from North America: a Presbyterian, Horace G. Underwood, and a Methodist, Henry G. Appenzeller. They, and many of their later colleagues, were influenced by Anglo-American revival movements that brought together "Puritan zeal and Wesleyan fervor," and by missionary movements that spanned denominations (Paik 1970 [1929]: 367, 95–97). They shared a common "holiness" tradition that emphasized the perfecting work of the Holy Spirit in the believer, and a conservative faith for which the Bible, the inspired word of God, was the pre-eminent authority (Williams 1990: 252–60). The missionaries' shared spirituality and common experience in Korea often overrode denominational differences, with the result that Protestant churches of different denominations have similar polity, share the same hymnbook and Bible, and have a remarkably similar pattern of worship (cf. Paik 1970 [1929]: 95, 107–108, 164, 362). The missionaries began by setting up hospitals and schools, and targeted the common people, especially women. Instead of pandering to the scholarly penchant for Chinese characters and literary style, the missionary educators adopted the Korean script, *Han'gŭl*, a highly scientific representation of the language that had lain largely neglected since its invention by King Sejong the Great in 1443 or 1444. By these means they vastly increased literacy and made it possible for the humblest of citizens to read the Bible. The impact of this was felt particularly in the lives of women, who had mostly been denied education, being expected, according to Confucian tradition, to follow first their father, then their husband, then their son. Women evangelists played a key role in spreading the faith across the country (for the case of Presbyterians, see Lee, Yon Ok 1998: 44–367). From the start, Protestantism was perceived as modern, and the hope it offered for national renewal was undoubtedly part of the attraction of Christian faith.

When they decided to follow Christ, Korean Protestants turned away from their religious traditions and embraced a new faith. This was most clearly expressed when they stopped the practice of ancestor veneration, which often meant that individuals cut themselves off from their families. Koreans have a reputation for zeal in many fields; earnestness and single-mindedness are noted features of Korean Christianity, probably because in Confucianism loyalty is so highly valued. The reflections of Yun Ch'iho (1865–1945), one of the early Korean Christian leaders, on his experience of the World's Parliament of Religions in Chicago in 1893, illustrate the prevailing attitude to religious pluralism: "I would rather be narrow and earnest than be broad and indifferent" (Yun Chi-ho's diary entry for 24 September 1893, quoted in Shin Ahn 2005). At the same time, for Korean Christians, other religions are not on the "outside" but "inside" (J. Park 1998: 41), in the sense that they are the heritage of Korean people, because they are "the cultural and philosophical mentors of the past" (Sang Jin Ahn 2001: 132). So pluralism in the sense of the influence of traditional religions on the Korean people is undeniable, but not usually in the sense of individuals practicing more than one religion (M. Lee 1999: 409).

The complex religious background of Korea has produced a rich variety of spiritual understandings, and resulted in a number of different terms for "spirit" and associated concepts. In the Korean Bible, the terms *sŏngshin* and *sŏngnyŏng* have been used to translate "Holy Spirit." Both are derived from Chinese. To contemporary Koreans, both Protestant and Catholics,[3] *sŏngshin* sounds dated and *sŏngnyŏng* is normally used, though this does represent a shift in meaning. *Sŏng* means "holy." The character *shin* alone denotes a god, deity or divinity, and is used of the Heavenly Spirit (*Ch'ŏnshin*) and other gods of primal Korean religion, as well as the one God of the monotheistic religions. The use of the same word for God, gods, Spirit and spirit(s) reveals the deep-rooted understanding that God is Spirit, or that God is the supreme Spirit among many others. *Yŏng* or *ryŏng* or *nyŏng* (depending on its relative position in a word) represents spirit more in the sense of "soul." *Yŏng* can refer to the human spirit or soul as distinguished from the body, as in the word *yŏnghon* (*hon* is another Chinese-derived word for soul) frequently used by Christians. This is the word used in the traditional rendering of Matthew 27:50, when Jesus "gave up his spirit" or "breathed his last." The current preference for *yŏng* over *shin* would seem to imply a more pietistic, and perhaps more philosophical, interpretation of the Holy Spirit.

Both *shin* and *yŏng* can sometimes be translated "spirit(s)" (Korean does not always distinguish between singular and plural). In Hebrews 1:14, where the angels are referred to as "ministering spirits," the word used is *yŏng*. In the Korean Bible, first completed in 1911, the word *guishin* (usu-

---

[3] Korean Roman Catholics did not have a separate Bible translation of their own until a new translation was authorized in 2005. From 1976, they shared the common (*kongdong*) translation with Protestants (see http://www.cbck.or.kr/eng/ccik/history.htm [accessed 9/21/2005]).

ally translated as "ghost") is used for both demons and evil or unclean spirits, despite the facts that these are distinguished in Greek, and that there are many other words used for spirits in Korean.[4] The words for spirits do not necessarily carry associations of fear and evil. Spirits of the ancestors are referred to as *yŏng* in Confucian ancestor veneration and *jŏngnyŏng* in more shamanistic ancestral rites; *jŏng* means "spirit" or "essence," and *jŏngshin* commonly means "mind." However, some departed spirits, by reason of the unfortunate circumstances of their death, still trouble the living—like "ghosts" in contemporary English usage. Without wishing to deny the generally evil effects of what are translated as demons and evil or unclean spirits in the Bible, the overuse of *guishin* in the translation of the Bible into Korean would seem to indicate a demonization of Korean tradition in the first reception of Christianity, and a failure to respect the differentiations of the spirit-world.

In the first Korean Bible, the spirit of God that moves over the waters in Genesis 1:2 is rendered *shin*. The 1956 revision, which is still the most widely used, retains this, but recent versions—both Protestant and Catholic—have opted for *yŏng*. However, neither term has the connotations of wind or breath implied in the Hebrew. It is interesting to note that Nestorian Christians in China in the seventh to ninth centuries used the character *p'ung*, meaning "wind," in referring to the Holy Spirit (the same character as in "typhoon").[5] The translators of the New Korean Standard Version (1993) tried to acknowledge the breadth of meaning of the word *rūach* in Genesis 1:2 by including a footnote giving an alternative rendering of "wind" (*param* in Korean). However, this was unacceptable to conservative theologians, who saw it as an attempt to weaken the divine nature and personhood of the Spirit, and thereby undermine doctrines of the inspiration of the Bible (e.g. K. S. Kim 2003: 205–206). *Ki*, also derived from Chinese, is another term that has been used to translate the word "spirit" in Genesis 1:2—by Chung Hyun Kyung, for example (1991b: 44–45)—to more closely represent the breadth of the Hebrew word. *Ki* is the Korean pronunciation of the Chinese *qi* (*ch'i*), and is one of the characters used in the word for the "breath" of life (*saeng'gi*) that God breathed into the first human being, according to Genesis 2:7. In contemporary Korean, *ki* can mean wind and breath, and also energy, temper, soul and spirit. It is used

---

[4] Departed spirits, for example, may be *mangnyŏng*, *jŏngnyŏng*, *wŏnhon*, *wŏn'nyong* or *aknyŏng*: these words are combinations of *shin*, *yŏng* and *hon* with *mang*, meaning "to die"; *jŏng*, meaning "spirit" or "essence"; *wŏn*, meaning "hatred"; and *ak*, meaning "evil."

[5] This is found, for example, in the Chinese inscription on the Nestorian monument discovered in Xi'an. The Chinese text is available in Saeki 1937 and a reliable translation can be found in A. C. Moule 1930: 34–47. I am indebted to Edmond Tang, University of Birmingham, for drawing this to my attention and also for his help in the transliteration of Chinese terms.

in compound words meteorologically, medically, psychologically and also philosophically. In Confucian philosophy, *ki* refers to the vital force, the rhythm of life. The vital force is responsible for the five elements—wood, fire, earth, metal and water—which are phases of the force; these basic units of nature, combined in different ways, are responsible for all phenomena. The relationship between *ki* and *ri* (*li* in Chinese), meaning "principle," "pattern" or "order," was a matter of great philosophical debate. Chu Hsi resolved this in his grand synthesis, which became the basis for neo-Confucianism in Korea, by postulating that in any particular thing or event *ri* and *ki* were held together in harmony by the Supreme Ultimate, *Tai Ji* (*T'ai Chi*). However, he tended to regard *ri* as superior to *ki* because he associated the latter with deviance and evil. Neo-Confucians in Korea were inclined to ascribe to *ki* all that threatened Confucian power; this is evident in the stress on discipline and organization in that tradition (Sang Jin Ahn 2001: 27, 32–34, 37–44). Today the spirit signified by *ki* is understood as the energy of the universe, but it does not include a transcendent meaning. For this reason, most Korean Christians would not consider *ki* a suitable vehicle to carry the meaning of the Spirit of God or the Holy Spirit.

The vital force *ki* oscillates between the energy modes of *ŭm* (female) and *yang* (male), better known by the Chinese pronunciation *yin* and *yang*. The concepts of *yin* and *yang* have been integrated into Confucian philosophy from more ancient Chinese religion. They are the complementary forces that explain the whole of life. As images of male and female, they correspond closely to stereotypes of masculine and feminine found in other societies; however, they are not only applied to gender distinctions but also used to explain, and therefore unite or distinguish, all other polarities. *Yin*, female, includes the concepts of earth, dark, cold, old, weak, passive and absorbing; *yang*, male, encompasses their opposites: heaven, light, hot, young, strong, active and penetrating. *Yin-yang* philosophy is so significant for Korean culture that a *yin-yang* symbol appears in the center of the South Korean flag as a circle divided exactly into *yin* (blue) and *yang* (red) halves by a wavy line. This representation of *yin-yang* is horizontal with the *yang*—red, meaning heaven and male—above the *yin*—blue, meaning earth and female. This is indicative of the way in which *yin-yang* philosophy has tended to be used in Korea, not to promote harmony and reconciliation, but to sanction oppressive rule and male domination (cf. J. Park 1998: 156). *Yin-yang* is also applied to religious differences. Shamanism is perceived as feminine not only because it is practiced largely by women, but because of its interest in the earth and natural forces, its preoccupation with domestic and family matters, and the unrestrained nature of its practice. By contrast, Confucianism's concern with the law of heaven, the centrality of the father-son relationship, its social and political agenda, its stress on order and book-learning, and the restriction of ritual practice to men all contribute to the perception that it is masculine.

Holy Spirit Movements in Korea: Paternal and Maternal

Korean Protestantism became indigenous relatively quickly. The first Koreans were ordained to the ministry in 1907 in the Presbyterian Church, with the Presbyterian Church of Korea being established in 1912 and the Korean Methodist Church in 1930. One of the primary reasons for the growth of the churches was that, from the first, Koreans themselves actively sought out Christianity and spread it. Other reasons include: the tangible benefits of modernity that the missionaries initiated; the shared missionary policy of encouraging self-support, self-governance and self-propagation of local churches (known in Korea as the Nevius method); the early adoption of some indigenous patterns of worship; and the early linking of Christianity with Korean nationalism and independence movements against the Japanese colonizers. Another important factor was that Protestant mission targeted the common people, who were suppressed by the Confucian hierarchy and oppressed by governmental corruption and other external powers, and whose standard of living was rapidly eroding. However, the popular religious answer to the question of why the church grew so rapidly is that this growth is the work of the Holy Spirit, which has been poured out on Korea (Ro 1995: 26; J. Kim 1995: 45–73; C. Han 1995: 74–77; Sam-Hwan Kim and Yoon-Su Kim 1995: 97–98).

The generally accepted view among historians is that the Korean church came into being as an indigenous body in a Holy Spirit movement or revival that began in 1907. In this way the masses were reached, and from this point on Korean church growth began (Paik 1970: 367–78; Ryu 2000: 416; Grayson 2002: 158). Therefore revivals, which are regarded as movements of the Holy Spirit, are essential to the nature of the Korean Protestant church, and doctrines of the Holy Spirit are central to Korean Christian self-understanding. The first revival began, significantly, shortly after Korea was made a protectorate of Japan (1905). It was initiated by the foreign missionaries, in the sense that they committed themselves to pray for revival in the Korean church amid the situation of frustration and despair in the country in general. However, the events, when they happened, clearly took the missionaries by surprise, and the movement took on a momentum of its own, beyond missionary control. The revival was stimulated by one of the foreign missionaries, Dr. Robert A. Hardie, a North American Methodist, who preached about his personal experience of being filled with the Holy Spirit through prayer and repentance. The missionaries also heard through their networks of the Welsh Revival of 1904 and the Indian Revival of 1905, and hoped for a similar outpouring of the Spirit in Korea. In 1907, a revival began at a Bible conference in P'yong'yang (now the capital of North Korea), which involved about fifteen hundred Korean men and was organized by the missionaries and Korean leaders. Missionaries described how the whole congregation began to pray out loud, all together in "a vast harmony of sound and spirit, a mingling together of souls moved by an irresistible impulse to prayer," which sounded "like the falling of many waters, an ocean of prayer beating against God's throne." This led to public confession of sin: "Man after man would rise, confess his sin, break down and weep, and then throw himself on the floor and beat the floor with his fists in a perfect agony of conviction" (quoted in Clark 1971: 161–62). Those whose lives were changed testified in the wider community to what had happened, with the result that others were drawn in, and the revival spread. From this time onwards, revival meetings became a regular feature of Korean Christianity, and there were many more such movements (see, for example, M. Park 2003, who examines the revival movement of 1907 and also those led by Kim Ik-du, Lee Myŏng-chik, Kim Ŭng-cho, Lee Sŏng-bong, and Yonggi Cho).

One of the founders of self-consciously Korean Christian theology, Ryu Tong-Shik (Yu Tong-shik) argues that there are two distinct patterns of revival, or "Holy Spirit movement," in Korean history: one linked with the movement led by Kil Sŏn-chu from 1907, which he calls "paternal," and the other with the movement led by Lee Yong-do of 1928–33, which he calls "maternal" (Ryu 2000: 414–26, using an idea taken from P. Park 1973: 28–48; see Ryu 2000: 415 n. 1). Though Ryu does not find it necessary to explain the background, this classification needs to be understood as a reflection of *yin-yang* philosophical distinctions in the religious sphere, as a Confucian pattern of religious expression versus a shamanistic one. The "paternal" pattern was established in the 1907 P'yong'yang revival. Kil Sŏn-chu (1869–1935), one of the first ordained Korean ministers, emerged as the main Korean leader of the revival, and he continued to lead revival meetings across the country until his death in 1935. Kil became the originator of dawn prayer meetings and repetitious Bible reading, which are characteristic of Korean Christianity. In their situation of national calamity and oppression by hostile ruling powers, Kil and others were particularly interested in the imagery of apocalyptic in the Bible, which encoded their feelings against the Japanese occupation. They saw themselves as living in the last age, and Kil himself spent much time reflecting on the book of Revelation (Y. Kim 1983: 110). To prevent the church from becoming a vehicle for political insurrection, the missionaries consciously promoted revival, in order for Koreans to internalize their faith, and even to make peace with their Japanese aggressors (Paik 1970 [1929]: 369, 416). Nevertheless, what Korean believers read in their Bibles was a message of political liberation, and though he actively dissuaded his fellow Christians from involvement in peasant uprisings, Kil signed the famous Declaration of Independence (from Japanese rule). Along with fourteen other Christians, fifteen leaders of Ch'ŏndo-gyo (*Tonghak*) and three Buddhists, he supported the nonviolent movement of March 1, 1919.

Kil and others read the story of Israel as meaning that their own weakness was the cause of their slavery, and so repentance of personal sin in the revival meetings was an important part of national recovery (J. Park 1998: 23). The language of regeneration by the Holy Spirit, used in the early revival, was directly connected by Kil and others with the restoration of the nation (Y. Kim 1983: 113–16). Kil's movement was Confucian—and therefore "paternal"—in its outlook in three main ways: first, in its concern for the national interest over and above the individual; second, in its conservative theology and repetitious way of reading the Bible; and third, in its disciplined and legalistic moral code for Christian living. In these last two aspects, Kil's Confucian approach also had much in common with the conservative theology and Puritanical ideas of many of the missionaries about what Christian conversion should entail, and Kil's emphasis on correct external behavior also went down well with the elite of the ruling class (see Choo 1998: 36–41; S. Han 1996: I 96–103). However, the revival that started in 1907 also broke out of a Confucian mold. In contrast to Confucianism, which emphasized self-cultivation or refinement, the Christian message of the Holy Spirit was one of transformation, and this was applied socially as well as individually (Y. Kim 1983: 113–16).

After the 1919 independence movement was suppressed and the Japanese grip on Korea tightened, so that social and political action became even more difficult, the revival meetings became more mystical in nature and more individualistic. Between 1928 and 1933, the preaching of a young revivalist called Lee Yong-do (1901–33) swept the nation; this was the archetype for Ryu's "maternal" pattern of Holy Spirit movement. Lee was a political activist who had been imprisoned by the Japanese several times. After being healed from illness in a miraculous way, he turned from politics to embrace what he believed was a true Christian life of "penitence, prayer, thankfulness, love and hope." After ten days of fasting and praying in the mountains, Lee saw a sacred vision of a heavenly flame and, soon afterwards, what was interpreted as the fire of the Holy Spirit descended on his church in the outbreak of revival. Lee began to lead mass meetings across the country, in which he encouraged crying and other emotional out-pouring. Evoking the vision of Ezekiel, of a valley of dry bones coming to life by the wind of God's Spirit, Lee invited Jesus to find his cross in the sufferings of the Korean people. He preached that by identifying with Jesus' sufferings, believers would experience his unlimited love, and in this way exchange the sin and materialism of earth for the life and holiness of heaven. Unlike Kil, Lee was highly critical of church leaders, who he felt were constrained by the conservative theology inherited from the missionaries; this criticism, together with his extreme mysticism, meant that some church bodies outlawed him. Lee's experience of imprisonment and torture had led him to the conclusion that there was no point in direct political action; any solution to the suffocating economic, social and cultural situation of Korea in this period would lie in an encounter with Christ in a mystical union. However, it may be misleading to describe his approach as "otherworldly," because his challenge to the established church retained an intensely political motive: to bring about national revival (J. Park 1998: 61, 64–72). Lee also advocated engagement in a spiritual struggle against the devil, calling upon the name of Jesus, in order to overcome evil (an activity he described as "victory over the devil," *sŭngma*). The similarities between Lee's testimony, the worship form of the movement, and its worldview, on the one hand, and Korean shamanism, on the other, have often been pointed out. Indeed, this continuity with the primordial values of Korean culture contributed greatly to the popularity of Lee's revival (Ryu 2000: 155–65), so that it indigenized the faith in the emotions of the masses (Choo 1998: 140).

In his analysis, which is based on religiocultural patterns and not on social statistics, Ryu compares and contrasts Kil's and Lee's movements after the paternal-maternal or Confucian/shamanistic patterns. The paternal movement is outward-looking and socially oriented, and the maternal one is interior-focused and individualistic. The former is politically active in fighting for social change, while the latter is politically tolerant, being a more therapeutic ministry. Furthermore, Ryu believes that the appeal of the paternal movement was to the educated middle classes, while the maternal movement appealed to the poor. Finally, he describes the paternal movement as "fundamentalist" in the rigidity of its teaching and in its conservative morality, whereas the maternal movement takes a mystical approach to faith (Ryu 2000: 423). Ryu is not arguing that Korean Christians are actually following Confucianism or shamanism in the name of Christianity, but that the way Christianity is practiced in Korea, unsurprisingly, reflects deep fault-lines in Korean society and religious traditions. Korean feminists agree that mainstream Korean Christianity has adopted the patriarchal structures of Confucianism, which have been reinforced by patriarchal conservative theologies from the West. Like Chung Hyun Kyung, they look to Korean primal religion, and especially shamanism, to provide an alternative for Korean women's spirituality, either outside or within the Christian faith (e.g. H. Chung 1991a; O. Lee 1994; Choi 2005).

Clearly the differences in the Holy Spirit movements are connected with deep divides in the way the Holy Spirit is understood in Korean Christian theology, the development of which began to take place alongside the dramatic events of twentieth-century Korean history (for introductions to Korean theology see Ryu 2000 [1982]; Choo 1998; S. Han 1996; in English, see also England et al. 2004: 475–651). In the first period, from the "germination" of Protestantism until the 1930s (the botanical analogy is due to Ryu 2000), the first Korean Protestants began to explore the implications of the gospel for Korea under the tutelage of foreign missionaries, and under the yoke of Japanese imperialism. Three founding fathers of Korean theology can be identified: the aforementioned Yun Ch'i-ho, an aristocrat who was motivated by the Christian gospel to progressive social involvement and, controversially, to cooperation with the Japanese; Ch'oi Byŏng-hŏn (1858–1927), who attempted to promote religious freedom and acceptance of Christianity by relating it to the existing religions of Korea; and the theologically conservative but politically active Kil Sŏn-chu (Ryu 2000: 49–72; cf. Choo 1998: 32–47; see also England et al. 2004: 509–513). The second period, from the 1930s through to the 1950s, was a period of enormous trauma and social disruption for Koreans, and a time of trial for Korean theology as it began to "take root in Korean soil" (Ryu 2000: 133–262; Choo 1998: 131–220). In the later period of Japanese colonization, the Korean people and resources were used and abused for the war effort, and a program of Japanization, including Shinto shrine worship, was imposed. The liberation of the peninsula by Russian and American forces in 1945 soon led to its division into North and South; the subsequent Korean War of 1950–53 was devastating, not only in its material destruction and the huge loss of human life, but also because it divided a people who had been unified in one nation for more than thirteen hundred years. The tensions caused by these events led to three splits in the Presbyterian Church in the 1950s. The excommunication in 1953 of Kim Chae-chun, founder of the Kijang group, is of particular interest here. On the basis of the Johannine writings, Kim taught that God is Spirit. The freedom of the Spirit led him to justify the use of higher criticism in biblical interpretation—which particularly upset the dominant conservatives—and to espouse liberalism in theological education. His reflection on the Spirit's activity in history resulted in a theology of democratization and social progress; and the cosmic dimensions of the Spirit's life led him to try to reconcile the Korean and the Christian, the primal and the new in "the community of universal love" that embraces heaven, earth and humanity (Ryu 2000: 257–62).

It was in the period from the 1960s through the 1980s, which was also the most rapid period of church growth, that Korean theology began to "unfold" like a lotus flower and develop in three main strands: a conservative wing interested in biblical theology and centered on salvation movements, a progressive theology concerned for political liberation and focused on sociohistorical problems, and a liberal strand seeking to inculturate the gospel in Korea in dialogue with the nation's other religious traditions (Ryu 2000: 31, 263–396; Choo 1998: 283–409). Two distinctive movements in Korean Christianity came to international attention: the *minjung* theology movement and the Full Gospel movement. Both arose to address the needs of the Korean people in a period of rapid national development and social change under military dictatorship, which was very costly in human terms. That is, both address the problem of poverty, but in radically different ways. The first is an example of a liberation theology, which addresses the structural problems of society that oppress the poor, the *minjung*. The second is a Pentecostal movement that primarily offers the poor hope of blessing, and power to cope with the suffering they endure. We shall examine these in turn through the work of their leading figures, to see how they represent two different pneumatologies; we will then introduce a third, less-known Korean pneumatology, *p'ungnyu* theology, which arose from a revival of interest in Korean religiocultural heritage in the wake of its widespread destruction. In our concluding discussion, we will relate these to one another and to other strands of Korean theology.

The Third Age of the Spirit and the *Minjung* Theology of Suh Nam-dong

Minjung theology was developed on behalf of the *minjung*—that is, the masses, the poor, the oppressed—in the 1970s and '80s by Christian intellectuals, many of whom were arrested and imprisoned as subversives, but whose liberation praxis had worldwide influence through ecumenical channels. Within Korea, Christian activists played a leading role in the movements for democratic reforms in Korea and in ameliorating the workers' conditions (J. Lee 1988: 7–8). A central figure of *minjung* theology was Suh Nam-dong (Sŏ Nam-dong; 1918–84), a Presbyterian, who studied theology in Japan, served as a pastor and, after further study in Canada, became professor of contemporary theology at Yonsei University in Seoul in 1966. During the 1970s he was active in opposing the government on issues of working conditions and human rights; he was arrested on several occasions and served twenty-two months of hard labor. His activities were inspired by pneumatology of liberation, developed in the context of Korean revolutionary history.

Suh was familiar with the Protestant theology of his time, with its particular interest in eschatology. He appreciated the future-oriented theology of the early Jürgen Moltmann especially, because Moltmann emphasized "the end in history" that inspired revolutionary and liberation theologies. However, Suh found Moltmann's approach too limited to the Christian community and human liberation, and felt the need to develop an "evolutionary eschatology" that encompassed the whole of human society and also the natural world. Looking back in Western history, he criticized Augustine's theology, arising out of the Constantinian settlement, for his equation of the kingdom of God with the reign of Christ through the church, beyond which remained only "the end of history" (1999a: 310). Suh regarded this theology of the kingdom of God as the theology of the rulers, and not the hope of the poor, and distinguished the kingdom of God—a heavenly, ultimate symbol of the place that believers enter when they die—from the millennium—a historical, earthly, penultimate symbol of the point at which history and society are renewed (1983a: 162).

Suh studied the thought of Joachim of Fiore at length, as the theologian who reintroduced belief in the millennium into Western theology (Suh 1999a:

310). He became convinced that "the third age of the Spirit" was now dawn-
ing, when human beings would be filled with the Spirit of God and become
friends of God. Theology of the Holy Spirit, he argued, transcended the historical limitations of christology, and the freedom of the Spirit would eventually burst out of the restrictions of the church. As he saw it, we were now
entering what Rosemary Radford Ruether described as a "post-Christian"
era, when Christians would recover the expectancy of the pre-Constantinian
church, and join hands with revolutionary movements outside the church,
to usher in a new social and economic order. In the new era, the category of
"religion," which he regarded as a personal, not a social concept, would also
be superseded by the "collective soul" (1999c [1979]: 370, 382). Following
Joachim, Suh understood the emergence of the third age to be the result of
a progressive increase in the presence of the Holy Spirit in history, and following R. P. C. Hanson, he stressed not only the presence but also the activity of the Spirit (Suh 1975: 39). So he understood the Spirit as the one who
brings about humanization in history.

Reflecting particularly on the *Tonghak* movement and the philosophy of
Ch'oe Che-u, Suh identified the people's rights movements as representing
the mission of God, that is, the activity of the Spirit in contemporary Korea.
He was also influenced by Paul Tillich, particularly by his emphasis on the
human condition as the starting point for theology, and on the need for
Christians to embrace collective action, and so he urged Christians to participate in them (Suh 1983a: 156–57; S. Han 1996: I 632). Suh believed that
the new era required a socioeconomic approach to theology, to clarify the
situation of the *minjung* and allow them to become "the subjects of their
own history and identity" rather than victims of exploitation (1983a: 157).
He drew on the recovery of *minjung* history by social historians, which
showed a progressive expansion of the social base of power, until in the
Tonghak movement the *minjung* first became politically active. This popular participation continued in the independence movement of 1919, the student movement of 1960, and the contemporary human rights struggle.
Furthermore, Suh saw a gradual humanization in Korean art and literature
as evidence of the emergence of the new age, when God's Spirit is poured
out on all people (1983a: 167–76).

Suh sought to develop a "pneumatological historical interpretation"—in
place of the traditional christological interpretation of history—which would
enable a "confluence" (*hapnyu*) between the Korean *minjung* tradition and
"the *minjung* tradition in Christianity" (Suh 1983a: 177). He cites as a parallel to the Korean *minjung* movements the way in which Thomas Müntzer
applied Joachim of Fiore's theology of the third age of the Spirit, and led
peasants and urban poor in sixteenth-century Germany in a movement for
social reform. Suh notes that Müntzer claimed to interpret the Bible by the
power of the Holy Spirit, which allowed for new prophecies and revelation. So Suh also understood certain events in history as a continuing rev-

elation: in particular, the emergence of democracy, the rise of social movements and the humanization of society and culture (: 165–66). Within the
Bible also, Suh was selective about what he regarded as inspired, ostensibly for historical-critical reasons, preferring to reflect on the Old
Testament prophetic tradition and on the life of Jesus Christ according to
Mark's Gospel and the hypothetical source "Q" (: 158–59). Suh saw two
main biblical events as crucial to his theology: the exodus, which was
emphasized by the Latin American liberation theologians of that time, and
the crucifixion-resurrection. He gave priority to the latter, because he saw
it as universal in its appeal, being repeated in the daily experience of suffering of the downtrodden (Suh 1999c [1979]: 356). Looking back over
Korean theological reflection on the cross, he observed the way in which
it had developed: from "an emergency prescription" to solve the problem
of sin in the early conservative tradition; through Lee Yong-do's theology
of identification with Christ's suffering on the cross; until, in the post-
Liberation period, Kim Chae-chun's school understood the cross as actual
and active in history as God continued to suffer with the oppressed (Suh
1999b). Suh came to understand that, by the action of the Holy Spirit, the
paradigmatic event of the cross undergoes "reactualization" or "reincar-
nation" in the events of history (1983a: 157). He believed that the suffering Christ is identified with the contemporary suffering *minjung*, and
that in their awakening to bring about their own liberation in revolutionary movements, the activity of the Spirit can once again be recognized
in history, as the Christ event is actualized here and now.

It was the writings of the Roman Catholic poet Kim Chi Ha (Kim Chi-
ha; 1941–) that inspired Suh and others to use the symbols and language of
the *minjung* in their reflections. Kim, a dissident and social activist, was tortured and eventually sentenced to life imprisonment by the military regime,
but he may have been the first Asian to combine Christian socialism with a
local spirituality (Chong Sun Kim and Killen 1978: xiii). His work was also
an inspiration to Samuel Rayan in India, and to others around the world
(see Rayan 1992: 11). Kim used the symbols of shamanism and reinvigo-
rated them with concern for the common good. He utilized particularly the
yearnings that prompt people to approach the shaman, and the shamanistic
sense that the desires of the individual cannot be thwarted but live on in that
person's spirit (Chong Sun Kim and Killen 1978: xviii). His writings vividly
portray the Korean Christ, who is brutally treated and suffers with the *minjung*, who is crowned and disempowered by the church, and for whose
release and revitalization the poor are longing and struggling. Suh borrowed
from Kim some elements of shamanism, beginning with the concept of *han*
that came to epitomize the situation of the *minjung* in his theology, and also
suggested the solution to their problems. *Han*—a pure Korean word and not
to be confused with the term for God—is the internalized sense of injustice
of the oppressed, which can break out in anger unless it is resolved. In Suh's

work, *han* takes the place of sin in conservative Presbyterian theology as the problem that Jesus Christ came to solve. He calls the church to "hear the cries of the *minjung*" (1983a: 68), often expressed in stories of supernatural occurences, and to address the problem of *han* by initiating a process of social change. In this way, through interaction with contemporary Western theology, liberation theology and Korean traditions, Suh developed a "theology arising out of today's secular world, which is based on hope, revolution, liberation, politics, the *minjung*, the Holy Spirit" (Suh 1983b: 166).

As far as the mainstream Korean church was concerned, Suh's critical approach to the Bible and his challenge to church and government authority put him beyond the pale of Christian orthodoxy. Furthermore, *minjung* theology as a whole was criticized for limiting theology to socioeconomic concerns, and for dualistically dividing society into good and bad (S. Han 1996: I 661). Suh intended his theology to oppose the tradition, and to challenge theological dogma with humanistic and secular thought (Suh 1999c [1979]: 379); he recognized its one-sidedness on behalf of the *minjung*. Nevertheless, in the long view, even a relatively conservative scholar like Han Sung-hong cannot help but be proud of Suh's "uniquely valuable" contribution to Korean theology and international stature among theologians (S. Han 1996: I 661). From the pneumatological point of view, Suh's contribution is to draw attention to the Spirit's activity in history, and especially in the Christ event, and at the same time to link Christian theology with wider social movements. Though he emphasized the freedom of the Spirit (often at the expense of the church), at the same time he tended to limit this by his single—though vitally important—criterion of socioeconomic justice for discerning the Spirit's work. Nevertheless, Suh established a theological framework for *minjung* theology that was explicitly pneumatological, and by relating this to Korean shamanism initiated a distinctive Korean contribution to pneumatology.

Ryu argues that Suh's *minjung* theology is a re-emergence in the post-Liberation period of the "paternal" model of Holy Spirit movement (Ryu 2000: 419–22). He makes this connection by noting the millennialism of both Kil and Suh and the political nature of both movements. In other respects, however, the 1907 revival and the *minjung* theology stand in different theological streams. Kil shared the conservative theology and literal approach to biblical interpretation of the missionaries, whereas Suh was theologically liberal. Kil addressed the problem of sin, and Suh, *han*. And, though fervent in prayer, the *minjung* movement was not expressed in revival-style meetings. Furthermore, Suh was certainly not Confucian in the sense of wishing to uphold the traditional, hierarchical society, though he was politically active. There is an implied criticism of *minjung* theology in labeling it "paternal": a suggestion that it is an elitist movement seeking to change society *for* the people rather than *with* them. Despite Suh's use of the language of *han*, it can be argued that *minjung* theology does not emerge from the traditions of the people themselves but only co-opts them into a Christian-socialist framework, or uses them to Koreanize liberation theology (Ryu 1999 [1979]: 389–90; cf. C. S. Song 1988: 122–26). Ryu also senses a rigidity of ideology that is more about economics than spirituality and human feeling (Ryu 2000 [1982]: 437–38). *Minjung* theology was a minority activity and not a mass movement, so it cannot claim to represent either the spirit of the masses or an outpouring of the Holy Spirit on all people. Defending himself, Suh points out that theologizing is always an elite activity, but he insists that *minjung* theology articulates the authentic voice of the oppressed—who are not to be identified with the masses—and works for a goal yet to be fully realized (Suh 1999c [1979]): 361, 369–70). For Suh, to listen to the cries of the *minjung* is to hear the sound of the Holy Spirit, and to respond is to join in the mission of God.

Feminist theologians have also criticized *minjung* theology as "paternal" in a negative sense because it is "andro-centric." Though Suh described women's experience as "*han* itself" (1983b: 58), feminists find that *minjung* theologians were preoccupied with anti-colonial and socioeconomic categories, and did not take patriarchal oppression seriously. Furthermore, women were not the subjects—in the sense of "the doers"—of *minjung* theology, and so their experience and spirituality were not recognized, yet they themselves are included among the *minjung* whom *minjung* theologians profess to be hearing (Choi 2005: 4–5, 98, 103–104; H. Chung 1991a: 109–111; 1994: 175–78). Consequently, though Korean feminist theology, which began in the late 1970s, also uses the terms *minjung* and *han*, feminist theologians do not generally express indebtedness to *minjung* theology. Though they also struggle for human rights in the framework of liberation theology, they claim to be recovering "a gut feeling" deriving from "our foremothers' spirituality" in the shamanistic tradition, rather than using "masculine" ideologies (O. Lee 1994; H. Chung 1991a; 1991b: 46), and so their "maternal" discourse is largely separate from the more "paternal" one.

The Power of the Holy Spirit and the Healing of the *Minjung* in the Theology of Yonggi Cho

In 1958, Yonggi Cho (Cho Yong-gi, also known as Paul or David Cho; 1936–), founded a church that met in an old GI tent pitched in a slum area of Seoul, among displaced people seeking to rebuild their lives after the devastation of the Korean War. Today Yoido Full Gospel Church (YFGC) claims the largest membership of any local church in the world: 760,000 people.[6] It occupies a large complex of buildings, including an enormous

---

[6] Figure given by Rev. Dr. Hong Young-Gi, President of the Institute for Church Growth, Hansei University and an ordained pastor of the Full Gospel Church, at a press

worship hall, office and education buildings, in a prominent location (Yoido) in the city, and has more than seven hundred full-time church workers. Yoido Church is part of the much wider ministry of Full Gospel Television, which includes six cable TV channels, mobile (cell) phone ministries, a highly-developed interactive website, a publishing house including particularly worship resources, and a national mass-distribution newspaper, *The People's Daily (Kukmin Ilbo)* (for details see the church's extensive website, www.fgtv.com). Cho is an international figure, and Yoido Full Gospel Church sends missionaries to every continent of the world, including North America. At home he has significant political influence, which he is using particularly to try to further the unification of North and South Korea. The secret of this success, he claims, is the work of the Holy Spirit (Myung and Hong 2003: ii) through the power of prayer (Cho 1984: 37–46).

Korean Pentecostalism needs to be understood both from within the Korean revival tradition (of which it is a part and not the whole) and also in terms of global Pentecostalism (Bae 1999: 160–63). Since he exercises such charismatic leadership, Cho's testimony, which is well known (Cho 1999b [1983]: xi–xix; Y. Lee 2004: 3; see also Cho's profile on the Full Gospel website), is also integral to the theology of his church. Cho was converted from Buddhism to Christianity while seriously ill with tuberculosis, and then experienced a miraculous recovery. Through the influence of American Pentecostal missionaries, and after three days of fasting, he had a vision of Jesus in which he experienced a call to dedicate his life to preaching the gospel. He studied at the Full Gospel Bible College, which is run by the Assemblies of God—a large, North American-based Pentecostal denomination—where he learned to derive the theological foundations of the Full Gospel Church "directly from the Bible in a literal sense."[7] Yoido Full Gospel Church shares many characteristics common to Korean Protestant churches. It uses the same version of the Bible and hymnbook, and follows a very similar order for Sunday worship. It has the same emphasis on Bible study and prayer inherited from the early Korean revivals; indeed, Cho aims at "365–day revival" (quoted in Chan 2004: 96). The cell structure of the church, by which the members of the congregation are all assigned to small groups meeting in different localities, and which is often hailed as the reason for its growth (Comiskey 2003), is also widespread in Korean churches, and may have originated in the subversive practices of resistance movements in Korean history (Lim 2004: 205).

The central message of the Church is the "five-fold gospel."[8] This follows the "four cardinal doctrines" of the Assemblies of God—regeneration,

---

conference of the World Council of Churches Conference on World Mission and Evangelism, Athens, May 2005. Such a large membership is possible by including "satellites," that is, congregations that regard themselves as under the same senior pastor and hear his sermons but meet in another locality and are ministered to by a junior pastor.

[7] http://english.fgtv.com/Gospel/main.asp [accessed 5/12/06].

[8] See http://english.fgtv.com/Gospel/Fivefold.asp [accessed 5/12/06].

baptism in the Spirit, divine healing and the return of Jesus Christ—but with one important addition, which we shall examine below. "Baptism in the Spirit" in Pentecostal theology is the experience of receiving the Holy Spirit, which is understood to be independent of water baptism. This expresses the Pentecostal critique of the established churches for having formal belief without spiritual life. For many Pentecostal churches the "initial physical evidence" of baptism in the Spirit is "speaking in tongues"; Cho also accepts this as normal but it is not stressed (cf. Cho 1989: 117). Though the teaching is essentially the same, Cho differs from the Assemblies of God in describing this second experience as "fullness of the Holy Spirit," rather than "baptism." In keeping with conservative Evangelicalism rather than with the holiness movements, Cho understands the fullness of the Holy Spirit primarily as equipping the believer for service rather than as directed toward the believer's sanctification (Menzies 2004: 30–31). The second feature that distinguishes Cho's teaching from the Assemblies of God doctrines is the addition of a fifth doctrine, "the Gospel of Blessing." This is expanded in his teaching of "three-fold blessing," which is based on John 2:3. In Cho's interpretation, this verse promises "spiritual well-being," "general well-being," and "bodily health." "Spiritual well-being" is the result of receiving the gift of the Holy Spirit, with the expectation that it is evidenced by the gift of tongues. This brings enhanced communication with God and the possibility of training the soul and controlling the greed of the body. "General well-being" refers to the expectation that, once the believer has received the Holy Spirit, not only will they have peace in their heart but all their worldly activities will prosper. Receiving material blessings and being successful in life is the result of cultivating the right attitudes of positive thinking, giving and vision. As for "bodily health," divine healing is given to those who yearn for it, are free from sin, and pray for it in faith. Health is maintained by not falling into sin and by releasing stress through unburdening oneself in prayer.[9]

Most of Cho's theology is widely available in English as well as Korean, and is translated into many other languages. He writes in a popular style, referring primarily to biblical texts and everyday experience to support his argument. Though Cho also preaches and writes about the person and work of Jesus Christ and the love of God the Father, much of his prolific output is devoted to his teaching on the Holy Spirit and the Spirit's blessing. He is credited with promoting the recognition of the personhood of the Holy Spirit, hitherto lacking in the Korean churches; in other words, Cho develops a theology of the Holy Spirit as one of the three persons of the Godhead, and also gives the Holy Spirit a personality (Y. Lee 2004: 17; Cho 1989: 35–43). He interprets 2 Corinthians 13:13 as invoking "communion with the Holy Spirit" rather than "communion in the Spirit." So the personhood

---

[9] See http://english.fgtv.com/Gospel/Threefold.asp [accessed 5/12/06].

of the Holy Spirit means that the believer relates personally to the Holy Spirit; it is not a concept expressed only in inner-trinitarian relations (Chan 2004: 102–104 disputes this view). He therefore encourages prayer not only *in* but to the Holy Spirit (Cho 1984: 37–46).

Cho refers to the Holy Spirit as his "senior partner" (Cho 1989). This description is primarily a business analogy; he sees the Holy Spirit as his partner in the work of evangelism because the Holy Spirit is the first witness and because the empowering of the Holy Spirit is necessary for effective witness (: 20–33). He also describes an intimate relationship in which the Holy Spirit is his friend, adviser and helper (: 7–13). Cho's message depends on a *Christus Victor* theology of release from bondage to sin, through the sacrifice of Jesus who judged and defeated Satan (: 70–76). As a result of this event, Cho believes the Holy Spirit is at work everywhere, in partnership with believers, to convict human hearts, witness to the good news and bring about the miracle of new birth into a life of faith (: 79–96). He sees a great urgency for the work of evangelism because, unless they accept the salvation of Jesus Christ, human beings will be destroyed. But once they do, they are granted "everlasting life" (: 67–78). However, in common with Pentecostal theology in general, Cho holds that believers only encounter the full power of the Holy Spirit through the second experience of receiving the fullness of the Holy Spirit, who gives gifts (: 97–127). Through these, Cho explains, "people and their environments are changed," for example by the planting of new churches, revival, and the establishment of schools and hospitals (: 140, 138). However, he argues that, in view of the fact that the spiritual forces that surround us are both good and evil, it is possible that faith and works are counterfeit. Therefore, Christians should beware of evil spirits, and apply tests to spiritual experience. Cho suggests examining the fruits of spiritual experience, as well as its christology and attitude, while also praying for the gift of discerning the spirits (: 129–36).

More recently, Cho has systematized his theology of the Holy Spirit, and emphasized that the Spirit is a member of the trinitarian Godhead, although with a particular character and work. In the first half of his book *Pneumatology* (1998a), he describes the history of the Holy Spirit through the Old Testament, in the ministry of Jesus Christ, and in the New Testament church. The second half considers the work of the Spirit, baptism and fullness of the Spirit, and the gifts and fruits of the Spirit. Cho's concern throughout is to help his readers to understand that the Spirit is not just a source of power or energy but a person, and therefore to realize the importance of cultivating personal fellowship with the Spirit (: 7). His teaching is set within an eschatological framework that understands the contemporary era of the Spirit as the prelude to the frozen "winter" of the end. Using Korean agricultural as well as biblical imagery, he describes the outpouring of the Spirit as the "latter rain" (Joel 2:23 etc.) brought by "the wind of the

Holy Spirit," which "is blowing strongly in the twilight over the open field awaiting the last harvest" (Cho 1998a: 4). Cho also gives greater emphasis to the Spirit's role in the church, and not just in individual believers' experience. He argues that it is particularly important for the church to welcome and honor the Holy Spirit because the Spirit is the one who establishes the church (on the foundation of Jesus Christ) and who is with the church in these last days, working with it, and bringing about the final events expected in dispensationalist theology. After the "rapture" of believers into heaven (1 Thess 4:13–18), the Spirit will withdraw to heaven during the rule of the "lawless one" on earth (2 Thess 2:6–8), returning with Jesus Christ at his second coming to judge the world, and fill it with God's glory (Cho 1998a: 211–23).

Cho's theology of blessing, which is often criticized as "prosperity theology," is undoubtedly influenced by Oral Roberts and other North American Pentecostal evangelists, who also use 3 John 2 as justification for believing that faith will be rewarded in a material way. However, its central place in Cho's theology originates in his ministry to a destitute congregation in the aftermath of the Korean War (Menzies 2004: 36–41; Anderson 2004b: 148–50). In these desperate times, he proclaimed hope for the suffering by his message that "God is good." He addressed their poverty by his doctrine of blessing and their sickness by his healing ministry (Anderson 2004b: 148–50, 153–56; Menzies 2004: 39–40). He offered spiritual power to the powerless that led to recovery of confidence and self-awareness, and he also created a community of the dispossessed, "a place prepared for the estranged masses," and a worship experience that allowed them to lay aside their problems, temporarily at least, and experience through worship "a corporate feeling of warmth" (Ryu 2000 [1982]: 425). The context of poverty does not make Cho's message correct (Chan 2004: 107–108) but, undoubtedly, many lives were turned around through contact with Cho and his congregation. From a purely sociological point of view, joining a Pentecostal church may encourage upward mobility because of a number of factors, such as the support of the community, moral discipline, opportunities in the church to exercise leadership and encouragement of education (cf. D. Martin 2002: 14–16; Hollenweger 1972: 11–17).

As South Korea became more prosperous, Cho's gospel for survival developed as a gospel for success, as reflected in book subtitles like "More Secrets for a Successful Faith Life" (1999b [1983]; 1999c [1989]). In Korea, as elsewhere, Pentecostal spirituality seems to engender attitudes consonant with success in the capitalist context of late- or post-modernity (D. Martin 2002: 14–16; H. Cox 1996: 213–41), and so Cho has been accused of linking the value of life with the pursuit of worldly gain (Ryu 2000: 425). However, he is unashamed to emphasize a material outlook, believing that the promise of material blessing is biblical (1998b: 27–41; International Theological Institute 1993: I 89–91). He sees no virtue in poverty—it is "a curse from Satan" (Cho 1999b: 137–38; 1999a: 121)—and he expects members of his congregations to prosper (1998b: 27–41; 1999a: 121). Cho has insisted on maintaining his theology of blessing, even though the Assemblies of God denomination in the USA has distanced itself from the teaching of the more extreme prosperity theologians. After all, the twentieth-century history of Korea appears to give strong evidence for the power of positive thinking, and the growth of Full Gospel Church is often held up as the pre-eminent example of this. Nevertheless, in the present context, Cho's "over-realized eschatology" (Chan 2004: 111) is deeply problematic for younger Full Gospel thinkers, who have attempted to divert attention from teaching on prosperity and to reinterpret Cho's emphasis on the material blessing. In interaction with theologians of the *minjung* tradition, they have linked theology of the Holy Spirit with ecological well-being, holism and harmony (see Bae 2005: 527–49). The overarching role of "the fourth dimension" is now described as a "holistic approach" that deals with people's *han* (Jeong 2005: 551–71).

The Full Gospel Church clearly falls into the shamanistic or "maternal" tradition of Holy Spirit movement (Ryu 2000: 422–25), and indeed Cho's supporters also see his movement in continuity with the revival tradition through Lee Yong-do and also through Kim Ick-Doo (Kim Ik-du; 1874–1950), whose revival movement particularly featured "signs and wonders," especially healing (Y. Lee 2005: 512; M. Park 2003: 65–94, 191–212). For example, like Lee, and in the shaman tradition, Cho's call was the result of miraculous healing from illness and a vision; both men encourage retreat to the mountains—where the ancient Koreans encountered *Hananim*—to pray; and they interact with the spiritual world of indigenous belief. As in shamanism, members of the Full Gospel Church approach the pastor—often as a last resort—in the hope that their personal problems will be solved (Cho 1998b; cf. M. Park 2004: 47–48). Therefore Cho has often been accused—from both within Korea and from outside— of syncretizing the Christian gospel and shamanism (e.g. C. Chung 1997: 33–35). Ryu believes Cho is in danger of "reducing the Holy Spirit to the power of shamanism" by using psychical rather than spiritual methods (Ryu 2000: 425); David Martin sees a fusion of "revivalism and prosperity theology with shamanistic practice" (2002: 161; cf. Hollenweger 1972: 161); and Harvey Cox thinks there is "a massive importation of shamanic practice into a Christian ritual" in Yoido Full Gospel Church (H. Cox 1996: 226). However, though Cho's ministry appeals in the context of shamanism and fulfils some of the role of the shaman with respect to spiritual power, any similarity to shaman practices is unconscious. Cho explicitly rejects "the evil spirit world" and does not adopt any of the language or cultural symbols of shamanism in the way that *minjung* theologians do (e.g. Cho 1999c: 46; Cho 1989: 129–30; cf. Anderson 2004b: 139–43).

Cho's theology is developed in the context of the spirit-world, but he regards the spirits of Korean tradition as evil, and exalts the Holy Spirit instead. Cho recognizes two or three spiritual forces, all evident in the first three chapters of the book of Genesis: the Holy Spirit of God with the angels, the spirit of Satan who sends unclean and evil spirits, and the human spirit of man (1999b: 38; 1989: 129; 1999c: 45). The realm of the Holy Spirit is "the fourth dimension," which, using the language of Genesis 1:2, "hovers over" the three-dimensional world. The world of evil spirits does not encroach on this, being only "supernatural" and not "spiritual." The spirits of all the other religions are included as evil spirits (1999c: 45–49, 72–73; 1999b: 35–37). Cho is suspicious of other religions, and particularly negative toward Zen Buddhism, from which he converted (1999b: 74–85). His attitude to other faiths is informed by the epistles of John, where Christians are encouraged to test the spirits in case they are of the antichrist (1999c: 44, 46, 72–73; 1999b: 74–85). In Cho's theology, the human spirit, which he equates with the subconscious, must be joined to one of the other spiritual forces; and the only way to be joined to the Holy Spirit—and therefore to "the heavenly Father, Creator of the Universe"—is through explicit confession of Jesus Christ (1999c: 47–49).

In Cho's teaching, the "fourth dimension" is the world of dreams and visions and, because it controls the other three dimensions, developing it in one's spiritual life is the way to "incubate" goals in the three-dimensional world. So he teaches his disciples to "see by faith" what they want to achieve; that is, to imagine the result and, if it is in accord with "the desire of the Holy Spirit"—measured by biblical texts—to then pray it into becoming reality (1999c: 51–73; 1999b: 50–57). Cho regards the Old Testament period as the age of the Father, the life of Jesus Christ as the age of the Son, and the age since Pentecost as dominated by the Holy Spirit (1999b: 1–3), though this is only now being realized. And he recognizes three corresponding levels of relationship with the Holy Spirit: first, the Holy Spirit, the wind of God, is at work everywhere in the world to accomplish God's desires. The Holy Spirit is sent into the world to convict of sin and bring people to Jesus Christ, at which point those who respond experience the second level, when God puts the Holy Spirit within them. The third level is the experience of the fullness of the Holy Spirit, a personal Pentecost (1999c: 5–8).

Whereas the paternal movements are conflictual in confronting injustice, Cho's movement is therapeutic in its approach, and operates primarily at a personal, rather than a political, level. Though the label "maternal" does not necessarily signal female leadership, Cho readily recognizes the tremendous influence of his mother-in-law, Choi Ja-shil, in his healing and his ministry. His wife, Sung-hae Kim, also has her own ministry, and is the only woman ordained by the Full Gospel Church. Though all the ordained clergy listed are men, Cho's cell group leaders are often women, and these are counted as church workers, so, taking all the employed leaders together, there are almost as many women leaders as men, which is unusual for Korean churches. On the other hand, Cho is affirming of Confucianism, believing it to be a way of life rather than a religion (Anderson 2004b: 145), and his leadership style and teaching also display many "paternal" characteristics, as indeed do most Korean social relations, in their emphasis on authority, discipline and order. Cho's vision for worldwide mission is decidedly imperialistic, and he founds it on the injunction to "enlarge the place of thy tent" (Isa 54:2–4) (1999a: 115–29, especially 115–16). Nevertheless, it is the informal grassroots evangelism that has been the basis of his church growth strategy, and this is by personal witness—mainly of women—in the power of the Spirit, after the pattern of the book of Acts (Lim 2004: 195; Cho 1989: 20–29).

Ryu criticizes Cho's gospel as "a Holy Spirit movement without a Trinitarian God," because it lacks theologies of creation, history, development of character, and judgment (Ryu 2000: 425). Cho certainly assumes his christology is orthodox and believes he holds a fully trinitarian theology (Cho 1989: 35, 133–34). However, it is true that he does little theologically to relate the Holy Spirit to Jesus Christ or to God the Father. When the Holy Spirit is envisaged as a business partner, it does not seem that the vision is of Jesus Christ as revealed in history. It is not always clear that the Holy Spirit has the character of Jesus Christ rather than that of the great Shaman, the Mountain Spirit. However, many of the criticisms directed at Cho for encouraging shamanistic attitudes and materialism could be—and are—leveled at revivalist movements in the mainstream churches as well (e.g. H. Lee 1999: 149, 157). It is too much to expect a rounded trinitarian approach, given that Cho's theology was originally simply a means of encouraging poor believers and giving them confidence for evangelism. However, now the International Theological Institute of Yoido Full Gospel Church is actively working to systematize and establish Cho's teaching in mainstream Christian doctrine and academic theology (W. Ma 2004: 260–61; see, for example, International Theological Institute 1993). As the membership approaches one million, and the church wields such influence through the media, Cho's stature is so high that the mission of the Full Gospel Church is no longer limited to solving domestic and personal problems. It has social programs, a political agenda, an environmental concern and a global outlook. The Full Gospel Church, which may well soon join the World Council of Churches,[10] is evolving into an ortho-

---

[10] Stated by Rev. Dr. Hong Young-Gi at a press conference of the World Council of Churches Conference on World Mission and Evangelism, Athens, May 2005: http://www.christianpost.com/article/20050514/3649.htm.

dox expression of Christian faith that has a particular emphasis on the power of the Holy Spirit to effect change in people's lives.

The Korean Spirit in History:
The Religiocultural Theology of Ryu Tong-Shik

Ryu Tong-Shik (b. 1922), whose typology of maternal and paternal Holy Spirit movements we have already looked at, is a Methodist minister and professor emeritus of the prestigious Yonsei University in Seoul. In dialogue with *minjung* theology and Full Gospel theology, Ryu put forward his own Korean pneumatology, in which the work of the Spirit of God is affirmed in Korean religion and culture. Ryu built on his earlier study of the inter-action of Christianity and Korean religions (Ryu 2001 [1965]), and in-depth study of shamanism, to trace certain common characteristics of Korean culture throughout Korean history. In *The Mineral Veins of Korean Theology*, he used this research to claim that a distinctively Korean Christian theology emerges from the long subterranean strata of Korean culture that stretch back through at least two thousand years of recorded history, and before that to the origins of the Korean people among the tribes of Central Asia. He explains this in terms of the preservation of the essential Korean spirit (*ŏl*) in the worship of God as *Hanŭnim* or *Hananim* in different religious forms in different ages. He suggests that "the true form of Korean theology must be found in *p'ungnyu* theology," a theology that represents the best of the Korean spirit. *P'ungnyu* literally means "wind and flow," evoking the inspiration of Korean thinkers through creative retreat in the fresh air and by the pure streams of the beautiful mountains. Ryu sees *p'ungnyu*, which he describes as "supreme perfect life," as the expression of Yahweh's *rūach* and the framework for Korean theology (Ryu 2000 [1982]: 357–58).

Ryu attempts to show how three basic elements of the Korean spirit (*ŏl*), which he defines as *han, mŏt* and *sam*, have been expressed in Korean life and thought through all the changes of religion and governance in Korean history (2000: 22–28). *Han*, meaning "absolute," "great," or "supreme" (and not to be confused with *han* meaning "pent-up feelings"), defines the religiocultural history of Korea, the understanding and appreciation of the natural world and creative forces. *Han* is used to name the sky and God, the Lord of Heaven, *Hanŭnim* or *Hananim*, whom Koreans have wor-shipped under all the different religious traditions. It is also the name given to the Korean people and land, and thus represents the faith of Koreans that they are the people of God.[11] Ryu sees *mŏt*, which represents the ideals and aesthetic sense of Koreans, as definitive of the art and culture of the nation,

---

[11] Note on the terms *Hanŭnim* and *Hananim*: *Hanŭnim* is the ancient name for God, but *Hananim*, literally "One Lord," was adopted by most Protestants because it was suf-ficiently similar to to be acceptable to those who insisted on continuity and sufficiently

classically expressed in the Three Kingdoms period (centuries CE), in particular in the sixth-century philosophy referred to as *p'ungnyu*. In this period, the finest young men were selected as *hwarang* (literally "flowers"), who were educated through *p'ungnyu* to be bodily fit and refined, to sing and dance for mutual enjoyment, and to appreciate their natural environment. *Sam*, meaning life, denotes the experience of the masses and the social movements that have contributed to Korean character and identity, including religious, nationalist and liberation movements (Ryu 2000: 20–22). Ryu also notes that the flowering of Korean culture and manhood in the Three Kingdoms period was the result of the cross-fertilization of the primal religion with Confucianism and Buddhism (: 17–18). In this view he follows in the footsteps of one of the founders of Korean Christian theology, Ch'oi Byŏng-hŏn, who envisaged the leaders of Korea's religious traditions enjoying *p'ungnyu* together on a holy mountain where, in a "spiritual pavilion," they "exchanged their hearts" in a dialogue that he interpreted as the fellowship of the Holy Spirit (cf. J. Park 1998: 38–41). In this way Ryu illustrates the spiritual life of Korea in three dimensions: religious (*han*), artistic and cultural (*mŏt*), and social (*sam*), all emanating from the essential Korean spirit (*ŏl*) (Ryu 2000: 28).

Ryu developed his *p'ungnyu* theology through the work of Lee Yong-do, Kim Chae-chun and Ham Sok Hon, who were all born in 1901 in what is now North Korea. Noting how Lee, the revivalist, proved to be in touch with the mood of the people, Ryu tries to ground his own theology in Korean consciousness by showing that Lee's thought reflects the founding spirit of Korean culture expressed as *han*, *mŏt* and *sam* (2000: 136–65). Ryu is inspired by Kim's views on the freedom of the Spirit, for which he was excommunicated from the Presbyterian Church in 1953, to produce a theology that reflects "national culture and cosmic community" rather than conforming to patterns from elsewhere (Ryu 2000: 248–62). Ham Sok Hon (Ham Sŏk-hŏn; 1901–1989), a Korean Christian thinker and cultural historian,[12] has been described as "a Korean Gandhi" because of the way in which he articulated a national vision derived from ancient Korean traditions. Imprisoned many times, both by the Japanese and by South Korean dictators, Ham sought to fathom the meaning of suffering and of Korean history, which appeared "nothing but a series of humiliations, frustrations, and failures" (Ham 1985; see ix). Looking back to the Three Kingdoms period, Ham encouraged the modern nation to find her salvation within, "from the depths of her spirit-mind," which is free, and to believe that Korea, the "Queen of suffering," would one day give birth to "the king of

different to meet the objections of those who resisted the former as a pagan term. See Paik 1970 [1929]: 252–53.

[12] Ham's work is not discussed in *The Mineral Veins of Korean Theology* since he was still theologically active when it was written.

a new day" (: 169). It is through Ham that Ryu discovers the Holy Spirit at work in Korean history.

Ryu advocates a "religio-cosmic" approach to theology that has an interconnected view of nature, a cosmic view of history, and a "pneumatic religion." In proposing an interconnected view of nature, he rejects what he calls a "Western" approach, which regards human beings as God's representatives ruling over the earth, and advocates an "Eastern" view that sees human beings as part of the creation, and all as organically connected to God. Accordingly, he argues that human beings should understand themselves as part of a cosmic history that is not limited to the sociopolitical realm, but embraces scientific and religious thought also. Therefore, religion should be pneumatic or spiritual, not in the sense of anti-material, but in the sense that, through self-denial, freedom, love and peace are embraced as the form of human existence. This, he believes, is the message of both Eastern religions and Christianity, and also the perspective of John's Gospel, which Asians find particularly inspiring. It leads beyond preoccupation with personal salvation and past the limitations of sociopolitical approaches to religio-cosmic questions (Ryu 2000: 438–40).

Ryu wishes to affirm the work of the Holy Spirit in the highest and best of Korean life, and to encourage Korean theologians to take the spirit of *han-mŏt-sam* as their starting point. In doing so, he suggests that, instead of being preoccupied with the sociopolitical, *minjung* theologians should give more attention to popular religious movements. He believes that what he sees as the contemporary manifestations of the paternal and maternal movements—*minjung* theology and the Full Gospel movement—both have their own particular strengths and weaknesses; they both agree and disagree; and, practically, they are both important pillars of the one faith movement of the Korean church (Ryu 2000: 426). Therefore, rather than try to eliminate or exclude each other, he believes they should both contribute, by mutual criticism and complementarity, to a healthy, united Korean church. Ryu hopes for a new movement of the Spirit in which the two will work together, in the spirit of *p'ungnyu*, to bring about the evolution of the whole creation toward spiritual life, the truly human life. Ryu discerns the work of the Spirit in Korea in all movements, whether religious, political or cultural, whether paternal or maternal, but only insofar as they can be regarded as sustaining the spirit of the Korean people through the tribulations of the last thirteen centuries.

Ryu's work is rich and insightful as he mines the veins of the holy mountains from which Korean religiosity draws its strength. As he relates the story of the inception, growth and flowering of Korean theological thought, he highlights the struggle to decide between conflicting loyalties to, on the one hand, the message as originally received from the missionaries, and on the other hand, to the thousands of years of growth of religious understanding of the Korean people themselves. In doing so he uncovers the depths of thought and cultural riches on which Koreans have to draw, and shows how Koreans—whether inclined to be conservative or reforming—cannot but respond to the Christian gospel from the perspective of the tradition of which they are a part. However, it is one thing to say that Korean theology should reflect Korean culture; it is another to assert that Korean culture is of the Holy Spirit. Suh, for example, criticized Ryu for not taking issues of justice seriously enough (1999d: 411–12). Because of the way Ryu begins his theology by uncritically affirming Korean heritage, it is open to the accusations leveled against other spirit theologies or philosophies that are optimistic about human progress, and encourage nationalist fervor. Identifying the Spirit of God with a particular national identity is as dangerous a step to take as identifying the Spirit with a particular ideology or religious movement (although these are common tendencies of theologians); it is perhaps less dangerous if that identity is one that challenges rather than supports the ruling authorities. The motive to encourage self-respect and national pride is understandable in the light of the history of Korean humiliation and suffering, and the affirmation of the spirituality of the poor is an important step in challenging the abuse of power of the elite. However, pneumatology needs to be more sophisticated than this if it is to reflect the historical fact that what are claimed to be movements of the Spirit often have consequences that are far from holy. It should allow for the possibility of disobedience to the Spirit or—using an image in keeping with the Korean traditional worldview—the interference of other, ungodly, spirits (K. Kim 2006a: 167). Furthermore, Korean Christianity—like any other—must preserve the memory that it would never have taken hold in the first place if the people had not also been open to recognize the Spirit of God outside their own experience.

Reconciling the Spirits:
The Mission of the Spirit on the Korean Peninsula

We have looked at three distinct Korean pneumatologies in the work of Suh, Cho and Ryu. Though each has a different theology of the Holy Spirit, they also exhibit a shared Korean-ness due to their common religiocultural heritage and shared national experience. The history of the Korean Protestant churches is almost universally understood in terms of the outpouring of the Holy Spirit, and revival or Holy Spirit movements; this provides the "matrix" for theological reflection and for church life and mission in Korea (J. Park 1998: 18–33). Because they understand the Spirit to be a missionary one, none of our three theologians confines the Spirit's work to the church. Cho places most emphasis on the outpouring of the Spirit on the church, but also understands the Holy Spirit or "Fourth Dimension" to be ruling over all aspects of life. Suh stresses the present realization of the Spirit's work in Jesus Christ in contemporary movements, and Ryu emphasizes the cosmic movement of the Spirit in creation. Nevertheless, the revival has created a sense that this is "the third age of the Spirit," which is reinforced in popular imagination by the national prosperity and success achieved in the twentieth century, which is unparalleled in all Korean history (Ryu 2000: 415). Jong Chun Park, a prominent Methodist theologian, describes a distinctively Korean perspective on the Spirit. Looking back over the troubled history of Korea, he sees God "crawling" with the people, as God did with the people of Israel in the Old Testament, and later in Christ. Using Romans 8:22–23, 26, he describes the Spirit of God "who crawled in Christ" as the Mother Spirit who groans with the children of God for liberation, and the *han*-cry of the whole earth (1998: 137–52). However, in a way analogous to a shamanistic outburst of energy (*shinmyŏng*) in the form of dance in order to solve *han*, in revival the grace of God turns crawling into dancing, through a burst of transforming energy that creates a new rhythm for life and work (: 166–67). Living in this new rhythm, Korean Christians have, from the early days, expressed great confidence that they have been chosen as a light not only to their nation, but also to Asia, and to the rest of the world (e.g. Paik 1970: 428; Ro 1995; Cho 1999a: 127).

Because our Christian theologians agree that the source of this new energy is the Holy Spirit, this gives a dynamic sense to their pneumatologies; the emphasis is on the Spirit's movement and activity rather than on the Spirit's presence and being. Cho strongly asserts that the Holy Spirit broke in from outside of Korean experience in revival, and that the way to access this power is through the name of Jesus Christ. At the other extreme, Ryu is emphatic that the work of the Spirit is present in all Korean history. Suh combines both views when he sees the liberation of the *minjung* in revival terms as the in-breaking of something new from outside, the new age of the Spirit and, at the same time, as the age of the Spirit emerging in history in *minjung* consciousness. Both Suh and Cho have a strong sense of the opportunities and urgency of the present age, and in view of this they advocate activism in either a social or an evangelistic way, whereas Ryu stresses the continuity of the ages of history, and wishes to affirm the Spirit's work in all the traditions of Korea. As a result, Ryu's theology is more concerned with achieving harmonious human relations through mutual appreciation in study and dialogue. Suh, on the other hand, challenges society and culture in the name of humanization, and Cho rejects the other traditions, believing that healing and the solutions to personal and social problems are found only through the Holy Spirit, and in the name of Jesus Christ. Cho therefore takes an exclusive and even antagonistic stance towards Korea's other religions—though not toward Korean culture as a whole—seeing them as the outworking of other spirits opposed to Christ.

Suh, by contrast, is anxious to transcend religious and communal differences in the name of cooperative action for social ends, and Ryu appears to
want to include all Korean traditions under the greater umbrella of indigenous Korean spirituality.

Each theologian encounters the Spirit through a different medium. For
Suh, the Holy Spirit is experienced in collective action to challenge injustice, realizing the death and resurrection of Jesus in the experience of the
minjung. Cho experiences the Holy Spirit in continuous prayer, visions and
dreams, and the power of signs and wonders. For Ryu, the Holy Spirit is
experienced through the best of Korean culture, its art, music, literature,
artifacts and religious traditions, as well as its social movements. As this
implies, Ryu and Suh tend to see the Spirit as arising from below, in the
sense that the Spirit is evidenced in Korean life and experience. In Ryu's view
the Spirit is a more or less constant or growing presence in "wind and flow,"
but for Suh the Spirit breaks out sporadically in challenges to the social
order, and with increasing frequency in the contemporary period. In other
words, Ryu holds an evolutionary and Suh a revolutionary perspective. Cho,
on the other hand, begins with the Spirit above, within whose sway all other
realities are found. His cosmology includes a dualistic world of supernatural spirits over which the power of the Holy Spirit, which comes from
beyond, is pre-eminent. Suh also has a strong sense of suffering and evil,
but his anger is mainly directed at the institutional faces of injustice. If Cho
tends to portray the Spirit as a transcendent power, Suh pictures the Spirit
as the social force of freedom, and Ryu images the Spirit as a shared national
consciousness.

In the Korean context, the person and work of the Spirit are well known,
and historically, the Spirit appears to be foundational to the Korean church
through the revival movement in recent history. Though many Korean theologians wish to be faithful to the message of the missionaries and to connect their theology with the wider traditions of the global church, because
our three theologians emphasize the direct experience of the Holy Spirit in
the Korean context, none of them has a particular interest in reading the
Church Fathers or developing a metaphysical doctrine of the Trinity. Suh's
main concern is with the historical Jesus, and the Holy Spirit is introduced
to explain how the suffering of Jesus and the power of his resurrection are
realized today, but this is not clearly related to God as Source of both Christ
and the Spirit. Cho formally adopts a trinitarian theology because he wishes
to be theologically orthodox, but he does little to connect this with his pneumatology. In his understanding, both the Holy Spirit and Jesus Christ are
sent from God, but the theology of the Holy Spirit is hardly connected with
the person of Jesus Christ, except as the key to accessing the Spirit's power.
Ryu's Holy Spirit is the Spirit of God who is at work in all the religions, and
is not necessarily to be thought of as the Spirit of Jesus Christ.

Ryu is correct when he suggests that Suh and Cho could learn from dialogue with one another (and with himself) (Ryu 2000: 426), but wider dialogue within the Christian community is necessary to address these differences. This is a problem, because none of the three theologians we have considered finds widespread acceptance in the mainstream Korean churches. Both *minjung* theology and the Full Gospel Church are minority movements in Korean Christianity, and Ryu's work represents an academic theology, not a church group. Each of of our three theologians has reasons for rejecting the conservative Evangelical mainstream of the Korean church: Suh accuses the majority of Christians of being bourgeois and unconcerned with the suffering of the *minjung*; Cho does not think they have experienced the fullness of the Holy Spirit; and Ryu is angry at their suppression of theological freedom. Consequently, their views are not reflected in mainstream theological education in Korea, which by and large teaches traditional Western theology, in which the main interest in the Holy Spirit is found under the categories of the inspiration of the Scriptures, the sanctification of believers and the fellowship of the church. However, the experience of the Spirit in local Korean Protestant churches continues to reflect the influence of the revival movement and to incorporate the paternal and maternal patterns of Holy Spirit movements we have described. In any one Korean church, the public face on Sunday morning contrasts with other services and meetings throughout the week. The Sunday service is Confucian in appearance and organization (even in Yoido Full Gospel Church), and male-led, and more Pentecostal-style worship and healing are practiced at other times, in which women may play a leading role. Particular churches and individuals may lean more toward one form of expression than the other, but they inherit both styles. There are signs that, as the Korean church continues to mature in theological reflection, mainstream theologians are seeking to integrate Korean theology and church life (see, for example, C. Lee et al. 2004).

The Evangelical churches preserve an element of the first revival that has not been very explicit in any of the three theologies we have studied, which is repentance of sin. This was a sign that people did not see themselves only as victims, as *minjung* theologians have tended to portray them. They understood the Holy Spirit convicting them of their complicity in their own personal and national failure, that they were sinners as well as sinned against (J. Park 1998: 61–62). It was also a recognition that Korean culture was not true to the Spirit of God, as religiocultural theologies might seem to suggest. And it was an admission of their own dependence upon God and inability to change their situation by positive thinking or any other means. This acceptance of individual and corporate responsibility for history has been the strength of the Korean people in the twentieth century, who have refused to indulge in victimhood. In addition to *han, mŏt* and *sam*, the Korean people have grasped hope of grace beyond their tragic circumstances, and held on to *ggum*, that is, a "dream" or "vision." In the midst of poverty and adversity, they have not lost hope of blessing from God in the form of a better life (S. Kim: forthcoming). However, the links between the spiritual vision and the person and work of Jesus Christ are weak in the theologies we have studied. Each could degenerate into something less than Christian theology: Suh's into a political program, Cho's into a handbook on power and Ryu's into a map of national consciousness. In a distinctively Christian theology, the third age of the Spirit cannot be allowed to eclipse the second age of Jesus Christ and the first age of the Father.

Chung Hyun Kyung's pneumatology, as exhibited at Canberra in 1991, is even less acceptable to the mainstream churches. The World Council of Churches' choice of someone whom Korean church leaders regarded as a "young, obscure . . . female theologian" (Ro 1993: 54) was enough to be provocative in a patriarchal society that is very formal in its public practices and that respects the wisdom of age. Furthermore, the content of the presentation made Chung infamous in many Christian circles, where it was regarded as symptomatic of the heretical tendencies that were already suspected of the Council, which most Korean denominations have not chosen to join. Bong Rin Ro is typical in criticizing Chung's approach as contrary to trinitarian teaching, negligent of human sinfulness, syncretistic and "intuitive" rather than "theological" (Ro 1993: 54, 55–58). Others were more direct in dismissing Chung's presentation as "not theology," "a one-day wonder," "without value for discussion or consideration" and "a prank" (S. Han 1996: II 517). In his *Streams of Korean Theological Thought*, which attempts to be comprehensive, Han Sung-hong, professor at the mainline Presbyterian College and Theological Seminary, dared to include a chapter on Chung's theology (: II 489–526). It is rare for women's voices to be heard at all in mainstream theology, and she is the only woman theologian listed in the entire two-volume work, but her presentation at Canberra is given lengthy treatment. However, contrary to the moderate tone of Han's work as a whole, Han's response to Chung is entirely negative. Far from hearing her plea for alternatives to oppressive, dogmatic theologies, Han accuses Chung of hurling "a bombshell to demolish theological dogma and the church's authority," and the tone of his chapter is indicative of the patriarchal attitudes against which her vehemence was directed. Han finds fault with Chung for "falling into" shamanism and Buddhism rather than developing Christian theology, and concludes by listing no less than seventeen undesirable characteristics of her way of thinking. He accuses her of bewitching the World Council of Churches with a portrayal of the Holy Spirit that is an "insult" to the Spirit of Christ, and that bears no resemblance to the testimony of the scriptures or to the trinitarian doctrine of the church (: II 517, 513, 497). It is true that Chung's theology is not orthodox, but the same can be said of several of the other theologians Han includes, such as Suh. It seems that the reasons for the vehemence of the attack have much to do with Chung's low status, and also her affirmation of the shamanistic elements of Korean faith, which are socially as well as religiously unacceptable.

In the light of our study so far, it is possible to locate Chung's theology as a development of the *minjung* theology of Suh in her concern for liberation, and also of Ryu's religiocultural and cosmic theology, in her emphasis that the Spirit is already present in Korean women's experience (H. Chung 1991b: 42–43, 46). However, her commitment to a feminist agenda means that she evidences a maternal approach, which in its spirit-language also relates, perhaps surprisingly, to the theology of Cho. Like Cho, Chung also recognizes the spirit-world—although not a supernatural one—and embraces an agenda of problem-solving for theology (H. Chung 1988). Both affirm the supremacy of the Holy Spirit or Spirit of life above all the others, condemn an evil force which is defeated though active, and recognize a multiplicity of other spirits. There is a significant difference between Chung's approach to the spirits and Cho's. While Cho rejects as evil all spirits that do not confess Jesus Christ as Lord, Chung maintains the ambiguity of many spirits in the shamanist traditions. She is sympathetic to those spirits who are victims of evil, invoking the Holy Spirit to release them from *han* and bring about their liberation. In other words, the difference mirrors their respective anthropologies.

In the late 1980s and early 1990s, Chung became a leader of the eco-feminist movement, which linked many feminist theologians across Asia and Africa (see H. Chung 1994). Her theology owes much to her Korean heritage of Christianity and other faiths. In her presentation at Canberra, Chung reflected the apocalyptic core of Korean theology when she compared the "unholy," "acquisitive" spirit of Babel, which brings death, with the Holy Spirit of life and liberation poured out on women and men at Pentecost, giving hope of new creation (1991b: 41–42). At the same time, she related the Spirit of life to the philosophical term *ki*, the life-force and interconnectedness of all beings, and to the "wild rhythm" of the shaman's dance (: 44–46). Moreover, she was in tune with the revival spirituality of the Korean church when she called for repentance as the prerequisite for experiencing the power of the Spirit in bringing about social change (: 42–43). Chung did not refer to traditional trinitarian theology; however, she did relate the Holy Spirit to the spirit and person of Jesus Christ, and particularly to the suffering of Jesus, with which Korean theologians of all persuasions have closely identified. The Spirit, she said, is that of the historical Jesus, "our brother Jesus, tortured and killed on the cross," and also the Spirit of the life he came to bring (: 39). Though she described her image of the Holy Spirit in relation to her Korean cultural background as the selfless goddess Kwan In of popular Buddhism, at the same time she suggested

Kwan In as a feminine image of Jesus Christ because both share a spirit of compassion and wisdom (: 47).

Though Chung did not present a distinctively Christian theology at Canberra, it could be argued that she made a major contribution to Christian theology of the Holy Spirit by setting the Holy Spirit in a plural context of many spirits, which led to several theological developments. Han makes the valid point that making the Holy Spirit appear one of a kind in this way was possible only because Chung gave her presentation in English, whereas in the Korean language various different meanings of the word "spirit" would be distinguished by different terms (S. Han 1996: II 497). However, despite the different terminology, all the spirits that she referred to are popularly understood to be part of one spirit-realm, whether they are benevolent or malevolent, so the Korean would convey the same sense of the Spirit moving in the spirit-world. This perspective enabled her to articulate a theology of mission as an encounter between the Spirit and the spirits (cf. J. Ma 2001). The response of many delegates at the Canberra Assembly to her presentation was to reflect that, where there are many spirits, the Spirit needs to be distinguished from the others by the adjective "holy," and so to call for a theology of discernment of spirits (Council for World Mission and Evangelism 1991a: 254). This is indeed necessary, but Chung made a further contribution to theology of the Spirit in the world by suggesting a theology for plural society; that is, a theology which acknowledges the diversity and complexity of human experience, and which understands that—on the ground—one spirit may appear like any other. We will return to these topics in the next chapter.

Korean society changed almost beyond all recognition during the twentieth century, and especially in the last fifty years. The issues for theologians today are as much to do with affluence, technology and the internet as with poverty and human rights. But one issue has remained at the forefront of Korean minds since the 1950s. The greatest cause of *han* is the twentieth-century tragedy of the division of Korea into two halves by the capitalist and communist powers, and the continuing separation of the two nations. Resolving this problem by the unification (*t'ong'il*) of the two Koreas is the fervent petition in the many prayer meetings of Korean Christians, and for many this event will be the greatest evidence of the outpouring of the Holy Spirit. In 1988 the Korean National Council of Churches took the initiative to overcome the division by declaring the mutual hatred of North and South and its justification to be sinful. The KNCC proclaimed 1995, the fiftieth anniversary of the liberation from Japan, a year of jubilee to express their "firm resolution to bring about the restoration of the covenanted community of peace" (National Council of Churches in Korea 1988). In his trinitarian theology of "interliving," which is in contrast to the Korean history of "interkilling," Jong Chun Park envisages reunification in pneumatological terms as a "Jubilee Pentecost," a combination of Leviticus 25 and Acts 2, a "positive [effect of] globalization" brought about by the power of the Spirit. In this paradigm, reunification is envisaged as a second Korean revival, like that of 1907—the spiritual reform of the nation leading to the restoration of national sovereignty (J. Park 1998: 128–135, 164–71, 44, 137–52).

The pneumatology of reconciliation developing in Korea has wider applications than just the political. What we have observed of maternal and paternal divides suggests that the reconciliation of Korean men and women in the one Spirit should be a high priority—as some women theologians pointed out in response to the Jubilee Declaration (Women's Forum for the International Christian Consultation on Justice and Peace in Inchon, Korea, which took place in 1988—quoted in J. Park 1998: 131). As we have seen, the gender issue is not unconnected with the need for reconciliation between different forms of religious expression, which is also a pressing issue. *T'ongchŏn* theology or "holistic theology" is a recent Presbyterian initiative to overcome these and other polarities in Korean theology. In introducing this approach, which owes a great deal to his work, theologian Lee Chong-sŏng stresses the importance of the development of pneumatology in the context of awareness of many spirits of different religions, and the experience of living in the third age of the Spirit (C. Lee 2004: 44–46). In his theology Lee tries to relate Pentecostal pneumatology to traditional Christian pneumatology by discussing the "special work" and the "ordinary work" of the Spirit. For him, the Spirit not only gives gifts of tongues, prophecy, healing and so on, but is also at work in society, history and even the natural world. In terms of the scope of the mission of the Spirit, parallels could be drawn between Lee's work and that of Jürgen Moltmann, but, whereas the latter's emphasis is on affirming the Spirit as the source of all life, Lee is more concerned with discerning the Spirit in the midst of all areas of life (see M. Kim 2004: 95–97). He stresses that the Spirit of God is not only the origin of life, but also of salvation (Hyŏn 2004: 266–67). That is, Lee is more anxious than Moltmann about distinguishing the Holy Spirit from the other spirits.

The willingness to recognize the Spirit at work in the ordinary and the unspectacular could be a sign that after the first excitement of revival and discovering faith in the midst of national and spiritual crisis, the Korean church is developing a theology for a more settled community, and that the apocalyptic no longer holds such a central place. In which case, there will be greater awareness of the unceasing "wind and flow" of the Spirit (*Yŏng*) on the lower slopes of the mountains of Korea (cf. C. Lee 2004: 51; Keum 2000: 65–80), and perhaps of the life-force of the Spirit (*ki*) as well. But it is to be hoped that the Korean people will continue to experience the outbreaks of the fire of the Spirit (*Shin*) on the rugged peaks that have given such hope and dynamic energy in mission.

CHAPTER 7

Theology of the Holy Spirit in a Plural World: Spirits, Spiritualities, Discernment

In preceding chapters, we have looked at several different ways of describing the relationship between mission and pneumatology: according to "the Spirit of mission" in the Western tradition, "the mission of the Spirit" in the Eastern Orthodox churches, "mission in the Spirit" in Indian Christian theology, and "mission among the spirits" in Korean Christianity. Each of these is an attempt to express how the Holy Spirit is at work in the world. In *The Spirit of Life*, Jürgen Moltmann lamented the fact that in the contemporary "flood" of writing about the Holy Spirit (in the West), no new paradigm in pneumatology had emerged beyond the Catholic doctrine of grace or the Protestant pattern of Word and Spirit (1992: 1). As we have seen, as far as missiology is concerned, there has been a considerable learning process in pneumatology taking place, that is, the development of mission pneumatology and interest in the Spirit's work in the world outside the Christian church. Moltmann himself articulates a new paradigm insofar as he describes the mission of the Spirit in creation. The catalyst for this, and for Moltmann's own work, has not only been conversations between theologians of different confessions—Protestant, Catholic, Orthodox and Pentecostal-charismatic—but also the reflections of Christians from different geographical locations and cultural contexts, particularly in Asia and Africa, on their profound and broad experience of the presence and activity of the Spirit of God. To develop a theology of the Spirit in the world, or mission pneumatology, it is important to continue this practice of global conversation (K. Kim 2004).

In one sense, Christians have to agree that the Holy Spirit's work is not confined within the visible boundaries of the church or the individual, because otherwise "mission itself would be impossible since it is the Spirit that brings people to Christ" (Oleska 1990: 331). In the Indian context it seemed obvious to our theologians that the Spirit's mission could not be limited to *preparatio evangelica*, because it was not clear that the Christian community alone represented the best hope for India's future. Furthermore, their shared perception—due to their Indian cultural background—was of a cosmic Spirit also involved in varied ways with the other communities of India, and not just for conviction of sin and conversion to Christianity. The sense that they were living in the third age of the Spirit led Korean leaders and theologians to expect the Spirit's power in dealing with social as well as personal problems, and in reviving the whole land. All the Asian theologians we have studied have a vision of the Spirit's work that is not limited by doctrines or institutions, and reaches beyond the Christian community into the whole creation.

In both India and Korea, the religious background understanding of "spirit" is seen to influence the expectations of what the Holy Spirit can do and how the Spirit will act. The way in which the Holy Spirit is understood and described is affected not only by confessional standpoints but also by the meaning of "spirit" in any particular cultural-linguistic context (Raiser 1991). In the West, renewed interest in the theology of the Holy Spirit has gone hand-in-hand with a revival of interest in spirituality and "spiritual" experiences in the wider society. In India, against a backdrop of fascination with spiritualities of all kinds and a pervasive consciousness of one universal Spirit, pneumatology has become both the "cornerstone" of Indian Christian theology, and the basis for many initiatives in interfaith relations. Korean theologians, on the other hand, are working with a prevailing tradition of belief in the many spirits of a shamanistic worldview, and expectation of the intervention of "the Great Spirit." These varied pre-understandings of "spirit" greatly enrich pneumatological reflection. They raise further questions about the background meaning of *rūach* in the Old Testament, *pneuma* in the New, and other terms in the Bible referring to spiritual beings. It is not possible to tackle these important biblical questions here directly, but we can approach them indirectly by exploring the range of interpretations further and by engaging in global conversation around the understanding of spirit, the Spirit, spirits and spiritualities. To put this negatively, if we do not do this, our approach to the biblical text will be limited by our own experience and worldview. Put positively, it is possible that Christian brothers and sisters coming from different cultural contexts have captured the meaning of the ancient text more fully.

One Spirit or Many?

The chief difference in religiocultural perception of "spirit" between the Indian theologians we have studied and those from Korea is the contrast in cosmologies: between the belief in the one universal Spirit, within which the universe has its being (or appears to have being), and the awareness of a world of many spirits, among which the Holy Spirit is believed to be pre-eminent. We could describe the dominant Indian perspective as a "one-Spirit" theology, in which the Holy Spirit is perceived to comprise what can be experienced of the spiritual world, and the dominant Korean perspective as a "many-spirits" theology, in which the spiritual world includes diverse spiritual entities. It may also be noted at this point that the strongly unitarian tendencies of Hindu philosophy emerged in a society that is racially and culturally very diverse, where religion has been an important binding force. In contrast, the plurality of Korean theology of the Spirit emerges from a setting that appears relatively racially homogeneous and mono-cultural, but in which religion is a differentiating factor. The Japanese theologian Kosuke Koyama also observes that Korea is distinguished among Asian nations for its sense of history and eschatology, which tends to override general Asian "cosmological universalism" (Koyama 1988: 141). This distinction between cosmologies of the one and of the many may be recognized as distinguishing different regions of the world as well, different paradigms of thought in history, and even the views of different groups within the same society. It is a major difference between theologies of a more catholic kind and those of a more pentecostal-charismatic nature. Within Korea, theologies of a paternal or Confucian nature have less time for the spirit-world than those of a shamanistic or maternal orientation.

Between the "one-Spirit" and "many-spirits" traditions, there is a difference of terminology: in contexts in which many spirits are recognized, there is a need to attach the adjective "holy," or some other qualifier, to the word "Spirit" when referring to the Third Person of the Christian Trinity. Where only one Spirit is in view, or the Spirit is more distanced from other spiritual entities, the qualifier is unnecessary and "the Spirit" or "Spirit" alone is enough to signify what is meant. This could be illustrated by the titles of two books on spiritual discernment: the first by a British Anglican is *Discerning Spirit* (Gorringe 1990), and the second by a North American Pentecostal pastor with a Malaysian-Chinese Buddhist background is *Discerning the Spirit(s)* (Yong 2000). A similar distinction between worldviews has been suggested by Aloysius Pieris, a Jesuit theologian from Sri Lanka, for which he uses the terms "cosmic" and "meta-cosmic." Primal, folk, or popular religions—or local spiritualities—deal with the somewhat chaotic world of many spirits at a cosmic level, but the world religions introduce a universal dimension and a higher level at which there is perceived to be an overarching unity. Thus a meta-cosmic worldview can incorporate a cosmic one, as seems to have happened in conversions of tribal people to Roman Catholicism in Latin America and other parts of the world in recent centuries, where aspects of indigenous religiosity have been absorbed into Catholic practice. Pieris also believes this explains why religious conversions almost always take place from a cosmic to a meta-cosmic religion, and not the other way round (Pieris 1990: 71–74). His point about conversion is not so convincing in the context of New Age and other emerging spiritualities in the West as it is in the Asian context, so it may be better to see cosmic and meta-cosmic as alternatives rather than as a hierarchy of belief systems.

Nevertheless, Pieris' model does further help to distinguish between "one-Spirit" theologies and "many-spirits" theologies.

The observation that there are broadly two different cosmologies at work here should not be understood as an attempt to reduce complex cultures and systems of thought to an essential core, or to synthesize different world-views into one. Each way of thinking has its own integrity, and there are many varieties of spirituality that could be included under each head. Nevertheless, the difference observed between the pneumatologies of India and Korea calls for some further reflection on the part of those developing theology of the Holy Spirit in the contemporary Western context, especially because the most obvious difference between modernity and what is called post-modernity is that for modernity the highest value is unity, whereas for post-modernity difference is most important (cf. Welker 2002: 438). Movements toward undifferentiated unity are therefore regarded with sus-picion in a post-modern age, where diversity and plurality are most appre-ciated. If it is to be heard in the current climate, mission theology for post-modernity must therefore recognize complexity and variety, and allow room for other theologies and modes of expression. In post-modernity, unity can only be discovered or inferred from within a particular context; it can-not be asserted a priori. It may be therefore that where "one-Spirit" pneu-matology was characteristic of modernity, "many-spirits" pneumatology may be more suited to post-modernity. This may be considered to be the theological import of the global rise of Pentecostal-charismatic spirituality.

Despite globalization, the contemporary West is dissimilar in many respects to the societies of India and Korea, but when it comes to dealing with plurality, there may be much the West can learn. Western seculariza-tion has not entirely extended to human consciousness, and the rediscovery of theological thought is a real possibility (Berger 1971). The rise of post-modernity has seen a resurgence of interest in what Berger called the "super-natural," and what now tends to be referred to as "spirituality" (Heelas and Woodhead 2005). Often, this does not conform to the old institutional pat-terns, but is expressed in conversion to Eastern religions, "New Age" eclec-ticism, or in other alternative movements. Within Christianity there are also alternative spiritual movements (see Tacey 2004), as well as new church movements that are Pentecostal-charismatic in type. The aim of this chap-ter is to reflect on Western theology in the light of the approaches of our Indian and Korean theologians, and especially the contrasting awareness of one Spirit and many spirits.

The One Spirit in a Plural World

Christians confess their unity in the one Spirit (1 Cor 12:13; Eph 4:4; Phil 1:27), but the nature of that unity has been the source of controversy since the Gentiles first became Christians (Acts 15:1–2; Gal 2:11–14). The one-Spirit theologies as we encountered them in India tended to emphasize unity rather than diversity. Rayan espoused unity to bring about revolution, and is a leading ecumenist; Vandana wanted to bring about oneness beyond religious differences; and Samartha aimed to encourage unity among communities. Vandana and Samartha in particular used Hindu philosophical frameworks to justify their position. However, many commentators are cautious of using philosophies of spirit, whether Indian or modern, to express the Holy Spirit's relation to the world, because they tend to impose a human construct on God's revelation. In the context of Europe, as Heron points out, idealist philosophies of spirit pose a "political menace" because of the ideological motivation behind them, which leads to totalitarianism (this criticism may be directed at both fascist and communist systems). On the other hand, some forms of idealism, he notes, have tended to pantheism, that is, "the reduction of God to a purely immanent Spirit working through the evolution of the cosmos" (1983: 147–48). Dialogue between philosophical systems and what is understood as God's revelation is necessary in every context, but capitulation of Christian theology to a particular philosophical system is neither necessary nor desirable (: 148; Hübner 1989: 326; Welker 2002: 447).

Michael Welker, professor of theology at the University of Heidelberg, sees Western theology and piety as captive to three forms of Western thought, none of which allows for the "reality of the Spirit" as encountered in the world (Welker 1994: 40–41, ix-xii). The first is the "old European metaphysics," in which religion is seen to establish one universal system of reference. Within this system the Spirit can be understood as ubiquitous, a totalizing universal force or structure (: 41–43). The second form of thought is "dialogical personalism," which attempts to comprehend the world in terms of I-Thou relations or subject-object interaction, as, for instance, in the theology of Barth and other dialectical theologians. In these constructs the Spirit is that which creates and sustains divine-human and human-to-human relationships (: 43–44). Third, there is "social moralism," originating with Kant, which sees religion as bringing about progress. In this category, which Welker believes is currently the most widely influential, the Spirit is that by which human beings participate in God's action (: 44–46). Welker finds almost no biblical basis for the first school of thought. Moreover, he finds that the old metaphysics does not allow for the specific actions of the Spirit recorded in Scripture. In Welker's view, the slightly stronger biblical basis for dialogical personalism does not justify the weight put on it and, furthermore, the complexity of human relations cannot be reduced to the I-Thou formula. Social moralism is established in Scripture and has proved open to pluralistic structures, but it may reduce the Spirit to a form of moral sensibility or to common humanity (: 46–49).

The Roman Catholic Church has seemed to exemplify the "old European metaphysics." Cardinal Walter Kasper, president of the Pontifical Council for Promoting Christian Unity, admits that Catholics have effectively "made the doctrine of the Church the living gospel" and tended to domesticate and monopolize the Spirit of God in ecclesiological terms, on the grounds that "Christ is the Head of the Church, the Holy Spirit her soul" (2004: 99–100). Kasper refutes the idea that traditional Catholic ecclesiology forgot the Holy Spirit, noting that Thomas Aquinas and other great theologians of the Middle Ages, together with the mystics, had a great deal to say about the Spirit (: 99). Furthermore, Aquinas taught that "the Spirit acts not only in the Church; he leads and brings to life all that is created and is at work in the whole of creation"; but Kasper accepts that, in their opposition to the reformers, Catholic theologians restricted the Spirit's work to the Catholic Church (: 98–99). He, like many others, sees the Second Vatican Council as ushering in a new Pentecost in the life and thought of the Roman Catholic Church, which allows for wider recognition of the presence and activity of the Holy Spirit (: 100–101). The Roman Catholic Church has always been fearful of pneumatocentrism and unbridled enthusiasm—this being the reason for adopting the *filioque* in the first place—and it has succeeded so far in keeping its charismatic movement and many emerging new movements across the world largely within its fold. One way this has been done is by setting limits to the movement of the Spirit; another way of achieving the same aim is to extend the ecclesial system to encompass the world, for example by Rahner's "anonymous Christians" theology. In other words, exclusivism and inclusivism may be closely related. Samartha regarded both inclusivism and exclusivism as "patronizing," since both express colonial mentalities and "seek to impose uniformity on a pluralist world" (1991a: 86, 3). Advaitic philosophy and the "old European metaphysics" are similar in the sense that the ubiquity of the Spirit leads to a tendency to subsume other points of view into its overarching system.

Despite the contributions of Rahner and others, the Council was reproached by the Orthodox, Anglican, Protestant and other observers for "christomonism," and one-sided christocentric ecclesiology. French Dominican Yves Congar argued that this was not the case, and attempted to draw out "the elements of true pneumatology" present in the Council documents (1983 [1979]: I 167). These he identified as: the Holy Spirit as the principle of the life of the church, the Holy Spirit as animator of the church, a trinitarian theology of creation and grace, recognition of charisms, attention to the local church as "called in the Holy Spirit," and mention of the Spirit's work in history (: I 167–73). In his three-volume pneumatology (1983 [1979]), Congar recognized both the revelation and the experience of the Spirit (volume 1) and conducted a dialogue with the Orthodox on the Trinity and the sacraments (volume 3), but his focus was on the Holy

Spirit as animator of the church and inspirer of personal life (volume 2). Congar succeeded in establishing Catholic pneumatology, but it still remained within the Holy-Spirit-in-the-human-heart and in-the-church models and did not discuss the wider work of the Spirit in the world (cf. Moltmann 1992: 1, 312 nn.4, 8).

Kasper further explains that Vatican II broke away from "a constricted and one-sided Christocentrism" (2004: 100) in several ways. First, the Council laid the groundwork for the development of Spirit christology by recognizing both the presence of the Holy Spirit in the saving work of Jesus Christ, and the church's sharing in this through participation in Christ's baptism (: 101–103). This had implications for the nature of the church, which is now seen more as an event of the Spirit and not only as an institution (: 103). As a "living tradition," the unity of the Church is seen as a unity of diversity, which embraces the gifts of the people as well as the hierarchy, and in which the interpretation of the scriptures by the Holy Spirit has been opened to the whole community (: 103–106). In another significant step, a result of dialogue with the Orthodox churches, the Roman Catholic Church since Vatican II has reintroduced into the liturgy an explicit prayer of invocation of the Holy Spirit upon the eucharistic elements (: 106–108). This amounts to recognition that the Church has an "epicletical structure"; that is, it does not "have" the Holy Spirit but asks for the Spirit, believing its plea will be heard (: 108). Kasper ascribes the ecumenical openness of the Catholic Church since Vatican II to this renewal of pneumatology, which has been accompanied by a renewed spirituality of the Church (: 104). Such has been the change that concrete steps have even been taken to overcome the problem of the *filioque* between East and West: the West would accept that the phrase "and the Son" in the Western version of the Nicene-Constantinopolitan Creed is an addition to the normative version originally agreed to by both sides, while the East would allow that it is a valid and important interpolation to solve a contextual theological problem (: 114).

This crucial recognition that the Spirit constitutes the church, rather than the other way around, pointed the way to open up Catholic pneumatology, so that in his *Dominum et vivificantem* (1986), Pope John Paul II could say, "We need to go further back [from the Spirit of the Father and of the Son, given to the Church], to embrace the whole of the action of the Holy Spirit even before Christ—from the beginning, throughout the world" (: paragraph 53). The pope reminded his hearers that "the wind blows where it wills," indicating that the Holy Spirit is also active "outside the visible body of the Church." Specifically, this justified an invitation to "all people of good will" and "all those who worship in spirit and truth" (: paragraphs 53–54). The encyclical further recognized that the Holy Spirit "is not only close to this world but present in it, and in a sense immanent, penetrating it and giving it life from within." This was applied to all life, though the focus was on human life and relations (: paragraph 54). On the other hand, the encyclical *Redemptoris missio* (1990), while affirming the "pre-eminence" of the Spirit's role as "the principal agent" of the church's mission *ad gentes* (John Paul II 1990: paragraphs 21–30), projected a more restricted view of the Spirit's work (see chapter 3). An officially endorsed mission pneumatology of the Catholic Church following the encyclical acknowledges that the Spirit gives life in creation and worked in the history of Israel, but stresses that this Spirit was not poured out on all the people of God until Pentecost (Federici 1995: 65–67). It emphasizes that the unity of the mission of the Son and the Spirit means there is "one divine mission in the New Testament," not two parallel ways through Son and Spirit. "True," Federici concludes, "the Spirit blows where he wills," but "[t]he Spirit blows only to bring about communion and establish God's Kingdom in the hearts of people through Jesus Christ," in such a way that the universal activity of the Spirit appears to be directed toward the (Roman Catholic) church (: 67–68, 71–73). This tension between humble recognition of the sovereignty of the Spirit and conviction of the centrality to God's purposes of the Roman Catholic Church, as the church of Jesus Christ, remains unresolved, so the tendency to make world, church and kingdom coterminous with one another remains.

Evangelical systems are more likely to fall into Welker's category of "dialogical personalism," and to assign to the Spirit the role of maintaining a dialectic or system of communication. John V. Taylor attempted to widen Evangelical appreciation of the Spirit's mission by extending I-Thou philosophy to the whole universe, so that the Spirit becomes "the go-between God," who facilitates every encounter in the universe. Taylor's mission pneumatology needs to be understood in the light of his earlier exploration of "the primal vision" in East Africa, which he interpreted as a "monistic totality" (Taylor 1963: 62–63, 72–73, 83–92, 201). In order to relate the Christian faith to the African worldview, he attempted to distinguish between "life-force" and "spirit" on the grounds that the two are distinguished in the Old Testament as *nephesh* and *rūach*, respectively, and that he believed the same distinction is also generally made by other tribal peoples (Taylor 1972: 7–8). So Taylor saw "spirit" not as the power of the monistic totality of life, but as the power of personhood and relatedness. Taylor's idea faces a number of difficulties: first, in translation of the Hebrew, because *nephesh*, usually rendered "soul," seems to be more closely connected with personhood than *rūach*, not the other way around (e.g. Gen 2.7; compare Brown 1971: 680 and 691); and second, because of the difficulties of generalizing about primal spiritualities. Furthermore, Taylor's Augustinian view of the Spirit as love needs to be balanced by an Orthodox understanding of the Spirit as life, otherwise, as we have seen, the personhood of the Spirit is diminished. If relations take place only "in the Spirit," then any relationship *with* the Spirit is impossible. Welker is right in saying that "dialogical personalism" cannot represent "the rich and complex relation between God and human beings and their fellow creatures" (1994: 41).

"Social moralism" is a tendency of theologies of liberation when they assume a universal consciousness and insist on a common vision. Until recently, European theologies (and philosophies) have maintained the traditional Latin or Augustinian pneumatological framework that connects the Spirit primarily with human consciousness and human redemption. So they have been mainly concerned with the future of humanity, rather than with the whole created order, and references to the Spirit in terms of natural forces such as wind, breath, water and fire are understood metaphorically. Moltmann observes how this "constriction" of the church to the world of human beings was tightened in modernity (Moltmann 1990: 31–39). Thus, for example, Congar did not venture to discuss the role of the Spirit in nature or creation (Moltmann 1992: 1, 312 nn. 4, 8). Kasper and Rahner were concerned with ecumenical and interfaith relations, and Welker's input is in the context of public life, from which perspective he uses "world" and "creation" in the sense of global society. This limited framework became especially apparent in the light of environmental crisis when some eco-theologians pointed to Western theological "anthropocentrism" (e.g. Kwok 1994: 109–10; Abraham 1994b: 69–70). At the Canberra Assembly, a creation-centered or life-centered approach was encouraged, and publications such as Jürgen Moltmann's God in Creation (1985) and Krister Stendahl's Energy for Life (1990) attempted to address this lacuna in ecumenical thinking. The key biblical text used was Romans 8, particularly verses 22–23: "We know that the whole creation has been groaning in labor pains until now; and not only the creation, but we ourselves, who have the first fruits of the Spirit groan inwardly while we wait for our adoption, the redemption of our bodies," which connects the redemption of humanity with the liberation of the whole created order in a birthing process. As was pointed out at the time, the Holy Spirit is not said to be at work in creation in this passage (Schweizer 1989: 408; Hübner 1989: 324, 332–33); it is the Spirit given to the community that is seen as the key to the wider renewal. The argument for the wider work of the Spirit in creation was based on the first chapters of Genesis, Ezekiel 37 and other passages in the Hebrew Bible, and on the assumed continuity of vocabulary and thought between the testaments (Hübner 1989: 336).

Eco-feminists narrowed the criticism of Western theology down from "anthropocentrism" to "androcentrism." The American feminist Mary Daly, for example, exposed masculine models of domination applied to the earth as well as to women, such as the use of the language of rape (Daly 1986: 114–22). Others, like Vandana (1991a: 56), Rayan (1994a) and Chung (1994), drew attention positively to the use of feminine terminology in primal religions to describe the earth and its energies—terms such as "Mother Earth," "Earth Mother," Shakti, Yin and Rūach. Chung's combination of eco-feminism and indigenous spirituality, which resulted in her representation of the energy of life as a shaman's dance, made her the leader of the eco-feminist theology movement in the early 1990s. Chung described her approach, and that of eco-feminism in general, as the search for "a spirituality which promotes the immanence of God, the sacredness of this world and the wholeness of body, sensuality and sexuality" (1994: 176). Rejecting the spirituality of traditional Western Christianity as not only androcentric but also "European" and "dualistic," she put forward the spirituality of the indigenous people in Asia and Africa as capturing "a cosmic interwovennness," a just and mutual relationship between human beings and nature (: 176–77). Chung's presentation at Canberra struck a chord with many other women, and encouraged the articulation of a feminist mission theology that aimed to move beyond masculine images of God, beyond paternalism, beyond patriarchy and beyond dualism, and to move toward a mission of love, mutuality and empowerment, of which the main symbol is bringing to birth, child-bearing (Rom 8:22–23; Jn 16:22). Mission was pictured as groaning in travail in solidarity with the Holy Spirit, with other women, and with the whole creation to bring about the new life of the gospel (K. Kim 2001). It was understood primarily as taking place by the feminine power of the Spirit, and in a way sensitive to the Spirit's movement in the whole creation as the Paraclete: the Spirit who "comes alongside as a sister inspiring and enlivening and drawing us into her activity" (: 23). Eco-feminism represented a rejection of the kingdom-of-God analogy for mission—by feminists because of its perceived authoritarian and patriarchal tones, and by third-world theologians because of its association with empire-building—and its replacement by the category of the Holy Spirit.

A Spirit-centered rather than kingdom-centered approach was seen by women as a less-threatening and a more personal and holistic way of doing mission (Oduyoye 1992: 174); it offered an alternative to totalitarian visions. However, Chung's attitude, as revealed at Canberra, was aggressive, and begged the question of whether replacement of "masculine" by "feminine" will necessarily end domination. Chung clearly espoused a social project, and was using both the Spirit and the spirits as imagery for a sociopolitical message. In her address, she called on the oppressed spirits as if they were all part of the same spirit, as if she was using a "metaphor of a universal Spirit calling us through the victims of the world" (Knitter 1995: 81). The spirit of "social moralism," whether Chung's or Moltmann's, appears more a human spirit that promotes life than the powerful, unpredictable Spirit of God encountered by the ancient Hebrews and the first Christians. Using the symbols of "indigenous spiritualities" to construct a "metaphor of a universal spirit" is also to misrepresent them, since they are essentially local and resist generalization into a philosophy of spirit (cf. J. Cox 1996). And fitting Christian theology into another framework only serves to restrict the distinctive Christian contribution to the debate, for the Spirit of God in the biblical tradition can no more be reduced to life than to love.

The shift from theologies of humanization to eco-theology had the effect of emphasizing that the Spirit is neither a human possession nor present only in human activity. Rather, the Spirit may be understood as part of the environment in which human beings live. It is another example of the shift in mission thinking toward "mission in the Spirit," which is an unfolding of the theology of *missio Dei*. However, in Christian theology, while it is true that "we live and move and have our being" in God (Acts 17:28), it is also true that the Son and the Spirit are sent into the world (17:31). The eco-feminist vision of the Spirit as the Mother of Life tends to be pantheistic, identifying God or the Spirit with the ecosystem (Moltmann 1992: 157–60; 1985: 98–103). Pantheism leaves little room for either Christian distinctiveness on the one hand or the Spirit's freedom on the other. In India, we saw that, despite the overwhelmingly pantheistic cultural background, Samartha, Vandana and Rayan generally—though not altogether—avoided it, insofar as being "in the Spirit" was understood not as a permanent state awaiting realization, but as the result of commitment to a particular mission: interfaith dialogue, mystical spirituality or social liberation. They distinguished the Spirit from creation and maintained a sense of transcendence or eschatological vision. Orthodox theologian Nikos Matsoukas points out that creation "is not the divine essence but a created essence" (Matsoukas 1989: 399), and so the Spirit is the Giver or Creator of life, not merely the life-force. It is in order to avoid such confusion that, as we have seen, the Orthodox talk in terms of human participation not "in the Spirit," but with the (uncreated) divine energies in the Holy Spirit.

Christian pneumatologies must avoid being totalitarian from above or pantheistic from below. As we saw in the context of Korea, a Christian theology must balance inculturation with liberation, evolution with revolution, and cosmology with eschatology. It must allow room for the Spirit to work "outside the box" (cf. Rayan 1976: 133), to come and to go (Jn 3:8). If the Spirit is all-encompassing or ubiquitous, the Spirit's absence is difficult to contemplate, but only if there is acceptance of the possibility that there may be places or occasions that God's Holy Spirit does not inhabit or endorse, is there the possibility of critical engagement with the world. In the next section we will move on to investigate how a many-spirits cosmology functions as a framework for pneumatological reflection.

The Spirit and the Spirits

Awareness of a spirit-world has been the norm in most societies in history and continues to be so (Arnold 1992: 198–205), but, particularly since the Enlightenment, Western Europeans have appeared to inhabit a simplified, sanitized world in which—in the historic Protestant churches at least—insofar as human beings have related to God at all, it has been without interference from or mediation of other spiritual beings. In modern theology, particularly Protestant theology, angels and demons alike are condemned to the realms of superstition, and what remains is "God and man." The German theologian Rudolf Bultmann famously remarked that "[i]t is impossible to use electric light and the wireless and to avail ourselves of modern medical and surgical discoveries, and at the same time to believe in the New Testament world of demons and spirits" (quoted in Dunn 1998: 67–68). Though Paul Tillich emphasized Spiritual Presence, for him the ambiguity of religion justified recognition of the demonic as well as the divine (1963: 102–106), but even he admitted that he found it difficult to accommodate "spirits" (plural) in his theology, because they implied the existence of a "spirit" realm that he associated with "ghosts" and rejected, because it stood apart from life as he understood it (: 23). The great twentieth-century Catholic theologians of the Spirit, Karl Rahner and Yves Congar, consider only the Spirit of God and the human spirit. Of the three Western theologians considered in chapter 3, only Karl Barth refers to "the spirits of the world" (e.g. Barth 1962: 129, 128, 134–35), and in his theology only evil spirits are contemplated.

In the context of India, advaitic Hinduism allows little room for a spirit-world, since spiritual life is more an internal matter of the heart than engagement with external forces. However, we have pointed out that the dismissal by Samartha and Vandana of the popular religion of many gods and spirits, under the influence of this philosophy, is a weakness of their theological approach, since such belief is so prevalent in the wider society. We have seen that for many Korean theologians the context is a more complex worldview of many spirits. Chung Hyun Kyung was exceptional at the Canberra Assembly in making the world of spirits the focus of her presentation, but many of the papers produced around the event referred to other spirits and used spirit-world language. The other opening plenary presentation by Parthenios, Patriarch of Alexandria and All Africa, made only passing reference to "the spirit of evil" from whom the Holy Spirit delivers us, but other Orthodox contributions seemed to assume multiple spirits as background to the debate. Orthodox reflections at Crete in 1989 warned that "spirits other than the Holy Spirit may act in the world" (1990: 92), a warning repeated in their statement of concerns after Canberra (Reflections of Orthodox participants 1991: 281). The statement also noted that, in Orthodox worship, the work of God in saving and redeeming from political and other forces is articulated as "a victory over the demonic principalities, forces and powers" (Orthodox reflections: 92, 95). African contributors Justin Ukpong (Catholic; 1990), Joseph Osei-Bonsu (Protestant; 1989) and John Pobee (Anglican; 1990) immediately related the topic of the Holy Spirit and creation with the spirits of African traditional religion, whereas others, such as the European Catholic Philip Rosato, discussed the whole range of "the mission of the Spirit within and beyond the Church" without finding it necessary to use the language of spirits or powers at all (Rosato 1990).

To go back to the Middle Ages in Europe by attempting to reinstate a hierarchy of angels, spirits and demons would not be desirable. Modernity delivered people from the fear of capricious activity and the need for fetishes and mantras that such a worldview can generate. Chung Hyun Kyung, for one, has written about how her Western education freed her from childhood fears of the ghosts and spirits her grandmother told her about (1988). Being released from this daily anxiety about unpredictable forces, Europeans developed modern science, which assumes the world is ordered and sees a bigger picture that has allowed them to control the environment in new and previously unimagined ways. Modernity has "demythologized" the "spirits" by revealing vested social and political interests behind religious doctrines and by finding social and psychological explanations for believing in the "spirits." Taylor's experience of "divination as practiced by mediums in Africa" led him to believe that, through the Holy Spirit, the voices of the spirits actually articulate "the subconscious awareness of the community" (1972: 67–68, 107–108, 166; 1963: 148–50). In the case of India, demons may speak what is otherwise unmentionable (Selvanayagam 2000). And we saw in Korea that shamanism may function as the "waste disposal" of the religious world (C. Kim 2003: 82–100, 189–91). However, consigning the spirit-world to fairyland and providing a logical explanation for belief in spirits does not necessarily solve the human problem. It has been the discovery of post-modernity that rationality is not the only or necessarily the best tool for dealing with "the absurdities of existence" (Suurmond 1994: 79, see 75–97). Religion and spirituality have a continuing role to play in helping human beings deal with the apparently inexplicable, the daily struggle, and the powerful—often unseen—forces they encounter. What is lost along with the spirit-world is a sense of the involvement of the Holy Spirit in the everyday world that "demons and spirits" inhabit, and the possibility of engagement with popular religion.

"One-spirit" religions tend to suppress local or primal spirituality. This is the case not only in Korea, where the later religions despised shamanism, and in India, where advaitic Hinduism relegated popular practices to a lower level of spirituality, but also in the modern West. Popular religion erodes any monopoly of the spiritual by introducing the struggle and competition of everyday life, as reflected in the gospel writings, into the theology of the Holy Spirit. It may well be that the suppression of popular religion and spirituality by elitist philosophies has contributed to a sense of the remoteness of the Spirit or a diminishing of the Spirit's personhood. The "Holy Spirit" without the many spirits can convey a sense of abstraction, distance and splendid isolation, which increases the alienation of academic theology from church life and popular belief, and inadvertently spurs the growth of new movements. At the very least, as one of the first scholars of Pentecostalism,

Walter Hollenweger, reflected after the Canberra Assembly, "The fact that [the issue of spirits] has produced so much dissension and discussion shows that it aggravates a weak spot in Western theology," which tends just "to label such beliefs 'psychological' or 'superstitious'" (Hollenweger 1997: 383).

Positive interest in what is termed in Catholic circles "popular religiosity," or in the ecumenical movement "indigenous spirituality," is a recent development, but several groups have been giving serious theological attention to the many-spirits perspective. The fact that the language of the spirit-world is found in the Bible makes it part of the shared heritage of all Christians. For the sake of better understanding of the biblical material, in recent years some New Testament scholars have shown the significance of the background of belief in the supernatural on the part of both Jews and Gentiles (for a summary of recent biblical scholarship, see Arnold 1992: 219–35). Since Wheeler Robinson in 1928, some have argued that it was the "spirit-world" that "formed the matrix of the idea of the Holy Spirit," and the absence of awareness of this context in the modern West makes interpretation of New Testament pneumatology particularly difficult (: 2). James Dunn, who has done particular work on the language of demons, spirits and exorcism in the New Testament, comments that "the New Testament world of demons and spirits," which Bultmann rejected, "is also the biblical world of the Holy Spirit." He fears that "in abandoning the dimension of the demonic we may find that we have abandoned also the dimension of the Spirit," since this is the milieu from which theology of the Holy Spirit arose (1998: 67–68).

By the nature of their engagement with spiritual power, Pentecostal-charismatic theologians have paid particular attention to passages of the Bible that concern "authorities," "cosmic powers," "spiritual forces" and "the heavenly places" (Eph 6:12). None of the major studies of the Pentecostal-charismatic movement considers awareness of a spirit-world to be a major characteristic. Bittlinger's early report contained only one reference to it (Hocken 1981); Hollenweger's definitive work included an eight-page chapter on "demonology" in a book of nearly six hundred pages (1972: 377–84); Martin discusses the spirit-world under the heading "Africanization" and in connection with shamanism, but not as inherent to Pentecostalism itself (2002: 138–43, 161–62); and Anderson does not list any references to spirits or demons, though he does refer several times to "exorcism" and "deliverance" (2004a: 197, 201, 211, 228, 230, 231, 233–34). Nevertheless, it can be said that Pentecostal-charismatic spirituality has a distinct advantage over traditional missiologies in parts of the world where people are familiar with phenomena from the spirit-world, because "the charismatic emphasis on the power of the name of Jesus Christ and His Spirit" could be used to relate to witchcraft, sorcery and other forms of the occult (Hocken 1981). The offer of healing by Pentecostal-charismatic forms of Christianity has been one of its major attractions to the poor, and especially in parts of the world least affected by moderniza- tion, secularization and scientific rationalism. There the Pentecostal-charis- matic message of "signs and wonders" meets popular hopes and expectations (Anderson 2004a: 210–14; cf. Yong 2000: 187). As we observed in the case of Yoido Full Gospel Church, the literal application of New Testament descriptions of Jesus' ministry of exorcism is part of the the- ology of Pentecostal-charismatic healing practices, in which demons or evil spirits are seen as the cause of disease, to be driven out by prayer "in the name of Jesus." In sub-Saharan Africa, for example, "Spirit-type" churches meet the need to deal with the fear of evil generated by the spirit-world, which Western theology has generally failed to address (Anderson 1991: 8–25; see also Daneel 1993).

In the 1970s and '80s three returned American Evangelical missionaries, Paul Hiebert, Alan Tippett and Charles Kraft, all of whom had backgrounds in anthropology, reflected together on their encounters overseas with the spirit-world in primal religious settings. They realized that they had not been trained theologically to deal with phenomena such as spirit possession, but were convinced of the reality of the realm of spirits. Paul Hiebert (1982) used the term "the middle zone" to refer to cosmic forces that had been dis- regarded, even eliminated, by the scientific mindset of modernity, and the group came to adopt a tribal religious understanding of the meeting of the gospel with the local culture as a "power encounter" (see Kraft 1992). Their work was applied to the United States in the 1980s, and became founda- tional to the so-called third wave of the Pentecostal-charismatic movement. Peter Wagner broadened the Pentecostal-charismatic healing ministry to deal not only with demonized individuals, but also with the "territorial spirits" that he believed were "assigned to every geopolitical unit in the world" (1989; for a critique of this from an Evangelical perspective, see Lowe 1998). This resulted in John Wimber's theology of "power evangelism," in which Christian witness consisted in demonstrating the power of the Holy Spirit over other spirits and thereby "conquering ground" (Wimber 1985; Lord 2005: 16–21), which was applied from Ecuador to Nigeria and Korea (Douglas 1990: 105–107). "Spiritual warfare" has provoked a great deal of discussion and criticism (e.g. Percy 1996; A. Scott Moreau et al. 2003), and the more politically correct "spiritual conflict" is now preferred in moder- ate circles (World Evangelical Alliance 1999: 20). Nevertheless, as Harvey Cox concludes after observing Pentecostalism in North America, it seems that "modern liberal theologians have too easily discarded the idea of transpersonal forces of evil" (1996: 286). As Cox (1996), Philip Jenkins (2002: 7–8), and others have highlighted, Pentecostal-charismatic move- ments are the fastest growing form of Christian expression today, and this is clearly an argument for developing a Christian theology of Spirit and spir-

its that is more representative of the biblical message and Christian tradition than is the theology of "spiritual warfare."

Like many Evangelicals and Pentecostal-charismatics, liberation theologians have used the biblical language of "the powers" or "evil spirits," but
in a rather different sense (McAlpine 1991). Liberation theology also pos-
tulates a spiritual struggle, but sees the "principalities and powers" as man-
made social structures rather than as supernatural in origin. So, for example,
one of the Canberra reports called for a new mission "not into foreign lands,
but into foreign structures" (World Council of Churches 1991: 66). And, in
a preparatory paper for the assembly, Indian theologian M. M. Thomas
called for "a spirituality for combat" for political struggles. He described
the Holy Spirit as the power of resistance against other spirits of destruction, self-righteousness and idolatry in the decisive battle ultimately won by
Christ on the cross (1990: 219). As we have seen, other liberation theologians, including Samuel Rayan and Suh Nam-Dong, see the Spirit as the
divine agent of social liberation. North American Walter Wink studied the
biblical language of the powers in depth, and then applied the biblical terminology of spirits, demons and angels to political powers and systems.
Wink sought to "name" and "unmask" the powers in societal structures;
that is, to address the spiritual dimension of institutions by "engaging" their
"fallen" spirits through nonviolent resistance, in order to bring about their
redemption (Wink 1984; 1986; 1992: 3–10).

The common language of the powers united liberal and Pentecostal-
charismatic theologies when "third-wave" theology found support in Wink's
biblical studies (see Wagner's endorsement in Wink 1992: ii), and Wink welcomed the insights of Wagner and others into "spiritual warfare" (e.g. Wink
1992: 313–14). Ostensibly the difference between them was not about the
reality of the "spirits," or their power over human life, but about whether
they were to be understood as "supernatural" (Arnold 1992: 198–205,
169–82; Wink 1992: 350 n. 44, 368 n. 19). Wink suggests that there is an
alternative to the natural-supernatural model in an "integral" or "panen-
theistic" worldview, which he claims is emerging from such diverse sources
as Jungian psychology, the new physics, Christian mysticism, liberation and
feminist theology, process philosophy, Buddhism and native American religions (Wink 1998: 13–36). The danger with an adversarial approach to
other spirits that are generally assumed to be evil—an approach that both
Pentecostal-charismatic and liberation theologians share—is a tendency to
oppose two equal and opposite worlds and to draw firm lines between good
and bad. This can encourage an aggressive approach in mission, which
degenerates into cosmic or spiritual "warfare." Both third-wave and liberation theology have been criticized for encouraging violent methods of
bringing about social change (e.g. A. Scott Moreau et al. 2003: 312;
Matthey 2004: 117). Wink tries to refute accusations of such dualism by

his sweeping assertion of eclectic holism, which seems to indicate that he is tending the other way, towards what Taylor described as "monistic total-ity" (1963: 81), instead. We saw how Yonggi Cho is at pains to point out in his doctrine of "the Fourth Dimension" that the spiritual world of the Holy Spirit encompasses all others, and so there is no question of a dualism of equal and opposite forces. He and other Pentecostal-charismatic theolo-gians have also tried to show that their theology is holistic in taking his-torical realities seriously and meeting bodily needs (see chapter 6; see also Sepúlveda 1993: 51–64; Land 1993; Petersen 1996; Wenk 2000).

The Holy Spirit in a World of Many Faiths

Various theologies of religion provide interesting examples of how the dif-ferent cosmologies of "one-Spirit" and "many-spirits" have been applied in pluralistic contexts. We have already considered some examples from India of how theologians have raised the question of the presence of the Spirit in other faiths, to counter those who see other faiths as "non-Christian," "anti-Christian" and even "demonic." Experiments in pneumatological approaches to interfaith dialogue show that consideration of "the (Holy) Spirit in a world of many faiths" opens new perspectives in theology of reli-gions. This not only raises questions internal to Christian theology, such as "Where and how is the Spirit present or active in other faiths?" "How can the Spirit of Christ be discerned among the many spirits of the world?" and "Can the theology of the Holy Spirit help Christians overcome barriers to dialogue with people of other faiths?" This pneumatological approach also raises the issue of whether concepts and experiences of spirit in other faiths can provide a starting point for interfaith discussions. The study of Christian theologies from different religious contexts, together with initial dialogue in the cases of Hinduism, Buddhism and Islam, suggest that this is a fruit-ful area that merits further investigation (K. Kim and Ipgrave 2003b).

Moonjang Lee argues convincingly that, because of distinctive Korean religious experience and sociocultural norms, Korean Christians have a per-spective on the other religions of the country that is significantly different from that which has recently become dominant in the West (M. Lee 1999). In Korea, Christianity is a new and minority religion, which other religions have found difficult to tolerate, and so Korean Christians do not feel the same guilt toward other religions that is detectable in Western theologies of religion, which carry with them a history of colonial domination (: 405–407). Furthermore, Lee argues, historically not only Christianity but also the traditional religions in Korea have been "exclusive in their religious commitment and missionary in their practice." Each religion, which is lit-erally "teaching" (gyo), represents a unique self-contained system that the disciple is expected to master. In Korean culture, loyalty is highly valued

and demands total commitment in the family, the workplace and also in religion. For the faithful believer to take an interest in another religion would
be disloyal, and to use elements of one religious system to correct another
would be misunderstood as diluting or compromising the tradition
(: 408–10). Though personal religious freedom is now constitutionally guar-
anteed, conversion from one religion to another may often cause expulsion
from the family, so it is a decisive step not to be undertaken lightly (: 410).
Lee concludes that pluralism in the sense of the influence of the different
religions on Korean culture is undeniable, but not in the sense of individuals practicing more than one religion. Korean religious identity is single, not
multiple; it is based on personal commitment, and religious boundaries are
clearly defined and respected (: 410–12).

Lee's concern is that Korean theology of religions should reflect Korean
experience of religious pluralism, and should not be a model imported from
the West, whether a pluralist (liberal) or exclusivist (Evangelical) model. In
their search for a theology of religious pluralism, which for them is a new
and recent experience, many Western theologians have looked to Asia to
provide a model; however, it is not Korea but India that has become their
"laboratory" (Knitter 1995: 157). The pluralist model—most closely associated with John Hick and Paul Knitter (Hick and Knitter 1987)—is like the
neo-Hindu view popularized by Mahatma Gandhi, in that it attempts to
unite diverse religious traditions under one umbrella, as different approaches
to the same ultimate truth, or different paths leading to the same goal. Such
a model has been criticized because it does not allow for contradictions
between religions and minimizes differences (e.g. Vroom 1989: 377–78).
Unease with Hick and Knitter's "theocentric" approach is articulated particularly clearly by the North American Mark Heim, who argues that a more
truly pluralistic approach is to recognize not only a plurality of paths but
also a plurality of salvations or goals among religions. In his view, the religions represent not only different paths but also different ends (1995: 6,
227). In India too, there is a renewed emphasis on the distinctiveness of religious traditions on the grounds that, "where communalism [sectarianism]
is mushrooming, not the emphasis on a common ultimate truth will lead to
a fruitful dialogue, but only the acceptance that the other is different"
(Nehring 1996).

Within the Roman Catholic Church, the starting point of a response to
religious plurality was the development of Spirit christology, but this provoked strong debate, particularly with respect to India. In a strongly worded
address at a meeting of Catholic missiologists in 1988, Cardinal Jozef
Tomko, Prefect (or head) of the Catholic Church's Congregation for the
Evangelization of Peoples, attacked theologians of interreligious dialogue,
and challenged them to say whether "the mystery of God" is "exhausted in
the revelation of Jesus Christ" or whether it is "revealed in other ways
through other religions" (Tomko 1990b: 240). Tomko specifically criticized

the work of Paul Knitter, who is a North American theolegian, and then moved on to "some Asian theologians," mentioning Michael Amaladoss, SJ and Jacob Kavunkal, SVD, both from India (1990a: 22–24). Tomko complained that these Indian theories, which recognized other ways of salvation, were now widespread and threatened what he saw as the real missionary enterprise of proclamation (: 24–25). Samuel Rayan was one who responded to Tomko, seeing in his address a "sense of superiority and exclusiveness" and of "political and partisan" motives associated with colonial missions, "which destroyed the credibility of the Christian name for decades to come in our land" (1990: 131, 133). Rayan noted that Tomko made no reference to the work of the Holy Spirit, and argued that his was a pre-Vatican II missiology in keeping with the "one-way mission" attitudes of the colonial era (: 131, 126–28; see K. Kim 2002).

The papal encyclical *Redemptoris missio* was interpreted in India and elsewhere as an attack on Indian theologies (Kanjamala 1993: 202; Burrows 1993: 244). Apparently sharing Cardinal Tomko's concerns about the reduction of mission, the pope emphasized the "permanent priority" of proclamation. Though recalling statements of Vatican II and *Dominum et vivificantem* (1986) about the Spirit's presence and activity "in every time and place," and recognizing this as an element in the foundations for interreligious dialogue, he stressed that the Spirit is "not an alternative to Christ," and resisted any separation of the work of the Spirit from Christ or the Church (John Paul II 1990: paragraph 29). Defending Indian methodology, Augustine Kanjamala identified in the encyclical "a certain opposition between the mission of Christ, which is mediated in and through the church, and the work of the Holy Spirit, which is present and operative in a less visible manner outside the church in the religions and cultures of the world" and suggested that it was the Vatican theologians, and not those of India, who were failing to keep Christ and the Spirit together (1993: 203). Indian theologians put forward several different views of the relation of christology and pneumatology. Rayan urged that pneumatology should not be seen as "a separate chapter" of theology in opposition to christology, but as a "comprehensive horizon" against which theology is done, "a methodology for all theology" that gives a new interpretive perspective (1999b). Felix Wilfred argued that a distinction—not a separation—between Jesus and Christ (acting through the Spirit) is necessary, in order to uphold the universal dimension of Christian salvation and the trinitarian character of Christian faith. This is to recognize an "interconnectedness of paths" of salvation in Christianity and other religions, but it is not to say that all paths lead to the same goal (1998: 909–912).

Belgian Jesuit Jacques Dupuis, who emerged as the leading exponent of Spirit christology in interreligious relations, acknowledged that "If I had not lived in India for 36 years, I would not preach the theology which I am preaching today" (*Times Online*, 12 Jan 2005). He experimented in India with the relationship of Jesus Christ and the Spirit, and was particularly influenced by the Christian *advaita* of Abhishiktananda (Dupuis 1977). Dupuis could not say, as Abhishiktananda and Vandana are inclined to do, that the difference between Jesus' self-consciousness and the experience of *advaita* is merely a matter of context and language. In the Son's oneness with the Father, he argues, the distinction of Father and Son remains, while at the same time being an absolute unity, whereas the advaitic concept of oneness is an identification in which the distinct self is lost. So for him, the unity of the Father and the Son fulfills Hindu aspirations to oneness, and not the other way around (Dupuis 1997: 269–74, 278–79). Dupuis wished to maintain an orthodox christocentric faith, while also recognizing religious plurality and entering into constructive dialogue with other faiths. He began from the affirmations in the documents of Vatican II that the Holy Spirit is at work universally to bring about salvation, and dismissed the earlier view that the salvific work of the Spirit is limited to the Church. On the other hand, he also rejected a pneumatocentric theology of religions that suggested that the Holy Spirit brings about the salvation of those of other faiths by other means than through Jesus Christ. He believed that there is only one economy of the Spirit and the Word, not, as Khodr suggested, two "hypostatically independent" economies (Dupuis 1995). Therefore his theology of religions is "Christian" or "christocentric," but is founded on a Spirit christology, that is, a christology that recognizes how the Spirit, who is operative in the history of humankind, is also actively present throughout the human history of Jesus. At the same time, he insists that Spirit christology is not an alternative to the traditional Logos or Word christology, otherwise "Jesus Christ would be reduced to a man in whom and through whom God is present and active" (Dupuis 1997: 196–98). Logos christology safeguards the divine nature of Jesus Christ, but Spirit christology explains how God's saving action in Christ is universally available.

Despite his evident desire to find a solution to the "impasse" in theology of religions that would be acceptable within Roman Catholic teaching, a "notification" was attached to Dupuis' book, *Toward a Christian Theology of Religious Pluralism* (1997), accusing him of "ambiguities" in the text, which might contravene Catholic teaching about the centrality of Christ, the completeness of his revelation and the importance of the church (Congregation for the Doctrine of the Faith 2001). Nevertheless, the legitimacy of Spirit christology seems to be accepted, as long as it is understood that it is complementary to traditional Logos Christology, not an alternative. In summary, since Vatican II, Catholic theology of religions has shifted: from a theory of the mystery of Christ's presence that regarded those being saved outside the church as "anonymous Christians," to one that explains salvation for those of other faiths more neutrally, in terms of the universal salvific work of the Holy Spirit, although even here the salvation that the Spirit brings about is understood to be none other than God's saving action in Jesus Christ.

Dupuis reached his conclusions working within the framework of Catholic and Hindu worldviews of the "one-Spirit" type, but we have already indicated in the case of Korea that Christian theology of religions can look very different if we begin instead from a different cultural context and a worldview of many spirits. Amos Yong is a North American Pentecostal pastor of Malaysian-Chinese parentage, who grew up with an awareness of the spirit-world of popular Mahayana Buddhism, and is troubled because in his Pentecostal tradition these spirits are indiscriminately labeled "evil" (Yong 2000: 140). Yong's conviction is that the Spirit "is at work in the religions, shaping and reshaping them, or else mollifying their resisting spirits" (: 324). He is not content with such "general theological affirmations about the Spirit's presence and activity in the non-Christian world," which seem to him to be undiscriminating in their application (: 64). Yong also finds existing pneumatologies (he considers the theologies of Rahner, Tillich and Alfred North Whitehead) unable to discern the Holy Spirit in the context of other faiths without either resorting to christological criteria—which he sees as divisive in interreligious relations—on the one hand, or holding a reduced understanding of the Trinity—which he wishes to uphold in its orthodox form—on the other (: 71–95, especially 94). Yong does not wish to avoid the christological questions, but hopes to postpone them to allow interreligious dialogue to progress further (: 58). He makes a novel contribution to theology of religions by attempting to construct a Pentecostal-charismatic model that he believes will enable discernment of just where and when the Holy Spirit is present, by application of certain general criteria (: 64–; see 255 n. 7).

Yong welcomes the attempts of Samartha, Knitter and Dupuis, whom he groups together, to follow through the "hypostatic independence" theory, and to approach theology of religions pneumatocentrically. He is disappointed that, after their initial experiments with pneumatology, all three return to christology. This is not, in his view, because the Spirit can only be discerned christologically, but because "they lacked the experiential and theological categories needed to sustain their efforts" in pneumatology (: 60–65). He hopes the Pentecostal-charismatic tradition can supply this missing dimension, and move theology of religions "beyond the impasse" created by the insistence on christological considerations as the only criteria for recognizing the presence and activity of the Holy Spirit (Yong 2003a). Yong is right in that the Pentecostal-charismatic movement does furnish an alternative approach, as he himself goes on to demonstrate, but the perspectives of Samartha, Knitter and Dupuis need to be differentiated from one another. If the Christian understanding that the salvation being worked by the Holy

Spirit in the world is available only through the work of Jesus Christ is understood as a confession of the distinctive Christian vision of salvation, not as an assertion to which all visions of salvation have to conform, then Dupuis' theology at least seems to meet Yong's desire for a theology of religions that is both orthodox and open.

Yong constructs his "foundational pneumatology" on the basis of Pentecostal-charismatic experience, incorporating trinitarian metaphysics in dialogue with Jesuit charismatic theologian Donald Gelpi; American pragmatist philosophy of symbolism; and emerging "comparative" or cross-cultural theology of the spirit (Yong 2000: 96–148). Then, taking as his starting point the suggestion of Harvey Cox that Pentecostal spirituality is the re-emergence in post-modernity of "primal spirituality" (H. Cox 1996), he proposes that the primary criterion for discerning the Spirit is the manifestation of "primal spirituality," as defined by Cox: ecstatic speech, mystical piety and millennial fervor (Yong 2000: 17–21). In his "comparative symbology of divine presence," Yong first attempts to use methods of comparative religion to identify similar phenomena in other religious traditions, then proceeds to seek comparable moral-ethical consequences of the Spirit's work, and finally looks for a cosmology that includes awareness of the demonic. The presence of all these three criteria together, to Yong's mind, would confirm that the phenomena are indeed evidence of the work of the Holy Spirit. In this way, he believes, Christians can recognize the Spirit in the symbols of other religions and establish dialogue, while leaving the question of "norms, ideals and values," including christology, to a later stage (: 220–55, cf. 143).

Yong believes he has found a way to maintain a Chalcedonian Trinity, while at the same time allowing for the wider work of the Spirit in the world, and this without subsuming the whole world into a Christian system (2000: 58). He regards himself as completing Wink's liberation approach by adding a metaphysical dimension (: 295, 128–30), and challenges third-wave theologians to a more holistic and theologically nuanced perspective (: 238–42). The success of Yong's project does not depend on acceptance of Harvey Cox's theory that Pentecostalism is part of a revival of a "primal spirituality" shared by all humanity. The characteristics Yong is looking for may be identified whether or not they are part of a common "primal" tradition. Whether the criteria and their order of priority can be endorsed by other Christians is a matter for further discussion (see below). A greater problem is that, as Yong points out, and as we saw in the Korean case, conservative Christians have not taken kindly the suggestion that their faith is similar to indigenous spirituality, since many of them have converted from this and demonized it (: 18). And, furthermore, from the point of view of those sympathetic to other faiths, Yong's model of Spirit and spirits can only provide a way forward if it is made clear that it does not imply paralleling Christianity with "the Spirit," and other religions with "the spirits."

The Spirit in a Plural Age

Amos Yong's investigations in the religious sphere using a many-spirits paradigm have implications for other plural contexts as well. In more recent, work he draws attention to the "unity in diversity" theme in the account of the first Pentecost, on which occasion the Holy Spirit is seen to be the ground of personal encounter and of personal identity in community, enabling eschatological reconciliation (2003b: 300). In so doing he points to the work of Jean-Jacques Suurmond, a Reformed minister in the Netherlands, and Michael Welker, mentioned earlier (: 300–301, 303–304). In his critical study, Suurmond, who also has a great deal of experience in North America, identifies the "essential contribution" of Pentecostalism to the world as its spirituality of celebration, which has its origins in third-world or black spirituality (Suurmond 1994: 19). This he characterizes as "play," which is neither disordered nor ordered, but brings Word and Spirit together (: 87–88). This baptism with Word and Spirit is the "beginning and principle" (quoting James Dunn) of all Christian life, and therefore has the sadly unrealized potential to unite diverse traditions (: 150, 160). The concrete expressions of this baptism are the gifts of the Spirit, which Suurmond argues—reflecting on the Pentecost event—become the ground of human encounter, because every gift of grace frees us to see the other as truly other (: 180–84). As Suurmond describes, it, in the play of Word and Spirit, identity (Word) interacts with the other (Spirit), making authentic relations of unity in difference possible (: 189–92). Since the gifts of the Spirit cannot be narrowly interpreted as "supernatural," these new modes of relationship extend into the wider society (: 198–202). As God's Wisdom, the Word and the Spirit are creatively present throughout the world (: 37–41). Suurmond urges that the church should discern this, and proclaim and celebrate that God's Wisdom in Christ has reconciled all things with himself and established this worldwide in the Spirit (202–203).

Welker also reflects on the pluralism in the Pentecost account, which is not subsumed into homogeneous unity by the outpouring of the Holy Spirit but, by the power of the Spirit, is differentiated into intersecting but distinct "force-fields" of giftedness (1994: 228, 240–41). As Welker sees it, "The one Spirit . . . makes use of diverse gifts of grace, diverse deeds and services (cf. 1 Cor 12:4–6) and of their interplay in order to reveal and attest to God's presence" (: 241). Thus, "in the force-field of the Spirit, concrete individuality and world-overarching universality are held together" (: 248). For him, the Spirit is "Christ's domain of resonance" (: 314). The Spirit is a "public person," whose "primary individual-human center of action" is Jesus Christ (: 312), but whose influence and effectiveness are worldwide and diverse. Suurmond's celebration of giftedness and Welker's recognition of force-fields of the Spirit contribute to Yong's Pentecostal vision of a

Christian theology that does not deny individual experiences and identities, but sees these as giving "particular testimony to the nature of humankind and humanity's relationship to God . . . in anticipation of the full reconciliation to be accomplished in the kingdom" (Yong 2003b: 308).

Speaking to the contemporary West, Michael Welker is suspicious that "[p]eople have emphasized over and over again that God's Spirit works union, unanimity, and unity among human beings," but that "[l]ess clarity and energy have been devoted to saying that 'the unity of the Spirit' not only tolerates differences and differentiation, but that it maintains and cultivates differences" in what Welker sees as a "powerful and invigorating" form of pluralism (1994: 22–23). He complains that the Western world has been shaped by a very different spirit, which has frequently been confused with the Spirit of God and has also spread all over the world; this spirit has attempted to define and regulate what is human, what is certain and what is meaningful across societies and cultures (: 279). Welker seeks a "realistic theology" that no longer attempts to fit God into a total metaphysical system, a theology that recognizes that the world cannot be explained solely in terms of bilateral relations, and escapes moralism and self-righteousness (: 40–41). His "realistic biblical theology" begins by giving up the illusion that a single system can explain God and by recognizing that God's revelation is mediated in diverse human attestations, each of which is partial. His theology therefore engages these attestations, in "testing them for interconnections and differences" in order to allow "the reality of God to come forward in ever-new ways" (: 46–47). This means being open to a plurality of experiences and constructions of experience, which are not necessarily compatible with each other, to express God's vitality and freedom and, resisting the temptation to harmonize and systematize them, to allow them to "mutually illuminate, strengthen, and clarify each other" (: 47, x). In addition, theology has the prophetic role of distinguishing between the Holy Spirit and the spirit of the world. Reflecting on the stories of the vision of Micaiah, the son of Imlah (1 Kings 22 and 2 Chr 18) and on the encounter between Balaam and Balak (Num 24:1–14), Welker defines this activity as constantly testing the spirit of the age against the Spirit of Truth as revealed in Jesus Christ, looking for integrity in political life and developing the theological capacity to relativize injustice (1994: 84–98).

Welker's vision of the interacting force-fields of the Holy Spirit and the spirits of the age in effect introduces a "many-spirits" cosmology into the Western context, to which, until recently, such a cosmology seemed so alien. In a preparatory paper for the Canberra Assembly, Nigerian Roman Catholic Justin Ukpong (1990) considered the discernment of the Holy Spirit in three contemporary situations of pluralism: where radically secular ideologies operate, in the context of other religions, and within the community of Christians (: 77). In keeping with his African background, Ukpong conceived of the plural society as a world of many spirits, and applied the spirit-language of the Bible to plural contexts. He noted that there are occasions when the term "spirit" is used in the Bible not to refer to the Holy Spirit, but to "entities which have separate existence and which can act on human beings." Crucially, and in contrast to most other commentators, Ukpong recognized there may be good spirits as well as evil spirits (: 80). He summarized that, in the Old Testament, broadly speaking, evil spirits come from God and are under God's control, while in the New Testament evil spirits are a kingdom opposed to God's kingdom. In the Old Testament, good spirits are sent from God to possess various people (e.g. 1 Chr 12:18; Judg 3:10; 6:34; 11:29; 14–16) or as charisms (1 Sam 10:1, 5–7; Isa 42:1; 61:1). The spirits of Moses (Num 11:25) and Elijah (2 Kings 2:9, 15) imparted power and authority to others. In the New Testament, divine activity is usually attributed to the Holy Spirit, but angels are described as "ministering spirits" (Heb 1:14), and other good spirits include "the spirits of the prophets" (Rev 22:6) (: 80–81; cf. Dunn 1978: 694–95).

Discerning the Spirit(s)

In such a world of many spirits, where it may not be immediately obvious which spirits are good and which are evil, Ukpong draws attention to the gift of "discernment of spirits," which is listed among other gifts of the Spirit in 1 Corinthians 12:10. He noted interest in discernment in three very different strands of Catholic tradition: the practice of the interior life (especially Ignatian spirituality), the social involvement of the religious orders and institutes as they adjust to modernity, and the experience of the contemporary charismatic renewal movement (Ukpong 1990: 78). Ukpong points to many examples of discerning the spirits in the biblical material, such as distinguishing true from false prophets (Num 11:26–29; Jer 5:28; Lam 2; Mic 3; 1 Jn 4:1), Peter's confession of faith (Mk 8:27–30) and identification of demon possession (Acts 13:10; 16:17). There are also examples of lack of discernment (e.g. Mt 9:1–8; 12:22–28). On occasion, God's action is also identified as taking place outside the community of God's people, for example in the cases of Abraham and Melchizedek (Gen 14:17–20), Moses and Jethro (Ex 18:1–26), Isaiah referring to Cyrus (44:24–28; 45:1; 2 Chr 36:22–23), Peter and Cornelius (Acts 10) and Jesus and the Syrophoenician woman (Mk 7:24–30). Ukpong regards all these stories as showing that God's Spirit is discerned in the lives of people regarded as pagans (1990: 81–82). Although, in the context of 1 Corinthians 12:10, "the spirits" means "spirits of persons as they may be under the influence of the Holy Spirit or other forces," Ukpong argues that in the Bible and in Christian experience, "discerning the spirits" is broadened to include "taking right decisions in accordance with God's will" and "recognizing God's action in the world at large" (: 78–79). Discernment, therefore, is "to identify God's action in the universe and in human affairs today" (: 81).

Before the Canberra Assembly, Samartha had expressed his hope that Christians could move on from the question of *"whether* or not the Spirit is at work among people of other faiths," and begin to discuss "how to *discern* the presence and work of the Spirit among those who live outside the visible boundary of the church" (1990: 59). In a one-Spirit cosmology, discernment amounts to recognizing the one Spirit, and "discerning the spirits [plural]" has little meaning. Unless a theology is very naive, discernment implies acknowledging the possibility of the Spirit's absence (cf. Yong 2000: 127). The Spirit's absence could be experienced in a number of ways: as a sense of abandonment, a yearning for something beyond, or awareness of the demonic, or of death and decay. One-spirit theologies like those of Vandana and Rayan differ in the extent to which this acknowledgement is made explicit. At Canberra, however, in the context of many spirits, and recognizing that "[The Holy Spirit] is distinct from other 'spirits' in this world, whether benign or demonic," the report called for a theology of discernment that would enable Christians both to identify the Spirit's presence and activity, and also to distinguish the Holy Spirit from other "spirits," however defined (World Council of Churches 1991e: 254).

The importance of discernment was raised even in the preparatory papers for Canberra (e.g. Hübner 1989: 335; Clapsis 1989: 344), which included the paper by Ukpong (1990) and another by Swiss Reformed theologian Eduard Schweizer (1989), both of which made "discerning the spirits" their particular focus. In contrast to Ukpong, Schweizer concentrated on recounting the events of the Holy Spirit in the Bible, which he sees as everywhere inseparable from Christ. He implied that, in the New Testament, discernment is an activity limited to Christians for the good of the Christian community, which consists in recognizing Christian truth, and that other spirits—being outside the new creation in Christ—are not a Christian concern (Schweizer 1989: 406, 408, 410–11, 413). However, as James Dunn has pointed out, if mission is understood as *missio Dei*, then mission amounts to participating in the mission of God carried out by the Spirit (Rom 8:14–17). If so, then the first act of mission is discernment, to discover the way in which the Spirit is moving in the world in order to join in (Dunn 1998: 72). If the church is to participate in the world, discernment must be directed at other movements, not just at the church. As Ukpong remarked, discernment of spirits is both a new question, in the context of the recognition of plurality, and also an old question, encountered in different forms in the church's mission history (1990: 77). Yong demonstrates—and indicates in the title of his book, *Discerning the Spirit(s)* (2000)—that there are many different approaches to the discussion of discernment: whether the aim is to discern one Spirit, or to distinguish between

many different spirits, within both "one-Spirit" and "many-spirits" cosmologies; whether all spirits are regarded as evil or some are regarded as
good; and whether spirits are understood to be psychological, societal or
supernatural. In the remainder of this section we will try to identify some
criteria by which to discern the Holy Spirit, which will, by implication, help
with the wider questions about the nature of the relationship of Spirit and
the world. But before discussing the criteria, there are some other preliminary considerations.

First, a decision needs to be made as to where to look for the Spirit. As
we have seen in this book, some look up to see the Spirit descending from
heaven, bestowing authority and sanctifying, whereas others experience the
Spirit below, as the ground of our being. Some expect the raw power of the
Spirit rushing in from outside to purify and transform, and others look
within to encounter the Spirit in the depths of their being. Some may look
primarily for the Spirit in those with whom they share the fellowship of the
Christian community; others may look beyond to see the Spirit in their
neighbors. The Spirit may be encountered in silent meditation or in charismatic worship, in movements of liberation or in interfaith dialogue. The
Spirit may simply be perceived as a presence, or seen as an event or activity. The fact that our three Indian theologians, for example, diverged so
much in their identification of where the Spirit is and how the Spirit works
suggests that we should keep an open mind on the issue. Indeed, given the
biblical freedom of the Spirit, it is unwise to limit expectations to any particular locus or *modus operandi*; on the contrary, we should be ready to be
surprised by the Spirit because, "The church can . . . never be sure where
the Holy Spirit is not" (Oleska 1990: 331).

A second consideration is the question of who defines the criteria for discerning the Spirit. This was the question Chung Hyun Kyung was raising at
Canberra. Instead of white Western men and Orthodox theologians, she
argued, it was time that third-world women discerned the Spirit (Kinnamon
1991b: 16). In retrospect, the controversy at Canberra was seen to represent a power struggle between "classical" and "contextual" modes of theologizing (World Council of Churches 1991e: 241). Heated debates on the
Gulf War at the Assembly also demonstrated the divisions, as people took
diametrically opposing views on the rightness or wrongness of the war
(Castro 1991: 162). No one is obliged to accept another person's identification of what is good or spiritual, no matter how strong that person's tradition is, how weighty the theology behind it, or how much power the
person wields—especially not if the individual's exercise of that authority is
incompatible with the Spirit of Christ (Mk 3:29; Mt 12:31–32). But at the
same time, Christians cannot presume or claim with certainty to have the
Spirit themselves, as individuals or as community. As Stanley Samartha once
wrote, "The claim that God's presence is with us is not for us to make. It is
for our neighbors to recognize" (Samartha 1981b: 670; cf. 1 Cor 14:20–25).

Discernment should not be a matter for individual conscience alone, but a community activity (see, for example, Acts 15:28) (World Council of Churches 1998b: 57). Discernment is "an ecumenical question," to be resolved through intra-Christian and even interreligious dialogue (Samartha 1990: 58). It is a serious matter to substitute another spirit for the Holy Spirit (Reflections of Orthodox participants 1991: 281); mistaking the Holy Spirit for an unclean spirit is described as blasphemy against the Holy Spirit, a sin which cannot be forgiven (Mk 3:29; Mt 12:31–32), because the sinner is cut off from the very means God has given of seeing the truth (see chapter 2).

Yong suggests a further word of caution: discernment is practiced only with regard to concrete situations, and never in general, and "[w]hat is discerned as the Holy Spirit or some other spirit in this or that particular situation today, may be decidedly reversed or no longer applicable when the situation is examined tomorrow" (Yong 2000: 287). This suggests that discernment is always provisional. Decisions and perspectives may need to be revised; the church is always reforming. And alliances of Christian mission with other movements on the basis that they share the same spirit will be temporary and for short-term goals only. The Spirit of Christ cannot be captive to any of the spirits of the world. Discernment requires wide horizons, in view of the breadth of the Spirit's mission; openness, because of the unpredictability of the Spirit's movements; and humility, since the Spirit is the Spirit of Almighty God.

Coming to criteria for discerning the Spirit(s), Yong is correct to say that the experience of the Holy Spirit need not be christologically perceived (2000: 68). The Spirit of God is at work in ways of which we are not aware. But for the Christian, the criteria for discernment of the Spirit cannot be other than christological. What defines Christians as Christians is that they understand the Spirit of God to be the Spirit of Jesus Christ, who is revealed in the Bible. This is the only criterion for discernment on which Christians can agree. Jesus Christ both received and gave the Spirit, he is revealed as the focus of the Spirit's activity and the channel of the Spirit's power of new creation. From the Christian perspective, the Spirit's nature is to testify to Jesus Christ (Jn 15:26): "The testimony of [or to] Jesus is the spirit of prophecy" (Rev 19:10). Jesus Christ is "the face of the Spirit" (Bevans 1998a: 103; 1998b: 108–109) and so Christian discernment amounts to seeing Jesus Christ. It is the characteristic and shared belief of Christians that the Spirit of God is the Spirit of Jesus Christ. But, as we have seen, people have different criteria for discerning the spirits according to their spiritual context. Christians differ greatly in their vision of Jesus Christ, and therefore in what they discern as the Spirit. Muslims, Hindus, Buddhists and those of other faiths will use their own criteria to recognize where God is at work, or what is holy or spiritual. Those of a secular persuasion may apply still other criteria to discern what is true and right. There is considerable overlap between these different value systems: we may not all be climbing completely different mountains, but at the same time we will not agree that we are climbing the same one. If Christians discern according to the criterion of Jesus Christ, it need not necessarily mean that Christians are imposing their faith on others or trying to make the whole world Christian, either explicitly or implicitly. The criteria used by any group are simply the expression of a particular commitment. The question of whose spiritual vision is most closely in touch with God or Ultimate Reality or the universe will only be answered at the end. In the meantime, if we are to live together in our common home—the earth—all communities need to respect one another's perceptions and share resources for discernment. The Christian contribution to this debate will always be Christ-centered.

At least four biblical criteria for discernment have been pointed out. The first is *ecclesial:* the confession of Jesus as Lord by the Christian community, which is made possible by the Holy Spirit (1 Cor 12:3; 1 Jn 4:2). The second criterion is *ethical:* the evidence of the fruits of the Spirit— love, joy, peace and so on (Gal 5:22)—in the up-building of the community. The Spirit changes lives, producing Christlikeness. The first two criteria are commonly acknowledged and were recognized immediately at the Canberra Assembly (World Council of Churches 1991e: 256; see also Clapsis 1991: 344; Oleska 1990: 331–33; Schweizer 1989: 411; cf. Dunn 1998: 71, 30–31, 323–27; Gorringe 1990: 38–39). The third criterion is *charismatic:* the practice of the gifts of the Spirit (1 Cor 12:4–11). Discerning the Spirit in this way is the particular contribution of the Pentecostal-charismatic movement. Where there is empowerment to prophecy, ministry, teaching, exhortation, giving, leading and compassion (Rom 12:6–8), there is good reason to believe God is at work (by the Spirit) (cf. Yong 2000: 224). The final criterion is *liberational*—being on the side of the poor. This is the contribution of liberation theology. The effect of the Spirit's anointing on Jesus Christ was that he announced good news to the poor (Lk 4:18), and so consideration for the poor must be a touchstone for all spiritual claims.

Any one of these four criteria could indicate the presence and activity of the Holy Spirit, but none constitutes conclusive proof of the Spirit's presence or activity, because for each criterion there is a qualification in Scripture. First, it is hoped that the Spirit is present in the Christian community; however, it is the Spirit that defines the church and the Christian, not the other way around. Calling "Lord, Lord" is not necessarily a guarantee of a spirit of obedience (Mt 7:21–22). Second, Christlike good works are not invariably a sign of the life of the Spirit; they may be the result of unregenerate legalism (Rom 7:6). Not only the works, but the whole character of faith is important (Jas 2:18). Third, exercise of a spiritual gift is not a sign of the Spirit's presence if it lacks love (1 Cor 13:1–3). And fourth, there is also a caveat to the criterion of liberation: the liberation struggle must be waged in a way that is loving to our enemies (Mt 5:43–48), and does not aim to crush them, but to live in peace with them (Rom 12:18) (Dorr 2000: 128). The criteria above should therefore be taken as indicators, rather than as concrete evidence, of the presence and activity of the Spirit of God, which Christians recognize as the Spirit of Christ (cf. Schweizer 1989: 40). Perhaps we are on surer ground when these all occur together.

Discernment is not an easy task: it is a complex process and an inexact science. The ability to discern is the fruit of wisdom; but it is God's wisdom, not human wisdom (1 Cor 2; Jas 3). When God gave Solomon wisdom, what he asked for and what he received was "an understanding mind . . . able to discern between good and evil" (1 Kings 3:9, 12). The ability to distinguish the spirits is itself a gift of the Holy Spirit, therefore it is not a mechanical activity (Schweizer 1989: 406; Hübner 1989: 335). Ukpong suggested that discernment may be "more a matter of experiencing rather than rationalizing on the action of God" (1990: 85). If the Holy Spirit is understood as a person with whom it is possible to have relationship, it is reasonable to suppose that it involves emotion and intuition, as well as intelligence. On the road to Emmaus, the eyes of the disciples were opened and they recognized Jesus (Lk 24:13–35). This incident provides a parable of discernment. Recognizing Jesus Christ involves both the heart (their hearts "burned within them"—verse 32) and the mind (they were "talking and discussing"—verse 15). It involved both the disciples' knowledge of the Scriptures (verse 27), and also their personal intimacy with Jesus Christ (he was known "in the breaking of the bread"—verse 35). It was a shared activity, the results of which were confirmed by the wider community (verses 33–35). And the disciples needed to be open to the possibility that Jesus Christ would be where they had not expected (verses 25–26), and at the same time true to Christian testimony (verses 22–23). Like Jesus, who appeared as a fellow traveler on the road, viewed from a perspective below, the Holy Spirit may at first be indistinguishable among many other spirits. In a plural world, the transcendent or eternal nature of the Spirit of Jesus Christ cannot be predetermined or assumed, but only discerned and experienced in the life of believers. Finally, though there is a process of discernment in the Emmaus account, in the last analysis this is a story of revelation: "he was made known to them" (: 35). As both Schweizer and Ukpong pointed out, the fact that "discernment of spirits" (1 Cor 12:10) is listed as a gift of the Holy Spirit shows that the Spirit is needed to discern the spirits. That is, discernment cannot be reduced to applying criteria and following procedures: it is an aspect of Christian spirituality, the result of "living by the Spirit" in relationship with Jesus Christ (Gal 5:13–26; Rom 8:1–17; Ukpong 1990: 82; Schweizer 1989: 40).

The Spirit of Reconciliation: Ethic and Ethos of Mission

Because in many Christian theologies other spirits are thought of as evil spirits, discerning the spirits tends to be seen as "exorcism," in the sense of casting out evil. However, James Dunn has shown that in the New Testament, discernment is connected with prophecy (1 Cor 12:8–10) rather than exorcism (Dunn 1998: 311–28). Discernment should therefore be understood primarily as "weighing up possibilities," rather than as rooting out falsehood in an act of spiritual warfare. Dunn has also broadened the meaning of exorcism in the New Testament, arguing that it "should not be bound to a particular conceptuality of demon-possession," but should be understood more broadly as "treatment of disordered humanity on the spiritual dimension appropriate to the disorder" (: 185). This therapeutic interpretation of exorcism appears closer to the Orthodox understanding. Boris Bobrinskoy explains the *epiklesis* in the Orthodox liturgy as an act of exorcism of the world, "freeing it from dark forces hidden in its depth" and "secretly breath[ing] into the whole cosmos its original glory" (1989: 361). And Michael Oleska, referring to Ephesians 6, writes, "It is the church's task to exorcise each person, each ideology, each movement, each political, social, economic program or structure, identifying its actual and potential evil and corruptibility, affirming whatever in it may be good, true, noble, honest, lovely, beautiful" (Oleska 1990: 331–33). Understanding exorcism as a reconciliatory activity is also closer to the practice of primal or local religions, for example the shaman's *kut* in Korea, as Chung Hyun Kyung demonstrated at Canberra. Indeed, an understanding of "exorcism" as placating spirits, rather than casting them out, has been recognized elsewhere in Asia and also in Africa (e.g. Yong 2000: 157; Anderson 1991: 120–25, 10).

The theme of reconciliation has to some extent superseded that of liberation in the discourse of the World Council of Churches and in other forums, because, after perhaps the most violent century on record, the need for both social and spiritual reconciliation is so very evident (Schreiter 1998: 3–4). In the New Testament, the word "reconciliation" (though not the idea) is almost exclusively Pauline. The verb *katallasso* (reconcile) and the noun *katallage* (reconciliation) are used by Paul eleven times, and are found in some of the central passages of his theology, in which he describes the new relationship we have with God as a result of the death of Jesus Christ (Rom 5:10–11; 11:15). This includes the reconciliation of Jew and Gentile with one another (Eph 2:14–16), which is cosmic in its scope (Col 1:19–22). Notwithstanding its prominence, the theme of reconciliation in Paul has received comparatively little attention until recently, largely because of a fixation in the Western church (Catholic and Protestant) on the doctrine of justification; this fixation may be traced back to Augustine, and was reinforced by the controversies of the Reformation. Recently, new perspectives have

contributed to freeing Pauline studies from captivity to Reformation controversies, by drawing attention to the facts that Paul was a missionary
before he was a theologian, and that his theological reflections stemmed
from his experience as a Jewish missionary to the Gentiles (Munck 1959;
Stendahl 1976: 78–96). Furthermore, first-century Judaism should not be
construed as a religion of works-righteousness (see Sanders 1991: 44–76).
It is now recognized that the center of the book of Romans is not only
Romans 8, from which Luther derived the assurance of salvation, but also
Romans 9–11, where the current rejection of the gospel by Israel is understood to be part of a process of "reconciliation of the world," which culminates in the final resurrection (Rom 11:15). Thus it is possible to regard
reconciliation as a central motif of Paul's theology, if not the central theme
(R. Martin 1981: 153; Dunn 1998: 387–88). Even Paul's initial conversion
experience on the road to Damascus, as recounted three times by Luke (Acts
9:1–8; 22:4–11; 26:12–15), was a personal experience of God's reconciliation of his enemy to himself, which laid the foundation for his theology of
the unity of the church as "the body of Christ" (1 Cor 1:13; 12:12–27) (S.
Y. Kim 1997; see also K. Kim 2005b).

At the same time, the new perspectives have revealed the role that pneumatology plays in Paul's theology, and the appropriateness of the theme of
reconciliation to express the Spirit's work. James Dunn shifts the center of
Paul's thought away from polemic about faith versus works, toward a discussion of the relationship between the law and the Spirit. He draws attention to the Pauline phrase "in the Spirit" and the extent to which it parallels
the equally Pauline term for church life: "in Christ." What is distinctive
about the Christian community is the Spirit of Christ, which Christians
are given as a foretaste, a guarantee or a down-payment of what is to
come (2 Cor 1:22; 5:5; Eph 1:13–14; Rom 8:23). The admittance of
Gentiles to the community was on the basis that they too had received the
gift of the Spirit (Gal 2:7–9; cf. Acts 10:47; 11:17; 15:8). So it is the
indwelling of the Spirit that defines the community, not outward signs of
the flesh (Gal 3:3; Rom 8:9; Dunn 1998: 419–425). For Paul it is not by
the marks of the flesh—circumcision or the keeping of food laws—but by
the Spirit that Christians recognize one another (Gal 3:1–5; 4:6–7). New
life in Christ is identified as "the unity of the Spirit in the bond of peace"
(Eph 4:3), and peace is characteristic of the Spirit-filled life (Rom 8:6; 14:17;
Gal 5:22).

Paul describes the participation of the church in God's reconciling mission to the world as a "ministry of reconciliation," modeled on that of Jesus
Christ (2 Cor 5:18–20); this appears in 2 Corinthians as a continuation of
what is earlier described as the "ministry of the Spirit" (2 Cor 3:8). The mission of reconciliation in the Spirit is therefore greatly concerned with human
relationships and right behavior toward God and neighbor; in other words,
it is ethical. New perspectives on Paul have highlighted the continuing

importance of good deeds in obedience to the law in Paul's theology of salvation, and in particular the practice of reconciliation (Wright 2003). Since
the process of the reconciliation of the cosmos is being worked out through
the practice of Christian love in the community (Eph 2:14–16), the paradigm of reconciliation has profound implications for the ethic of mission.
The reconciled community, practicing the requirements of the law—love of
God and neighbor—is at the heart of the mission of reconciliation, since
"reconciliation with others is the only convincing evidence that we are reconciled with God" (Dorr 2000: 133; see Mt 5:23–24). The ministry of the
Spirit that is reconciliation is like that of the ambassador, one who builds
human relationships: "God making his appeal through us" (2 Cor 5:20).
However, "the ultimate goal of God in reconciliation is broader than human
attempts at conflict resolution" (Burrows 1998: 82). The vision of reconciliation encompasses the whole creation (2 Cor 5:19, 17; Col 1:20). Romans
8 begins with life in the Spirit, and goes on to the reconciliation of creation
before returning to the Spirit again (Rom 8:1–27). So the reconciling work
of the Spirit extends from the resurrection of Christ, through the ethics of
church life, until it pervades the whole of the created order (Gunton 2002).

Paul urged upon the churches not only an ethic of reconciliation, but also
an ethos of reconciliation, an attitude or spirit that refrains from provoca-
tion and revenge and, as far as possible, aims to be at peace with all (Rom
12:16–18). He warns that ministry or missionary work is ineffective unless
it is done in a spirit of love, which is patient and kind and does not insist
on its own way (1 Cor 13). So Paul seeks to convince the Galatians that the
Spirit of Christ, who saves them, should also guide them to live in reconciled community (Gal 5:25–26; cf. 5:16–24). What is regarded as
"Christian" is often a contentious issue now, as it was then, and is often
defined by cultural, legal, or theological considerations. Reconciliation can
only take place when such issues are overridden by a shared ethos that
respects and aims to love one another. Reconciliation is achieved by the
"spirit of gentleness," not by compulsion (Gal 6:1, 12). The image of the
ambassador that Paul chooses to use in second Corinthians implies an ethos
of persuasion, not force. If we are reconciled in the Spirit of Christ, this will
be demonstrated in the ethical way in which Christian mission is carried
out, and in the peaceable ethos of Christian mission (K. Kim 2004d).

Toward a New Mission Theology of the Holy Spirit

Reconciliation can be shown to encompass almost all aspects of mission (see
examples in K. Kim 2005a) but, by its very nature, it cannot be used to
imprison all other mission theologies. As we have seen, there are many different ways of understanding mission. David Bosch's *Transforming Mission*,
which so masterfully gathered many of these perspectives together, has not yet

been surpassed as *summa missiologica*, and has fulfilled Lesslie Newbigin's prediction that it would become "the indispensable foundation for the teaching of missiology for many years to come" (Bosch 1991: back cover). However, the weakness of Bosch's "emerging ecumenical consensus" on mission was apparent in its very year of publication—1991—when the Seventh Assembly of the World Council of Churches at Canberra famously failed to come to consensus. We noted in chapter 3 that Bosch's book, which deals with the Old Testament in less than five pages, did not anticipate the interest in creation theology at Canberra. It did not reflect the interest in ecology, feminism and "indigenous spiritualities" of the "Justice, Peace, and the Integrity of Creation" program either. By its very nature, *Transforming Mission* is retrospective; it documents what had already been resolved by the late 1980s, not the debates of today. In the words of Robert Schreiter, it "tells us where we have come in mission at the end of the twentieth century" (Schreiter 1991: 181). New approaches are needed, and this is particularly true of Bosch's pneumatology of mission.

Bosch has been praised for his emphasis on the work of the Holy Spirit in mission (see, for example, Shenk 1996: 89). In highlighting the Orthodox contribution to theology of mission and the theology of Luke, Bosch draws attention to the missionary nature of the Spirit (see especially Bosch 1991: 113–115, 516–517), and taking account of Pentecostal-charismatic perspectives, he stresses the crucial importance of Pentecost for missions. But, as we saw in chapter 3, his pneumatology is limited to consideration of the eschatological Spirit of mission, poured out on the church at Pentecost to "initiate," "guide" and "empower" its mission (: 113–114). The presence and activity of the Spirit before Pentecost, even in the mission of Jesus, is hardly considered, partly because he does not include John's Gospel in his biblical foundations. Bosch does not link the Spirit that descended on Jesus Christ, and was poured out at Pentecost, with the "breath" or "wind" of God in the Old Testament. Though he does occasionally allow for the wider work of the Spirit in the world and is prepared to be surprised by the Spirit (: 379, 489, 494; see also 150, 517), this broader pneumatology cannot easily be integrated with the rest of the book and with its structure, which is based firmly around the historical activity of Jesus Christ. The result of Bosch's exclusive interest in the post-Pentecost Spirit is a "jesusological pneumatology" in which the Spirit is an "afterthought used to explain God's activity in the church in connection with Jesus, ignoring the mystery of the Spirit as an equal modality or *persona* of the divine nature" (Burrows 1996: 129). So, although he propounds the theology of *missio Dei*, in which the church participates in the mission of God by the Spirit, Bosch binds the mission of the Spirit very closely to the missionary activity of the church. Thus, when he seeks to broaden mission to take account of the "comprehensive" nature of salvation, he can do so only by increasing the scope of the church's missionary activity (see Bosch 1991: 393–400). In this way mission still appears to be in the mold of the Enlightenment project (cf. Schreiter 1991: 181) as a *work* to be achieved by organization and strategy, rather than as a participation in the Spirit.

A corollary of Bosch's close association of the Spirit with the established church is the un-contextual nature of his missiology. Though he names theologians from the global South (and he himself is South African), his interlocutors are almost all of European descent. So he does not hear the suspicions of third-world theologians about global theologizing, but follows the traditional ecumenical approach of thinking globally and applying this locally (cf. Saayman 1996: 50–51; Verstraelen 1996: 12–14; Mofokeng 1990: 173–75; see also van Butselaar 1992). As the outline of *Transforming Mission* makes clear, it is within the Bible and (Western) Christian tradition that Bosch looks for the wind of the Spirit to renew the church in mission. The use of extra-biblical and extra-ecclesial sources from contextual experience is not contemplated. In his discussion of mission as dialogue, Bosch acknowledges the role of the Spirit in other faiths in *preparatio evangelica* (1991: 484), but he hesitates to give any value to the faiths in themselves. His attitude of "bold humility" in the context of religious plurality recognizes an "unresolved tension": "we cannot point to any other way of salvation than Jesus Christ; at the same time we cannot set limits to the saving power of God" (: 489). Bosch's approach has been highly acclaimed (cf. Saayman and Kritzinger 1996: title), but whereas this combination of "ultimate commitment to one's own religion and genuine openness to another's" (Bosch 1991: 483) is laudable, in a pluralistic context, those who claim to have the Spirit of Christ may need to go further to engage with other faiths and worldviews, while exercising the gift of discernment.

David Bosch calls his approach "the postmodern paradigm" for mission (1991: 349), and this is true in the sense that it recognizes many different approaches ("elements") in mission, appropriate to different contexts (: 368–510). But in view of his lack of attention to essential issues in postmodernity—feminism, ecology and indigenous spiritualities—and also because of his modernist desire to unify mission theology and set it within the history, largely, of the Western church, it must be questioned whether Bosch's paradigm is as post-modern as he claims (K. Kim 2000). The development of mission pneumatology implies understanding mission differently than does David Bosch, though such an understanding is greatly indebted to his work. It suggests a mission theology whose starting point can be none other than a particular experience of the Spirit in the world, which interacts with other contextual theologies arising in different geographical locations, social conditions and religious milieus, where the Spirit is at work. The result of such an approach would be a theology that sees mission more as an attempt to live in the Holy Spirit than as a task to be accomplished. This involves a willingness to trust an intuitive sense of the Spirit's presence and activity in creation, in many contemporary movements, in many spiritualities and in many individuals. This will not be naïve optimism, but will be accompanied by the practice of discernment. The concern of mission will be with the whole creation, with all movements and with all spiritualities, and yet it will also be delimited by the Christian confession that the Spirit is the Spirit of Jesus Christ. This condition will not be imposed on others; it is the result of personal or community choice. Those of other persuasions could, just as legitimately, claim ultimacy for another spirit.

Therefore, it may be useful in post-modernity to assume that, in the course of mission, we will encounter many diverse spirits and powers in the world, whether we regard these as supernatural entities or natural forces, or simply use this language as a metaphor for socioeconomic powers. A model that allows for both good and evil (or neutral or fallen) spirits at work in the world could perhaps help mission to steer a course between a priori rejection of other traditions and naive embrace of movements that do not share the Christian vision. It would allow for both conflict and cooperation of Christians with other groups, within a plural perception of reality. Christians can have confidence that, however powerful and threatening they may be, all "thrones," "dominions," "rulers" and "powers" are only creatures of God and, at the end, will be reconciled in Christ (Col 1:15–20). We do not have to maintain the attitude that "whoever is not with me is against me" (Mt 12:30)—it may be that "whoever is not against us is for us" (Mk 9:40). At the very least, we may need to give others the benefit of the doubt, and perhaps cooperate with them for specific purposes. In showing hospitality to strangers, we may be entertaining angels without knowing it (Heb 1:14; 13:2). There are good as well as bad forces at work. A mission theology of the Holy Spirit should allow us to appreciate creativity and love wherever it is found, and affirm whatever is true, honorable, just, pure, pleasing and commendable (Phil 4:8).

In this scenario, what is discerned in mission is not the Spirit of Jesus Christ as such, but the affinity (or lack thereof) between a particular spirit—through which the Holy Spirit may or may not be mediated to us—and pertinent characteristics of Christ. On the basis of this criterion, decisions can be made about whether and to what extent Christian mission can ally itself with a particular group or movement. Since discernment is an ongoing and provisional process, alliances with others would never be permanent, and the mission would always be changing within the broad framework of faithfulness to Christ. Such an approach could avoid the implicit co-option of others into Christian faith, and also make clear that, while being committed to their own mission, Christians acknowledge other missions and support those whose temporal aims coincide with theirs. Mission will be both chastened and invigorated by awareness that there are many spirits abroad. In any truly missionary encounter, these spirits will be recognized and their natures discerned by the Spirit of Christ. They will be seen and appreciated for what they are, without being rejected on the one hand or subsumed into Christianity on the other. Living together in the Spirit of Jesus Christ, among many spirits, we discern the Spirit of mission in order to participate in the mission of the Spirit.

Conciliation at Athens 2005

When the apostle Paul stood in front of the Areopagus, he began by connecting with the spirituality of the ancient Athenians. He affirmed their search for God and the spiritual awareness of their poets, who proclaimed that God is Spirit "in whom we live and move and have our being," and that, as God's "offspring," we are spiritual beings. Paul attempted to use the Athenians' spiritual language to talk about the Creator God and the Christian gospel. At the same time he discerned a spirit of idolatry, which distracted them and prevented them from repentance and practical obedience to the Holy Spirit of God, as manifested in Jesus and his resurrection (Acts 17:16–34). It was difficult for Paul to bridge the spiritualities of the Jewish and Greek worlds in this way—there was a lot of misunderstanding and he had limited immediate success in terms of new converts to Christianity—but two thousand years later, Athens remains a Christian city, and the use of Greek thought and language has contributed greatly to the formation of Christian theology, particularly to the understanding of God the Holy Spirit. So it was doubly appropriate that in 2005 the Thirteenth Conference on World Mission and Evangelism of the World Council of Churches met in Athens, at the invitation of the Greek Orthodox Church, it dared to pray again "Come, Holy Spirit!"

Come, Holy Spirit, Heal and Reconcile!

Mindful of the furor of the Canberra Assembly, and seeking to move forward together fourteen years after that event, the organizers petitioned the Holy Spirit to "heal and reconcile!" Furthermore, the event was organized more as an exercise in healing and reconciliation than as a theological debate. Billed as the widest gathering of Christians yet, twenty-five percent of the participants were from non-member churches and organizations, which included many Evangelicals and representatives of Pentecostal and other new churches. The older Protestant churches provided most of the support, a large delegation represented the Vatican and, as the hosts, the Orthodox Church was fully engaged. Living together for a week in chalets by the seaside, Christians from around the world had the opportunity to experience the fellowship of the Spirit, and learn something of how their brothers and sisters in Christ understood the presence and activity of the Holy Spirit in the world.[1]

Healing and reconciliation are very closely related terms and, since the theology of healing had already been given attention by the World Council of Churches' "Health, healing, and wholeness" desk,[2] and in the context of the council's "Decade to Overcome Violence,"[3] reconciliation became the overriding theme. Current awareness of violence and its harmful effects had made peacemaking and reconstruction major priorities, and all the more so for Christians, given that the link of violence with religion often gives it greater virulence (Schreiter 2004: 11–15). Roman Catholic mission theologian Robert Schreiter, a plenary speaker at Athens, developed a mission paradigm of reconciliation out of a critique of the paradigm of liberation, which does not aim at reconstruction or making peace (: 12, 14), and even tends to justify violence, or at least aggressive tactics, to achieve revolutionary change (Schreiter 1998: 3). In his description of the ministry of reconciliation in his book of that title, the main point that he makes, and reflects in the subtitle, is that reconciliation is "more a spirituality than a strategy" (Schreiter 1998). This precludes violence (: vi) and gives priority to religious and spiritual considerations over political and legal concerns (: 4). As Schreiter explains it, in Christian tradition, reconciliation comes about when the reconciliation with God that Jesus Christ brought about sets us free to be reconciled to one another. It is in God working through the believer, to bring about resurrection to new life, that reconciliation takes place, and not by mechanical performance of a task or slavish obedience to a set of rules (: 4). Among the early liberation theologians, Samuel Rayan was particularly quick to realize that the mission enterprise of liberation had to be accompanied by a spirituality (see chapter 5). Unless God's mission is done in God's way, mission movements are discredited, or else they alienate others before their aims, however worthy, can be achieved. Miroslav Volf insists on "the primacy of love over freedom," so that we "insert the project of liberation into . . . 'a theology of embrace'" (Volf 1996: 105). If we have a view to future reconciliation with our enemy, we will resist violence and unjust means in our struggle, because we hope to live with our neighbor afterwards (Dorr 2000: 128). In other words, if the goal is reconciliation, the means will also be reconciliatory, and this has implications for processes and attitudes in mission. The Holy Spirit delimits the strategies of mission since not all methods are compatible with the Spirit of Christ.

Reconciliation, particularly the declaration of God's purpose in Ephesians

---

[1] See the conference website, http://www.mission2005.org.

[2] See website at http://wcc-coe.org/wcc/what/mission/hhw.html.

[3] See website at http://overcomingviolence.org/.

1:9–10 "to unite all things in him [Christ], things in heaven and things on earth," had been highlighted before in connection with mission—at the very first assembly in Amsterdam in 1948 and in New Delhi in 1961. But former World Council of Churches General Secretary Philip Potter notes that even in the cosmic sweep of Joseph Sittler's interpretation in Delhi, reconciliation was not connected with the Holy Spirit, except insofar as the Spirit empowered the church to proclaim the reconciliation wrought in the Christ event (Potter 1991: 307). However, in the Spirit christology of the Canberra Assembly, the reconciling event of Jesus Christ itself was understood as taking place "in the Spirit" (2 Cor 3:6, 17); and the assembly clearly defined the basis of mission as God's reconciliation of the world through Christ crucified and risen, and understood the goal of mission to be a reconciled and renewed creation. In other words, Canberra connected the reconciling ministry of Jesus Christ and the ministry of the church within the ministry of the Spirit, which is reconciliation (World Council of Churches 1991c: 100; Potter 1991: 305–306). In focusing attention on the Spirit's role as healer and reconciler, the Athens conference covered not only the societal and political aspects, but reconciliation in all aspects of life—it bridged "paternal" and "maternal" spiritualities. Seeing the Holy Spirit as healer and reconciler encouraged a comprehensive understanding of the Holy Spirit's work. In Christian healing, the Spirit's presence and the Spirit's activity are held together as comforter (e.g. Jn 16:6–7) and curer (e.g. Mt 12:22, 28). Moreover, reconciliation balances truth-telling with listening, justice with peace, because the Spirit is the Spirit of truth (Jn 16:12–13) and also the Spirit of love (Rom 5:5). In practice, healing and reconciliation each link the creative and redemptive roles of the Spirit together (cf. Taylor 1972: 25–41), as God is at work by the Spirit to bring well-being and joy in our hearts, in the church, and in the world (Acts 14:17).

The Reconciling Spirit: Dove with Color and Strength[4]

However, reconciliation can be misunderstood or misrepresented to mean that all Christians everywhere must follow some preordained pattern of faith, or sacrifice their distinctive identity by passively conforming in church or society. The most common depiction of the Holy Spirit is as the dove of peace. The use of the dove to represent the Holy Spirit is a reminder of the descent of the Holy Spirit on Jesus Christ on the occasion of his baptism in the River Jordan (Mk 1:9–11; Mt 3:13–17; Lk 3:21–22; cf. Jn 1:29–34). Many Christian churches and organizations use a dove on their logos—often alongside the cross or the open Bible—to signify their belief in the Holy

---

[4] Material for this section is drawn from K. Kim 2005c.

Spirit. The dove is also a symbol of peace and reconciliation. Doves are used on Christmas cards with the message "peace on earth," and on the badges and banners of organizations working for peace; doves are even released en masse at peace rallies. This is not a direct reference to the revelation of Jesus Christ as Son of God at his baptism, but to the dove that Noah sent out from the ark as the flood waters began to subside. The book of Genesis tells how the dove returned with an olive leaf in its beak, and thus became the sign of peace after the deluge (Gen 8:10–11; 9:1–17). By association of these two doves, the Holy Spirit is often thought of as the harbinger of peace and reconciliation.

However, despite its biblical pedigree as the symbol of God's presence that descended on Jesus at his baptism, use of the dove alone is distinctly unhelpful in communicating the reality of the Spirit of God—and also the meaning of reconciliation. In many cases, the symbol of the dove represents either inner tranquility and purity—without a community connection—or else the kind of peace on earth that we sometimes dream of at Christmas, which is merely the cessation of conflict without the activity of reconstruction. The dove is very white and sometimes comes close to looking like the fat turkey of consumerism, or else it resembles the eagle of empire. In the scriptures, the peace that comes in Jesus Christ is not a blanket of snow that covers over everything and makes the world colorless, nor is it the kind of absence of activity that makes the waters still. It is represented by the colorful community of believers striving to live together in the Spirit of Christ, and experiencing reconciliation as the result of deep prayer life, strenuous activity, fearless witness, agonizing suffering, sacrificial sharing and living together in a complex world full of competing spirits of one sort or another. The image of the dove as popularly portrayed does not do justice to all the dimensions of the Holy Spirit or to the nature of the reconciliation that the Spirit brings. The dove seems hardly compatible with the raw power and vibrant color of the Spirit, who brooded over the creation, inspired the prophets, propelled the infant church into mission, transformed lives and freed people from all kinds of bondage. In our imagery, we have captured the dove of freedom and power and caged it. The heavenly dove has become like the doves in the temple that were being sold for sacrifice (Mt 21:12–13).

The Canberra theme harked back to another biblical image of a bird: the Spirit that in the beginning hovered over the waters to bring about creation (Gen 1:2). Surely this bird was not white and delicate, but a multicolored fire-bird that brought forth the multifarious creation in all its brilliant and varied hues. It is as if the (assumed to be) white dove that brought the leaf signifying tranquility to Noah after the flood transforms into the rainbow, bringer of the promise, under which Noah's sons and daughters set about building a new world (Gen 8:10–12; 9:8–19). Under the rainbow, Noah's descendants discovered the true meaning of community through the trauma of the rise and fall of the Tower of Babel. They learned to prize their linguistic and cultural diversity, and became a family of nations ever in need of reconciliation (Gen 10–11). Reconciliation takes place under the wings of the dynamic and vigorous Spirit of God, who brooded over the waters to bring forth creation, and hovers still today. The task of reconciliation involves a spiritual struggle (2 Cor 4:7–12; 5:18–20; Eph 6:10–20). It is not for the faint-hearted, but requires courage and strength. Agents of reconciliation need to be as innocent as doves but also as wise as serpents (Mt 10:16–20). The Spirit is also the empowering mother eagle, who bears her young on her wings, who teaches them to overcome their weariness and rise up like she does (Ex 19:4; Isa 40:31).

In many religious traditions, including Christianity, birds symbolize divine presence (J. Park 1998: 160). The reason is not hard to find: birds come down from heaven and rise up there again. Like the Spirit of God, birds are go-betweens, connecting heaven and earth. They appear as messengers of God, like the angels. The descent of the dove on Jesus at his baptism is a reminder that, in Christ, God is reconciling the world (2 Cor 5:19) and that, in the Spirit, heaven and earth are connected. Participating in God's mission is catching onto—and being caught up by—the wings of the Spirit as she moves in the world. However, the heavenly bird is not limited in the biblical record to the dove, nor is the imagery of the Holy Spirit restricted to the dove. As Samuel Rayan once said, with a hint of exasperation, "The Spirit is not only dove" (1979: 7). Nor is reconciliation the only paradigm of mission. David Bosch was right when he described a multiplicity of entry points to mission, from evangelism to common witness, from action for justice to being with others (Bosch 1991: 368–510). We have seen in this book that the mission of the Spirit encompasses the whole breadth and depth of God's purposes in the world. I do not feel the need, as a result of this research, to come to some overarching definition of that mission, which would in any case be impossible. Nor can we arrive at unanimous expressions of Christian doctrines or theologies of how the Holy Spirit relates to the other spirits in the world. However, we need to keep up the global conversation on these matters, and Christians must continue to confess that, wherever and however the Spirit is present and active, the Spirit leads to Jesus Christ, the Son who reveals the Father, the origin of all things.

BIBLIOGRAPHY

Abhishiktananda 1984. *Saccidananda: a Christian approach to advaitic experience.* Rvsd edn. Delhi: ISPCK.

Abraham, K. C. 1991. "Syncretism is not the issue: a response to Professor Chung Hyun Kyung," *International Review of Mission* 80/319-320 (Jul–Dec), 339–46.

—— 1994a. "Taking the poor seriously: an interpretative report" in K. C. Abraham and Bernadette Mbuy-Beya (eds.), *Spirituality of the third world.* Ecumenical Association of Third-World Theologians 1992 assembly, Nairobi, Kenya. Maryknoll, NY: Orbis Books, 207–210.

—— 1994b. "A theological response to the ecological crisis" in David C. Hallman (ed.), *Ecotheology: voices from South and North.* Geneva: World Council of Churches/ Maryknoll, NY: Orbis Books, 65–78.

—— and T. K. Thomas 2004. "Asia" in John Briggs, Mercy Amba Oduyoye and George Tsetsis (eds.), *A history of the ecumenical movement.* Vol. 3: *1968–2000.* Geneva: World Council of Churches, 495–522.

Ahn, Sang Jin 2001. *Continuity and transformation: religious synthesis in East Asia.* New York: Peter Lang Publishing.

Ahn, Shin 2005. "Yun Chi-ho's international religious network: mission or dialogue?" Paper presented at the British-Scandinavian Conference of Historians of Christianity, Lund, 8–11 September.

Allen, Roland 1962 [1912]. *Missionary methods: St. Paul's or ours?* Grand Rapids, MI: Wm B. Eerdmans.

—— 1964 [c1910]. *Missionary principles.* Grand Rapids, MI: Wm B. Eerdmans.

Anastasios of Androussa, Bishop 1989. "Orthodox mission—past, present and future" in George Lemopoulos (ed.), *Your will be done: orthodoxy in mission.* Geneva: World Council of Churches.

Anderson, Allan 1991. *Moya: the Holy Spirit in an African context.* Pretoria: University of South Africa.

—— 2004a. *An introduction to Pentecostalism.* Cambridge: Cambridge University Press.

—— 2004b. "The contextual theology of David Yonggi Cho" in Wonsuk Ma, William W. Menzies and Hyeon-sung Bae (eds.), *David Yonggi Cho: a close look at his theology and ministry.* Baguio, Philippines: APTS Press, 133–59.

Appasamy, A. J. 1928. *Christianity as bhakti marga: a study of the Johannine doctrine of love.* Madras: Christian Literature Society.

Arnold, Clinton E. 1992. *Powers of darkness: a thoughtful biblical look at an urgent challenge facing the church.* Leicester: InterVarsity Press.

Athappilly, Andrew 1984. "Response to Samuel Rayan, 'The ecclesiology at work in the Indian Church'" in Gerwin Van Leeuwen (ed.), *Searchings for an Indian ecclesiology.* Bangalore: Asia Trading Corporation, 213–16.

Augustine of Hippo 1991. *The works of St. Augustine: a translation for the twenty-first century I/5 The Trinity* (trans. Edmund Hill). Brooklyn, NY: New City Press.

Augustine of Hippo 1993. *The works of St. Augustine: a translation for the twenty-first century* III/7 *Sermons* (trans. Edmund Hill). Brooklyn, NY: New City Press.

Baago, Kaj 1969. *Pioneers of indigenous Christianity.* Bangalore: CISRS/Madras: Christian Literature Society.

Bae, Hyoen Sung 1999. "Response" in Allan H. Anderson and Walter Hollenweger (eds.), *Pentecostals after a century: global perspectives on a movement in transition.* Sheffield: Sheffield Academic Press, 160–63.

—— 2005. "Full Gospel theology and a Korean Pentecostal identity" in Allan Anderson and Edmond Tang (eds.), *Asian and Pentecostal: the charismatic face of Christianity in Asia.* Oxford: Regnum Books, 527–49.

Barrett, David B., George T. Kurian and Todd M. Johnson, *World Christian encyclopedia* 2nd edn. Vol. 1: *The world by countries: religionists, churches, ministries.* Oxford: Oxford University Press, 2001.

Barth, Karl 1962 [1935]. *Credo.* New York: Charles Scribner's Sons.

Basu, Raj Sekhar 2000. "Dalitization and a new version of Christianity from below: some preliminary observations on the belief patterns of Christian Paraiyars in Tamilnadu" in Roger E. Hedlund (ed.), *Christianity is Indian: the emergence of an indigenous community.* Mylapore: MIIS/Delhi: ISPCK, 87–99.

Bauckham, Richard 1987. *Moltmann—messianic theology in the making.* Basingstoke, UK: Marshall Pickering.

Berger, Peter L. 1971. *A rumour of angels: modern society and the rediscovery of the supernatural.* Harmondsworth, Middlesex: Pelican Books.

Bergunder, Michael 2001. "Miracle healing and exorcism: the South Indian Pentecostal movement in the context of popular Hinduism," *International Review of Mission* 90/356-57 (Jan–April), 103–112.

Berkhof, Hendrikus 1965. *The doctrine of the Holy Spirit.* The Annie Kinkead Warfield lectures 1963–64. London: Epworth Press.

Berthrong, John H. and Evelyn Nagai Berthrong 2000. *Confucianism: a short introduction.* Oxford: Oneworld.

Bevans, Stephen B. 1998a. "God inside out: toward a missionary theology of the Holy Spirit," *International Bulletin of Missionary Research* 22/3 (Jul), 102–105.

—— 1998b. "Jesus, face of the Spirit: reply to Dale Bruner," *International Bulletin of Missionary Research* 22/3 (Jul), 108–109.

Bevans, Stephen B. and Roger P. Schroeder 2004. *Constants in context: a theology of mission for today.* Maryknoll, NY: Orbis Books.

Bobrinskoy, Boris 1989. "The Holy Spirit—in the Bible and the Church," *Ecumenical Review* 41/3 (Jul) 357–362.

Boer, Harry R. 1961. *Pentecost and missions.* Grand Rapids, MI: Wm B. Eerdmans.

Bosch, David J. 1991. *Transforming mission: paradigm shifts in theology of mission.* Maryknoll, NY: Orbis Books.

Boyd, Robin H. S. 1975 [1969]. *An introduction to Indian Christian theology.* Rvsd edn. Delhi: ISPCK; first published in 1969.

Bria, Ion 1980. "Introduction" in Ion Bria (ed.), *Martyria/mission: the witness of the Orthodox churches today.* Geneva: World Council of Churches, 3–9.

—— (ed.) 1986. *Go forth in peace: Orthodox perspectives on mission.* Geneva: World Council of Churches.

—— 1996. *The liturgy after the Liturgy: mission and witness from an Orthodox perspective.* Geneva: World Council of Churches.

Brown, Colin (ed.) 1971. *The new international dictionary of New Testament theology*, Vol. 3. Exeter: Paternoster Press.

Brown, John 1991. "Mission impulses from Canberra: some reflections," guest editorial, *International Review of Mission* 80/319-320 (Jul/Oct) 299–304.

Burgess, Stanley M. 1989. *The Holy Spirit: Eastern Christian traditions*. Peabody, MA: Hendrickson Publishers.

—— 1997. *The Holy Spirit: medieval Roman Catholic and Reformation traditions*. Peabody, MA: Hendrickson Publishers.

Burrows, William R. (ed.) 1993. *Redemption and dialogue: Reading* Redemptoris missio *and* Dialogue and proclamation. Maryknoll, NY: Orbis Books.

—— 1996. "A seventh paradigm? Catholics and radical inculturation" in Willem Saayman and Klippies Kritzinger (eds.), *Mission in bold humility: David Bosch's work considered*. Maryknoll, NY: Orbis Books, 121–138.

—— 1998. "Reconciling all in Christ: an old new paradigm for mission," *Mission Studies* 15-1/29, 79–98.

Casaldáliga, Pedro 1990. "Fire and Ashes in the Wind" in Emilio Castro (comp.), *To the wind of God's Spirit: reflections on the Canberra theme*. Geneva: World Council of Churches, 1–2.

Castro, Emilio 1991. Editorial, *Ecumenical Review* 43/2 (April), 161–64.

Chakkarai, Vengal 1981 [1932]. *Jesus the Avatar* (Madras, 1932); reproduced in P. T. Thomas (ed.), *Vengal Chakkarai*, Vol. 1. Madras: Christian Literature Society for the United Theological College, 42–198.

Chan, Simon K. H. 1994. "Jürgen Moltmann's *The Spirit of life: a universal affirmation:* an Asian review," *Journal of Pentecostal Theology* 4 (Apr) 35–40.

—— 2004. "The pneumatology of Paul Yonggi Cho" in Wonsuk Ma, William W. Menzies and Hyeon-sung Bae (eds.), *David Yonggi Cho: a close look at his theology and ministry*. Baguio, Philippines: APTS Press, 95–119.

Chenchiah, P. 1938. "Jesus and non-Christian faiths" in G. V. Job, P. Chenchiah, V. Chakkarai, D. M. Devasahayam, S. Jesudason, Eddy Asirvatham and A. N. Sudarisanam, *Rethinking Christianity in India*. Madras: A. N. Sudarisanam, 47–62.

Cho, Yonggi (Paul) 1984. *Prayer: the key to revival*. USA: Word Incorporated.

—— 1989. *The Holy Spirit, my senior partner: understanding the Holy Spirit and His gifts*. Milton Keynes, UK: Word Publishing.

—— 1998a. *Pneumatology (Sŏngnyŏn'non)*. Seoul: Sŏulmalssŭmsa.

—— 1998b [1980]. *Solving life's problems*. Secunderabad, India: Ben Publishing.

—— 1999a [1993]. *Born to be blessed*. Secunderabad, India: Ben Publishing.

—— (David) 1999b [1983]. *The fourth dimension: more secrets for a successful faith life*, Vol. 2. Secunderabad, India: Ben Publishing.

—— 1999c [1989]. *The fourth dimension: the key to putting your faith to work for a successful life*. Secunderabad, India: Ben Publishing.

Choi, Hee An 2005. *Korean women and God: experiencing God in a multi-religious colonial context*. Maryknoll, NY: Orbis Books.

Choo, Chai-yong (Chu Chae-yong) 1998. *A history of Christian theology in Korea (Han'guk krisdo-gyo shinhak-sa)*. Seoul: Christian Literature Society of Korea.

Chung, Chai-Sik 1997. *Korea: the encounter between the gospel and neo-Confucian culture*. Geneva: World Council of Churches.

Chung Hyun Kyung 1988. "'Han-pu-ri': doing theology from a Korean women's perspective," *Ecumenical Review* 40/1 (Jan), 27–36.

——— 1991a. *Struggle to be the sun again: introducing Asian women's theology.* London: SCM Press.

——— 1991b. "Come, Holy Spirit—renew the whole creation" in Michael Kinnamon (ed.), *Signs of the Spirit.* Official report of the seventh assembly of the World Council of Churches, Canberra, 1991. Geneva: World Council of Churches, 37–47.

——— 1994. "Ecology, feminism and African and Asian spirituality: towards a spirituality of eco-feminism" in David G. Hallman (ed.), *Ecotheology: voices from South and North.* Geneva: World Council of Churches, 175–178.

CIA 2005. Country file: South Korea. http://www.cia.gov/cia/publications/factbook/geos/ks.html [accessed 12/16/05].

Clapsis, Emmanuel 1989. "The Holy Spirit in the Church," *Ecumenical Review* 41/3 (Jul), 339–47.

——— 1991. "What does the Spirit say to the churches? Missiological implications of the seventh assembly of the World Council of Churches," *International Review of Mission* 80/319-320 (Jul/Oct) 327–37.

Clark, Allen D. 1971. *A history of the church in Korea.* Seoul: Christian Literature Society of Korea.

Clarke, Sathianathan 1999. *Dalits and Christianity: subaltern religion and liberation theology in India.* Delhi & Oxford: Oxford University Press, 43–48.

Comblin, José 1989 [1987]. *The Holy Spirit and liberation.* Tunbridge Wells: Burns & Oates; original edition published in Brazil in 1987.

Congar, Yves 1983 [1979]. *I believe in the Holy Spirit.* 3 vols. (trans. David Smith). London: Geoffrey Chapman, 1983; first published in French in 1979.

Congregation for the Doctrine of the Faith 2001. Notification on the book *Toward a Christian theology of religious pluralism* (Orbis Books: Maryknoll, NY 1997) by Father Jacques Dupuis, SJ http://www.vatican.va/roman_curia/congregations/cfaith/documents/rc_con_cfaith_doc_20010124_dupuis_en.htm [accessed 9/6/01].

Comiskey, Joel 2003. "Rev. Cho's cell groups and dynamics of church growth" in Myung Sung-Hoon and Hong Young-Gi (eds.). *Charis and charisma: David Yonggi Cho and the growth of Yoido Full Gospel Church.* Oxford: Regnum Books, 143–57.

Cox, Harvey 1996. *Fire from heaven: the rise of Pentecostal spirituality and the reshaping of religion in the twenty-first century.* London: Cassell.

Cox, James L. 1996. "The classification of 'primal religions' as a non-empirical Christian theological construct," *Studies in World Christianity* 2/1, 55–76.

Daly, Mary 1986 [1973]. *Beyond God the Father: toward a philosophy of women's liberation.* London: The Women's Press; first published 1973.

Daneel, M. L. 1993. "African Independent Church pneumatology and the salvation of all creation" in Harold D. Hunter and Peter D. Hocken (eds.), *All together in one place: theological papers from the Brighton conference on world evangelization.* Sheffield: Sheffield Academic Press, 96–126.

Deane-Drummond, Celia E. 1997. *Ecology in Jürgen Moltmann's theology.* Lampter, UK: Edwin Mellen Press.

Devasahayam, V. 1998. "Conflicting roles of the Bible and culture in shaping Asian theology: a tale of two theologies," *Transformation* (Oxford Centre for Mission Studies) 15/3 (Jul/Sept), 21–27.

Di Noia, J. A. 1997. "Karl Rahner" in David F. Ford, *The modern theologians: an introduction to Christian theology in the twentieth century.* 2nd edn. Oxford: Blackwell Publishers, 118–33.

Dorr, Donal 2000. *Mission in today's world.* Blackrock, Co. Dublin: Columba Press.

Douglas, J. D. (ed.) 1990. *Proclaim Christ until He comes: calling the whole church to take the whole gospel to the whole world.* Report of Lausanne II International Congress on World Evangelization, Manila, 1989. Minneapolis: World Wide Publications.

Dunn, James D. G. 1975. *Jesus and the Spirit: a study of the religious and charismatic experience of Jesus and the first Christians as reflected in the New Testament.* London: SCM Press.

—— 1978. "Spirit, Holy Spirit" in Colin Brown (ed.), *Dictionary of New Testament theology* Vol. 3. Exeter: Paternoster Press, 689–709.

—— 1998. *The Christ and the Spirit: collected essays.* Vol. 2: *Pneumatology.* Edinburgh: T & T Clark.

Dupuis, Jacques 1977. *Jesus Christ and His Spirit: theological approaches.* Bangalore: Theological Publications in India.

—— 1995. "Religious plurality and the Christological debate," *SEDOS Bulletin* 15/2–3 (1995) http://www.sedos.org/english/dupuis.htm [accessed 6/28/00].

—— 1997. *Toward a Christian theology of religious pluralism.* Maryknoll, NY: Orbis Books.

Duraisingh, Christopher 1995. Editorial, *International Review of Mission* 84/334, 203–209.

—— (ed.) 1998. *Called to one hope: the gospel in diverse cultures.* Report of the conference of the Commission on World Mission and Evangelism, Salvador, Brazil, 1996. Geneva: World Council of Churches.

England, John C. et al. 2004. *Asian Christian theologies: a research guide to authors, movements, sources.* Vol. 3: *Northeast Asia.* Delhi: ISPCK.

Evangelical perspectives from Canberra 1991 in Michael Kinnamon (ed.), *Signs of the Spirit.* Official report of the seventh assembly of the World Council of Churches, Canberra, 1991. Geneva: World Council of Churches, 282–86.

Federici, Tommaso 1995. "Pneumatological foundation of mission" in Sebastian Karotemprel, *Following Christ in mission: a foundational course in missiology.* Bombay, Paulines Publications, 64–74.

Fitzgerald, Michael 1991. "Mission in Canberra," *International Review of Mission* 80/319-320 (Jul/Oct) 315–26.

Francis, T. Dayanandan (ed.) 1992. *The Christian bhakti of A. J. Appasamy: a collection of his writings.* Madras: Christian Literature Society.

Fung, Raymond 1993. "The spirit world" in Bong Rin Ro and Bruce J. Nicholls (eds.), *Beyond Canberra: Evangelical responses to contemporary ecumenical issues.* Oxford: Regnum Books, 60–63.

Gnanadason, Aruna 1993. "Towards a feminist eco-theology for India" in Prasanna Kumari (ed.), *A reader in feminist theology.* Madras: Gurukul, 95–105.

Gordon, A. J. 1893. *The Holy Spirit in missions.* New York and Chicago: Fleming H. Revell Company.

Gorringe, Timothy 1990. *Discerning Spirit: a theology of revelation.* London: SCM Press.

Grayson, James Huntley 1985. *Early Buddhism and Christianity in Korea: a study in the emplantation of religion.* Leiden: E.J. Brill.

—— 2002. *Korea—a religious history.* Rvsd edn. Abingdon, Oxon: Routledge-Curzon.

Grenz, Stanley J. and Roger E. Olson 1992. *Twentieth-century theology: God and the world in a transitional age.* Downers Grove, IL: InterVarsity Press.

Gunkel, Hermann 1979 [1888]. *The influence of the Holy Spirit: the popular view of the apostolic age and the teaching of the Apostle Paul* (trans. Roy A. Harrisville and Philip A. Quanbeck II). Philadelphia: Fortress Press.

Gunton, Colin 2002. "The Spirit moved over the face of the waters: the Holy Spirit and the created order," *International Journal of Systematic Theology* 4/2 (July), 190–204.

Gutiérrez, Gustavo 1991. "Theology as wisdom" in T. K. John (ed.), *Bread and breath: essays in honor of Samuel Rayan.* Anand, Gujarat: Gujarat Sahitya Prakash, 3–5.

Hallman, David G. (ed.) 1994. *Ecotheology: voices from South and North.* Geneva: World Council of Churches.

Ham, Sok Hon 1985. *Queen of suffering: a spiritual history of Korea* (trans. E. Sang Yu; edited and abridged by John A. Sullivan). London: Friends World Committee for Consultation.

Han, Chul-Ha, 1995. "Involvement of the Korean church in the evangelization of Asia" in Bong Rin Ro and Marlin L. Nelson (eds.), *Korean church growth explosion.* Rvsd edn. Seoul: Word of Life Press, 74–95.

Han, Sung-hong 1996. *Streams of Korean theological thought (Hang'guk-shinhak-sasang-ŭi hŭrŭm).* 2 vols. Seoul: Presbyterian College and Theological Seminary Press.

Heelas, Paul and Linda Woodhead 2005. *The spiritual revolution: why religion is giving way to spirituality.* Oxford: Blackwell Publishers.

Heim, S. Mark 1995. *Salvations: truth and difference in religion.* Maryknoll, NY: Orbis Books.

Hennecke, Susanne 2003. "Related by freedom: the impact of third-world theologians on the thinking of Jürgen Moltmann," *Exchange: Journal of Missiological and Ecumenical Research* (Leiden: Brill Academic Publishers) 32/4, 292–309.

Heron, Alasdair I. C. 1981. "The *filioque* in recent Reformed theology" in Lukas Vischer (ed.), *Spirit of God, Spirit of Christ: ecumenical reflections on the filioque controversy.* Geneva: World Council of Churches, 110–117.

——— 1983. *The Holy Spirit: the Holy Spirit in the Bible, in the history of Christian thought, and in recent theology.* London: Marshall Morgan & Scott.

Hick, John and Paul F. Knitter (eds.) 1987. *The myth of Christian uniqueness: toward a pluralistic theology of religions.* Maryknoll, NY: Orbis Books.

Hiebert, Paul G. 1982. "The flaw of the excluded middle," *Missiology: An International Review* 10/1 (Jan), 35–47.

Hocken, Peter D. 1981. "A survey of the worldwide charismatic movement" in Arnold Bittlinger (ed.), *The church is charismatic: the World Council of Churches and the charismatic renewal.* Geneva: World Council of Churches, 117–47.

Hollenweger, Walter 1972. *The Pentecostals* (trans. R. W. Wilson). London: SCM Press.

——— 1997. *Pentecostalism: origins and developments worldwide.* Peabody, MA: Hendrickson Publishers.

Hrangkhuma, F. (ed.) 1998. *Christianity in India: search for liberation and identity.* Delhi/Pune: ISPCK/CMS.

Hübner, Hans 1989. "The Holy Spirit in holy scripture," *Ecumenical Review* 41/3 (1989), 324–38.

Hyŏn, Yo-han 2004. "The Spirit of life that is the origin of life" (Saengmyŏng-ŭi kŭnwŏnin saengmyŏng-ŭi yŏng) in Lee Chong-sŏng et al., *Holistic theology (T'ongchŏnchŏk shinhak)*. Seoul: Changnohoe Shinhakdaehakkyo Publishing House, 233–67.

Idowu, E. Bolaji 1974. "The Spirit of God in the natural world" in Dow Kirkpatrick (ed.), *The Holy Spirit*. Nashville, TN: Tidings, 9–19.

International Missionary Council (IMC) 1953a. "A statement on the missionary calling of the Church" in Norman Goodall (ed.), *Missions under the cross*. Addresses and reports from the enlarged meeting of the committee of the International Missionary Council, Willingen, Germany, 1952. London: Edinburgh House Press, 188–192.

——— 1953b. "A statement on the calling of the church to mission and unity" in Norman Goodall (ed.), *Missions under the cross*. Addresses and reports from the enlarged meeting of the committee of the International Missionary Council, Willingen, Germany, 1952. London: Edinburgh House Press, 193–94.

——— 1953c. "The theological basis of the missionary obligation (an interim report)" in Norman Goodall (ed.), *Missions under the cross*. Addresses and reports from the enlarged meeting of the committee of the International Missionary Council, Willingen, Germany, 1952. London: Edinburgh House Press, 238–45.

International Theological Institute (Kukche shinhak yŏn'guwŏn) 1993. *Faith and theology of Yoido Full Gospel Church (Yŏdo sunbokŭm kyohoe-ŭi shinanggwa shinhak)* Vol. 1. Seoul: Seoul Sŏchŏk.

Janelli, Roger L. and Dawnhee Yim Janelli 1982. *Ancestor worship and Korean society*. Stanford, CA: Stanford University Press.

Jenson, Robert W. 1997. "Karl Barth" in David F. Ford, *The modern theologians: an introduction to Christian theology in the twentieth century*. 2nd edn. Oxford: Blackwell Publishers, 21–36.

Jeong, Chong Hee 2005. "The Korean charismatic movement as indigenous Pentecostalism" in Allan Anderson and Edmond Tang (eds.), *Asian and Pentecostal: the charismatic face of Christianity in Asia*. Oxford: Regnum Books, 551–71.

John Paul II 1986. *Dominum et vivificantem* http://www.vatican.va/edocs/Eng0142/__pg.htm (On the Holy Spirit in the life of the church and the world). [accessed 5/22/06].

——— 1990. *Redemptoris missio* http://www.vatican.va/edocs/Eng0219/_index.htm (On the permanent validity of the Church's missionary mandate). [accessed 7/24/06].

John, T. K. (ed.) 1991. *Bread and breath: essays in honor of Samuel Rayan*. Anand, Gujarat: Gujarat Sahitya Prakash.

Johnson, Elizabeth A. 1992. *She who is: the mystery of God in feminist theological discourse*. New York: Crossroad.

Kanjamala, Augustine 1993. "*Redemptoris missio* and mission in India" in William R. Burrows (ed.), *Redemption and dialogue: reading* Redemptoris missio *and* Dialogue and proclamation. Maryknoll, NY: Orbis Books, 195–205.

Kärkkäinen, Veli-Matti 2002. *Pneumatology: the Holy Spirit in ecumenical, international, and contextual perspective*. Grand Rapids, MI: Baker Academic.

Kasper, Walter 2004. *That they may be one: the call to unity*. London: Burns & Oates.

Kavunkal, Jacob 1998. "Neo-pentecostalism: a missionary reading," *Vidyajyoti: Journal of Theological Reflection* 62/6 (Jun), 407–22.

Kay, William K. 2004. "Introduction to Pentecostal eschatology" in William K. Kay and Anne E. Dyer, *Pentecostal and charismatic studies: a reader*. London: SCM Press.

Kelsey, David H. 1997. "Paul Tillich" in David F. Ford, *The modern theologians: an introduction to Christian theology in the twentieth century*. 2nd edn. Oxford: Blackwell Publishers, 87–102.

Kendall, Laurel 1985. *Shamans, housewives, and other restless Spirits: women in Korean ritual life*. Honolulu: University of Hawaii Press.

Keshishian, Aram 1992. *Orthodox perspectives in mission*. Oxford: Regnum Lynx.

Kessler, Diane (ed.) 1999. *Together on the Way*. Official report of the eighth assembly of the World Council of Churches. Geneva: World Council of Churches.

Keum, Jang-tae 2000. *Confucianism and Korean thoughts*. Seoul: Jimoondang Publishing Company.

Kim, Chongho 2003. *Korean shamanism: the cultural paradox*. Aldershot, UK: Ashgate.

Kim, Chong Sun and Shelly Killen 1978. "Preface" in Kim Chi Ha, *The gold-crowned Jesus and other writings*, edited by Chong Sun Kim and Shelly Killen. Maryknoll, NY: Orbis Books, ix–xl.

Kim, Joon-Gon 1995. "Korea's total evangelization movement" in Bong Rin Ro and Marlin L. Nelson (eds.), *Korean church growth explosion*. Rvsd edn. Seoul: Word of Life Press, 45–73.

Kim, Kil-sŏn 2003. "A theological examination of the New Korean Standard Version of the Bible," *Shinhak Jinam* (late summer issue) 198–224.

Kim, Kirsteen 2000. "Post-modern mission: a paradigm shift in David Bosch's theology of mission?" *International Review of Mission* 89/353 (Apr) 172–79.

——— 2001. "Mission in feminist perspective," *Dharma Deepika* (Chennai/Madras) 5/1 (Jan–Jun), 17–26.

——— 2002. "India and the Vatican: does Christ exhaust the mystery of God?" in Israel Selvanayagam (ed.), *Moving forms of theology: faith talk's changing contexts*. Delhi: ISPCK, 107–111.

——— 2003a. *Mission in the Spirit: the Holy Spirit in Indian Christian theologies*. Delhi: ISPCK.

——— and Michael Ipgrave 2003b. "*Yr Ysbryd*: more questions and some answers" in papers from the conference held at the University of Wales College Newport, Caerleon, 14–17 Jul 2003, 90–93 (unpublished).

——— 2004a. "India" in John Parratt (ed.), *Introduction to third world theologies*. Cambridge: Cambridge University Press, 44–73.

——— 2004b. "Missiology as global conversation of (contextual) theologies," *Mission Studies* 21/1, 39–53.

——— 2004c. "Spirit and 'spirits' at the Canberra Assembly of the World Council of Churches, 1991," *Missiology: an international review* 32/3 (July), 349–365.

——— 2004d. "Reconciliation, integrity and the Holy Spirit: ethic and ethos of mission." Paper presented at the International Association for Mission Studies conference, Port Dickson, Malaysia, 1–8 August.

——— (ed.) 2005a. *Reconciling mission: the ministry of healing and reconciliation in the church worldwide*. Delhi: ISPCK.

——— 2005b. "Reconciliation as the ministry of the Spirit: neither Jew nor Gentile" in Kirsteen Kim (ed.), *Reconciling mission: the ministry of healing and reconciliation in the church worldwide*. Delhi: ISPCK, 62–82.

——— 2005c. "The reconciling Spirit: the dove with colour and strength," *International Review of Mission* 94/372 (Jan), 20–29.

——— 2006a. "Holy Spirit movements in Korea—paternal or maternal? Reflections on the analysis of Ryu Tong-Shik," *Exchange: Journal of Missiological and Ecumenical Research* (Leiden: Brill Academic Publishers) 35/2, 147–68.

——— 2006b. "Come, Holy Spirit": Who? Why? How? So what?" in report of the World Council of Churches' Conference on Mission and Evangelism, Athens, 9–16 May 2005.

Kim, Myŏng-yong 2004. "The holistic theology of Lee Chong-sŏng" (Lee Chong-sŏng ŭi t'ongchŏnchŏk shinhak) in Lee Chong-sŏng et al. *Holistic theology (T'ongchŏnchŏk shinhak)*. Seoul: Changnohoe Shinhakdaehakkyo Publishing House, 83–116.

Kim, Sam-Hwan and Kim Yoon-Su 1995. "Church growth through early dawn prayer meetings" in Bong Rin Ro and Marlin L. Nelson (eds.), *Korean church growth explosion*. Rvsd edn. Seoul: Word of Life Press, 96–110.

Kim, Sebastian C.H. 2003. *In search of identity: debates on religious conversion in India*. Oxford/Delhi: Oxford University Press.

——— forthcoming. "The problem of the poor in post-war Korean Christianity: *kibock sinang* or *minjung* theology?" in *Transformation* (Oxford Centre for Mission Studies).

Kim, Seyoon (S. Y.) 1997. "God reconciled his enemy to himself: the origin of Paul's concept of reconciliation" in R. N. Longenecker (ed.), *The road from Damascus: the impact of Paul's conversion on his life*. Grand Rapids: Wm B. Eerdmans, 102–124.

Kim, Yong-Bock 1983. "Korean Christianity as a messianic movement of the people" in Commission on Theological Concerns of the Christian Conference of Asia (ed.), *Minjung theology: people as the subjects of history*. London: Zed Press, 80–119.

Kinnamon, Michael (ed.) 1991a. *Signs of the Spirit*. Official report of the seventh assembly of the World Council of Churches, Canberra, 1991. Geneva: World Council of Churches.

——— 1991b. "Canberra 1991: personal overview and introduction" in Michael Kinnamon (ed.) 1991. *Signs of the Spirit*. Official report of the seventh assembly of the World Council of Churches, Canberra, 1991. Geneva: World Council of Churches, 5–26.

Knitter, Paul F. 1991. "Stanley Samartha's *One Christ—many religions*—plaudits and problems," *Current Dialogue* 21 (Dec) 25–30.

——— 1995. *One earth, many religions: multifaith dialogue and global responsibility*. Maryknoll, NY: Orbis Books.

Korean Buddhist Research Institute (ed.) 1993. *The history and culture of Buddhism in Korea*. Seoul: Dongguk University Press.

Koyama, Kosuke 1988. " 'Building the house by righteousness': the ecumenical horizons of *minjung* theology" in Jung Young Lee (ed.), *An emerging theology in world perspective: commentary on Korean* minjung *theology*. Mystic, CT: Twenty-third Publications, 137–52.

Kraemer, Hendrik 1938. *The Christian message in a non-Christian world*. London: Edinburgh House.

Kraft, Charles H. 1992. "Allegiance, truth and power encounters in Christian witness" in Jan A. B. Jongeneel, *Pentecost, mission and ecumenism: essays on intercultural theology*. Festschrift in honor of Prof. Walter J. Hollenweger. Frankfurt am Main: Peter Lang, 215–30.

Kuzmic, Peter 1994. "Jürgen Moltmann's *The Spirit of life: a universal affirmation:* a Croatian war-time reading," *Journal of Pentecostal Theology* 4 (Apr) 17–24.

Kwok Pui-lan 1994. "Ecology and the recycling of Christianity" in David C. Hallman (ed.), *Ecotheology: voices from South and North*. Geneva: World Council of Churches Maryknoll NY: Orbis Books, 107–111.

Land, Steven J. 1993. *Pentecostal spirituality: a passion for the kingdom*. Sheffield: Sheffield Academic Press.

Lausanne Committee for World Evangelization 1974. "The Lausanne covenant" http://www.lausanne.org/ [accessed 7/23/06].

Le Guillou, Marie-Joseph 1975. "Church" in Karl Rahner (ed.), *Encyclopedia of theology*. London: Burns and Oates, 205–209.

Lee, Chong-sŏng et al. 2004. *Holistic theology (T'ongchŏnchŏk shinhak)*. Seoul: Changnohoe Shinhakdaehakkyo Publishing House.

—— 2004, "Introduction to Holistic Theology" (T'ongchŏnchŏk shinhak sŏsŏl) in Lee Chong-sŏng et al. *Holistic theology (T'ongchŏnchŏk shinhak)*. Seoul: Changnohoe Shinhakdaehakkyo Publishing House, 13–52.

Lee, Hong Jung 1999. "*Minjung* and Pentecostal movements in Korea" in Allan H. Anderson and Walter Hollenweger (eds.), *Pentecostals after a century: global perspectives on a movement in transition*. Sheffield: Sheffield Academic Press, 138–60.

Lee, Jung Young 1988. "*Minjung* theology: a critical introduction" in Jung-Young Lee (ed.), *An emerging theology in world perspective: commentary on Korean minjung theology*. Mystic CT: Twenty-third Publications, 3–29.

Lee, Moonjang 1999. "Experience of religious plurality in Korea: its theological implications," *International Review of Mission* 88/351 (Oct), 399–413.

Lee, Oo Chung 1994. *In search of our foremothers' spirituality*. Seoul: Asian Women's Resource Centre for Culture and Theology.

Lee, Yon Ok (Li Yŏn-ok) 1998. *Centennial history of the National Organization of Korean Presbyterian Women (Yŏchŏndohoe 100 nyŏnsa)*. Seoul: Editorial committee of the National Organization of Korean Presbyterian Women.

Lee, Young-hoon 2004. "The life and ministry of David Yonggi Cho and the Yoido Full Gospel Church" in Wonsuk Ma, William W. Menzies and Hyeon-sung Bae (eds.), *David Yonggi Cho: a close look at his theology and ministry*. Baguio, Philippines: APTS Press, 3–23.

—— 2005, "The Korean Holy Spirit movement in relation to Pentecostalism" in Allan Anderson and Edmond Tang (eds.), *Asian and Pentecostal: the charismatic face of Christianity in Asia*. Oxford: Regnum Books, 509–26.

Lim, David S. 2004. "A missiological evaluation of David Yonggi Cho's church growth" in Wonsuk Ma, William W. Menzies and Hyeon-sung Bae (eds.), *David Yonggi Cho: a close look at his theology and ministry*. Baguio, Philippines: APTS Press, 181–207.

Lipner, Julius 1994. *Hindus: their religious beliefs and practices*. London and New York: Routledge.

—— 1999. *Brahmabandhab Upadhyay: The life and thought of a revolutionary*. Delhi: Oxford University Press.

Lord, Andrew 2003. "The Pentecostal-Moltmann dialogue: implications for mission," *Journal of Pentecostal Theology* 2 (Feb), 271–287.

Lossky, Vladimir 1957. *The mystical theology of the Eastern Church.* London: James Clark.

Lowe, Chuck 1998. *Territorial spirits and world evangelization? A biblical, historical and missiological critique of "strategic level spiritual warfare."* Sevenoaks, UK: Mentor/OMF.

Ma, Julie C. 2001. *When the Spirit meets the spirits: Pentecostal ministry among the Kankana-ey tribe in the Philippines.* Rvsd edn. Frankfurt am Main: Peter Lang.

Ma, Wonsuk 2004. "Toward the future of David Yonggi Cho's theological tradition" in Wonsuk Ma, William W. Menzies and Hyeon-sung Bae (eds.), *David Yonggi Cho: a close look at his theology and ministry.* Baguio, Philippines: APTS Press, 255–72.

Macchia, Frank D. 1994. "Jürgen Moltmann's *The Spirit of life: a universal affirmation:* a North American response," *Journal of Pentecostal Theology* 4 (Apr) 25–33.

Manning, Henry Edward 1865. *The temporal mission of the Holy Ghost.* London: Longmans, Green.

Martin, Ralph P. 1981. *Reconciliation: A study of Paul's theology.* London: Marshall, Morgan & Scott.

Martin, David 2002. *Pentecostalism: the world their parish.* Oxford: Blackwell Publishers.

Matsoukas, Nikos 1989. "The economy of the Holy Spirit: the standpoint of Orthodox theology," *Ecumenical Review* 41/3 (Jul), 398–405.

Matthey, Jacques 2004. "Reconciliation, *missio Dei* and the church's mission" in Howard Mellor & Timothy Yates (eds.), *Mission, violence, and reconciliation.* Sheffield: Cliff College Publishing, 113–37.

McAlpine, Thomas H. 1991. *Facing the powers: What are the options?* Monrovia, CA: MARC.

"Memorandum: the filioque clause in ecumenical perspective" 1979 in Lukas Vischer (ed.), *Spirit of God, Spirit of Christ: ecumenical reflections on the filioque controversy.* Geneva: World Council of Churches, 3–18.

Menzies, William W. 2004. "David Yonggi Cho's theology of the fullness of the Spirit: a Pentecostal perspective" in Wonsuk Ma, William W. Menzies and Hyeon-sung Bae (eds.), *David Yonggi Cho: a close look at his theology and ministry.* Baguio, Philippines: APTS Press, 27–42.

Moffett, Samuel Hugh 1998. *A history of Christianity in Asia.* Vol. 1: *Beginnings to 1500.* Maryknoll, NY: Orbis Books.

Mofokeng, T. A. 1990. "Mission theology from an African perspective: a dialogue with David Bosch" in J. N. J. Kritzinger and Willem Saayman (eds.), *Mission in creative tension: a dialogue with David Bosch.* Pretoria: South African Missiological Society, 168–176.

Moltmann, Jürgen 1967 [1965]. *Theology of hope: on the ground and the implications of a Christian eschatology* (trans. James W. Leitch). London: SCM Press.

—— 1974 [1972]. *The crucified God: the cross of Christ as the foundation and criticism of Christian thelogy.* NY: Harper & Row.

—— 1977 [1975]. *The church in the power of the Spirit: a contribution to messianic ecclesiology* (trans. Margaret Kohl). London: SCM Press.

—— 1981a [1980]. *The Trinity and the kingdom of God* (trans. Margaret Kohl). London: SCM Press.

—— 1981b. "Theological proposals towards the resolution of the filioque controversy" in Lukas Vischer (ed.), *Spirit of God, Spirit of Christ: ecumenical reflections on the filioque controversy*. Geneva: World Council of Churches, 164–73.

—— 1985 [1985]. *God in creation: an ecological doctrine of creation* (trans. Margaret Kohl). The Gifford lectures 1984–85. London: SCM Press.

—— 1990. "The scope of renewal in the Spirit" in Emilio Castro (comp.), *To the wind of God's Spirit: reflections on the Canberra theme*. Geneva: World Council of Churches, 31–39.

—— 1992 [1991]. *The Spirit of life: a universal affirmation* (trans. Margaret Kohl) London: SCM Press.

—— 1993. *God in creation: new theology of creation and the Spirit of God* (trans. Margaret Kohl). The Gifford lectures 1984–85. Minneapolis: Fortress Press.

—— 2000. "The mission of the Spirit: the gospel of life" in Timothy Yates (ed.), *Mission—an invitation to God's future*. Papers of the conference of the British and Irish Association for Mission Studies, Oxford, 1999. Sheffield: Cliff College Press, 19–34.

Moreau, A. Scott et al. (eds.) 2003. *Deliver us from evil: an uneasy frontier in Christian mission*. Monrovia, CA: MARC.

Mott, John R. 1910. "The opportunity and the urgency of carrying the gospel to all the non-Christian world" in World Missionary Conference, *Carrying the gospel to all the non-Christian world: report of Commission I of the World Missionary Conference, Edinburgh 1910*. Edinburgh: Oliphant, Anderson & Ferrier, 5–49.

Moule, A. C. 1930. *Christians in China before the year 1550*. London: SPCK.

Moule, C. F. D. 2000 [1978]. *The Holy Spirit*, 2nd edn. London and New York: Continuum.

Müller-Fahrenholz, Geiko 1995. *God's Spirit: transforming a world in crisis*. Geneva: World Council of Churches.

Munck, Johannes 1959. *Paul and the salvation of mankind*. London: SCM Press.

Myung, Sung-Hoon and Hong Young-Gi (eds.) 2003. *Charis and charisma: David Yonggi Cho and the growth of Yoido Full Gospel Church*. Oxford: Regnum Books.

National Council of Churches in Korea (NCCK) 1988. "Declaration of the churches of Korea on national reunification and peace," unanimously adopted at the 37th general meeting of the National Council of Churches in Korea, held in the Yondong Presbyterian Church, Seoul on February 29, http://www.warc. ch/pc/20th/03.html [accessed 5/16/06].

Nehring, Andreas 1996. "The prodigal son's religious grounding: questioning pluralist theologies" in David C. Scott and Israel Selvanayagam (eds.), *Re-visioning India's religious traditions. Essays in honor of Eric Lott*. Delhi: ISPCK for United Theological College, Bangalore, 173–86.

Neill, Stephen 1970. *The story of the Christian church in India and Pakistan*. Madras: Christian Literature Society.

Newbigin, Lesslie 1982. *The Light has come: an exposition of the fourth Gospel*. Edinburgh: Handsel Press.

—— 1994. "Reply to Konrad Raiser," *International Bulletin of Missionary Research* 18/3 (Apr), 51–52.

—— 1995. *The open secret: an introduction to the theology of mission.* Rvsd edn (1st edn 1978). Grand Rapids, MI: Wm B. Eerdmans.

Nirmal, A. P. 1994 [1988]. "Towards a Dalit Christian theology" in R. S. Sugirtharajah (ed.), *Frontiers in Asian Christian theology: emerging trends.* Maryknoll, NY: Orbis Books, 27–40; first published as Arvind P. Nirmal, "Towards a Christian Dalit theology" in Arvind P. Nirmal (ed.) 1988. *A reader in Dalit theology.* Madras: Gurukul, n.d., 53–70.

Noreen, Barbara 1994. *Crossroads of the Spirit.* Delhi: ISPCK.

Oduyoye, Mercy Amba 1992. Guest editorial, *International Review of Mission* 81/322 (Apr) 173–75.

Oleska, Michael J. 1990. "The Holy Spirit's action in human society: an Orthodox perspective," *International Review of Mission* 79/515 (Jul), 311–37.

"Orthodox reflections on the assembly theme" 1990 in Emilio Castro (comp.), *To the wind of God's Spirit: reflections on the Canberra theme.* Geneva: World Council of Churches, 87–98.

Osei-Bonsu, Joseph 1989. "The Spirit as agent of renewal: the New Testament testimony," *Ecumenical Review* 41/3 (Jul), 454–60.

Paik, Lak-Geoon George 1970 [1929]. *The history of Protestant missions in Korea 1832–1910.* Seoul: Yonsei University Press; first published in 1929.

Painadath, Sebastian 1993. "Towards an Indian Christian spirituality in the context of religious pluralism" in Dominic Veliath (ed.), *Towards an Indian Christian spirituality in a pluralistic context.* Papers and statement of the 14th meeting of the Indian Theological Association, Pune, Dec 1990. Bangalore: Dharmaram Publications, 3–14.

Panikkar, Raimundo 1973. *The Trinity and the religious experience of man.* Maryknoll, NY: Orbis Books/London: Darton, Longman & Todd.

Park, Jong Chun 1998. *Crawl with God, dance in the Spirit! A creative formation of Korean theology of the Spirit.* Nashville, TN: Abingdon Press.

Park, Myung Soo 2003. *Research into revival movements in the Korean church (Han'guk kyohoe puhŭng undong yŏnku).* Seoul: Han'guk kidokyo Yŏksa Yŏn'guso.

—— 2004. "Korean Pentecostal spirituality as manifested in the testimonies of members of Yoido Full Gospel Church" in Wonsuk Ma, William W. Menzies and Hyeon-sung Bae (eds.), *David Yonggi Cho: a close look at his theology and ministry.* Baguio, Philippines: APTS Press, 43–67.

Park, Pong-pae 1973. "Is it compromising or reforming?" (T'ahyŏp inga pyŏnhyŏk in ga), *Shinhak sasang* 1 (Aug) 28–48.

Parthenios, Patriarch of Alexandria and All Africa 1991. "The Holy Spirit" in Michael Kinnamon (ed.), *Signs of the Spirit.* Official report of the seventh assembly of the World Council of Churches, Canberra, 1991. Geneva: World Council of Churches, 28–37.

Percy, Martyn 1996. *Words, wonders and power: understanding contemporary Christian fundamentalism and revivalism.* London: SPCK.

Petersen, Douglas 1996. *Not by might nor by power: a Pentecostal theology of social concern in Latin America.* Oxford: Regnum/Paternoster.

Pieris, Aloysius 1990. *An Asian theology of liberation.* Maryknoll, NY: Orbis Books.

Pobee, John S. 1990. "Lord, Creator Spirit, renew and sustain the whole creation: some missiological perspectives," *International Review of Mission* 79/314 (Apr), 151–58.

Porter, Muriel 1990. *Land of the Spirit? The Australian religious experience*. Geneva: World Council of Churches.

Potter, Philip 1991. "Mission as reconciliation in the power of the Spirit: impulse from Canberra," *International Review of Mission* 80/319–20 (Jul/Oct), 305–314.

Putney, Michael E. 1991. "Come, Holy Spirit, renew the whole creation: seventh assembly of the World Council of Churches," *Theological Studies* 52 (Dec), 607–635.

Rahner, Karl 1968 [1939]. *Spirit in the world* (trans. William Dych). London and Sydney: Sheed & Ward; first published 1939.

—— 1971. *Theological investigations* (trans. David Bourke). Vol. 7: *Further theology of the spiritual life I*. London: Darton, Longman & Todd.

—— 1975a. "Trinity, divine" in Karl Rahner (ed.), *Encyclopedia of theology: a concise* sacramentum mundi. London: Burns & Oates, 1755–64.

—— 1975b. "Trinity in theology" in Karl Rahner (ed.), *Encyclopedia of theology: a concise* sacramentum mundi. London: Burns & Oates, 1764–75.

—— 1979. *Theological investigations* (trans. David Morland). Vol. 16: *Experience of the Spirit, source of theology*. London: Darton, Longman & Todd.

Raiser, Konrad 1991. "Beyond tradition and context: in search of an ecumenical framework of mission hermeneutics," *International Review of Mission* 80/319–320 (Jul–Oct), 347–54.

Ramachandra, Vinoth 1996. *The recovery of mission*. Carlisle: Paternoster.

Rayan, Samuel 1970. "Mission after Vatican II: problems and positions," *International Review of Mission* 59 (Oct) 414–26.

—— 1971. "The basic dilemma" in Tony Byrne, *The church and development dilemma*. Eldoret, Kenya: Gaba Publications, 41–46.

—— 1972. "Human well-being on earth and the gospel of Jesus," *Jeevadhara* 5/7 (Jan–Feb) 35–46.

—— 1974a. "Christian participation in the struggle for social justice: some theological reflections," *The Clergy Monthly* (Aug) 282–96.

—— 1974b. "Interpreting Christ to India: contributions of Roman Catholic theological seminaries," *Indian Journal of Theology* 23/4, 223–31.

—— 1975. "Evangelization and development" in Gerald H. Anderson and Thomas F. Stransky (eds.), *Evangelization*. Mission trends no. 2. Grand Rapids, MI: Wm B. Eerdmans, 87–105.

—— 1976. "'The ultimate blasphemy.' On putting God in a box," *International Review of Mission* 65/257 (Jan) 129–33.

—— 1977. Review of S. Samartha, *The Hindu response to the unbound Christ*, *International Review of Mission* 66/262 (Apr) 187–89.

—— 1978. "Jesus and the poor in the fourth Gospel," *Bible Bhashyam* 4/3 (Sep) 213–28.

—— 1979. *Breath of fire—the Holy Spirit: heart of the Christian gospel*. London: Geoffrey Chapman. First published as Samuel Rayan, *The Holy Spirit: heart of the gospel and Christian hope*. Maryknoll, NY: Orbis Books, 1978; re-published as Samuel Rayan, *Come, Holy Spirit*. Delhi: Media House, 1998 and Samuel Rayan, *Come, Holy Spirit and renew the face of the earth*. Delhi: Media House, 1998.

—— 1980 [1976]. "Indian Christian theology and the problem of history" in Douglas J. Elwood (ed.), *Asian Christian theology: emerging themes*. Philadelphia: Westminster Press, 125–132. First published as "An Indian theology and the problem of history" in Richard W. Taylor (ed.), *Society and religion: essays in honor of M. M. Thomas*. Madras: Christian Literature Society/Bangalore: CISRS, 1976, 167–93.

——— 1982a. "How will the Hindu hear?," *International Review of Mission* 71/281 (Jan) 49–59.

——— 1982b. "The irruption of the third world—a challenge to theology," *Vidyajyoti: Journal of Theological Reflection* 46/3 (Mar) 106–27.

——— 1985a. "Baptism and conversion: the Lima text in the Indian context" in Godwin Singh (ed.), *A call to discipleship*. Delhi: ISPCK, 167–87.

——— 1985b. "Jesus and imperialism" in Sebastian Kappen (ed.), *Jesus today*. Madras: AICUF Publications, 98–117.

——— 1989a. "Spirituality for inter-faith social action" in Xavier Irudayaraj (ed.), *Liberation and dialogue*. Bangalore: Claretian Publications, 64–73.

——— 1989b. "Wrestling in the night" in Mark H. Ellis and Otto Maduro (eds.), *The future of liberation theology*. Essays in honour of Gustavo Gutiérrez. Maryknoll, NY: Orbis Books, 450–69.

——— 1990. "Religions, salvation, mission" in Paul Mojzes and Leonard Swidler (eds.), *Christian mission and interreligious dialogue*. Lewiston, NY: The Edwin Mellen Press, 126–39.

——— 1992. "The search for an Asian spirituality of liberation" in Virginia Fabella, Peter K. H. Lee and David Kwang-sun Suh (eds.), *Asian Christian spirituality: reclaiming traditions*. Maryknoll, NY: Orbis Books, 11–30.

——— 1994a. "The earth is the Lord's" in David C. Hallman (ed.), *Ecotheology: voices from South and North*. Geneva: World Council of Churches/Maryknoll, NY: Orbis Books, 130–148.

——— 1994b. "how lovely . . . !" *Vidyajyoti: Journal of Theological Reflection* 58/2 (Feb) 65–73.

——— 1999a. "Decolonization of theology," http://www.sedos.org/english/Rayan. html [accessed 6/7/99].

——— 1999b. "New efforts in pneumatology." Paper delivered at Jesuit Congress on Ecumenism, 1999, courtesy of Fr. Thomas Michael, SJ, Secretary of the Secretariat for Inter-Religious Dialogue, Rome.

——— 1999c. "A spirituality of mission in an Asian context," http://www.sedos.org/ english/rayan2.htm [accessed 6/7/99].

——— 1999d. "Local cultures: instruments of incarnated Christian spirituality," http://www.sedos.org/english/rayan1.htm [accessed: 07/06/99].

Razu, I. John Mohan (ed.) 2001. *Struggle for human rights: towards a new humanity. Theological and ethical perspectives*. Nagpur: National Council of Churches of India.

"Reflections of Orthodox participants" 1991 in Michael Kinnamon (ed.), *Signs of the Spirit*. Official report of the seventh assembly of the World Council of Churches, Canberra, 1991. Geneva: World Council of Churches, 279–82.

Ridderbos, Herman 1975. *Paul—an outline of his theology* (trans. John Richard de Witt). Grand Rapids, MI: Wm B. Eerdmans.

Ritschl, Dietrich 1981. "Historical development and implications of the filioque controversy" in Lukas Vischer (ed.), *Spirit of God, Spirit of Christ: ecumenical reflections on the filioque controversy*. Geneva: World Council of Churches, 46–65.

Ro, Bong Rin 1993. "Theological debates in Korea after Canberra" in Bong Rin Ro and Bruce J. Nicholls (eds.), *Beyond Canberra: evangelical responses to contemporary ecumenical issues*. Oxford: Regnum Books, 53–59.

———— 1995. "The Korean Church: God's chosen people for evangelism" in Bong Rin Ro and Marlin L. Nelson (eds.), *Korean church growth explosion*. Rvsd edn. Seoul: Word of Life Press, 11–44.

Robeck, Cecil M. 1993. "A Pentecostal reflects on Canberra" in Bong Rin Ro and Bruce J. Nicholls (eds.), *Beyond Canberra: Evangelical responses to contemporary ecumenical issues*. Oxford: Regnum Books, 108–20.

Robinson, H. Wheeler 1928. *The Christian experience of the Holy Spirit*. Digswell Place, Herts: James Nisbet & Co.

Rosato, Philip J. 1981. *The Spirit as Lord: the pneumatology of Karl Barth*. Edinburgh: T & T Clark.

———— 1990. "The mission of the Spirit within and beyond the church" in Emilio Castro (comp.), *To the wind of God's Spirit: reflections on the Canberra theme*. Geneva: World Council of Churches, 21–30. Also in *Ecumenical Review* 41/3 (Jul 1989), 388–97.

Ryu, Tong-Shik 1999 [1979]. "The question of theology of the *minjung* in Korean theology" Hanguk-shinhak-ŭrosŏ-ui minjung-shinhak-ui kwacha; debate held in 1979 including Suh Nam-dong and Ryu Tong-Shik, in Chukchai Suh Nam-dong moksa yukojip p'yŏnjip-wiwŏnhoe (comp.), *Suh Nam-dong shinhak-ŭi isak-chupki*. Seoul: Taehan-kidokkyo-sŏhoe, 356–90.

———— 2000 [1982]. *The mineral veins of Korean theology (Han'guk shinhak-ŭi kwangmaek)*. Rvsd edn. Seoul: Tasan Kulbang.

———— 2001 [1965], *The Christian faith encounters the religions of Korea Han'guk chong'gyo wa kidok'kyo*. Seoul: Christian Literature Society of Korea; first published in 1965.

Saayman, Willem 1996. "A South African perspective on *Transforming mission*" in Willem Saayman and Klippies Kritzinger (eds.), *Mission in bold humility: David Bosch's work considered*. Maryknoll, NY: Orbis Books, 40–52.

Saayman, Willem and Klippies Kritzinger (eds.) 1996. *Mission in bold humility: David Bosch's work considered*. Maryknoll, NY: Orbis Books.

Sabev, Todor (ed.) 1982. *The Sofia consultation: Orthodox involvement in the World Council of Churches*. Geneva: World Council of Churches.

Saeki, P. Y. 1937. *Nestorian documents and relics in China*. Tokyo: Maruzen Co.

Samartha, Stanley J. 1974a. *The Hindu response to the unbound Christ: towards a christology in India*. Bangalore: CISRS.

———— (ed.) 1974b. *Living faiths and ultimate goals: a continuing dialogue*. Geneva: World Council of Churches.

———— 1974c. "The Holy Spirit and people of various faiths, cultures and ideologies" in Dow Kirkpatrick (ed.), *The Holy Spirit*. Nashville, TN: Tidings, 20–39; republished in Stanley J. Samartha, *Courage for dialogue: ecumenical issues in inter-religious relationships*. Geneva: World Council of Churches, 63–77.

———— 1979. *Guidelines on dialogue*. Geneva: World Council of Churches.

———— 1981a. *Courage for dialogue: ecumenical issues in inter-religious relationships*. Geneva: World Council of Churches.

———— 1981b. "Milk and honey—without the Lord?" *National Council of Churches Review* 101/12 (Dec), 662–71.

———— 1990. "The Holy Spirit and people of other faiths" in Emilio Castro (comp.), *To the wind of God's Spirit: reflections on the Canberra theme*. Geneva: World

Council of Churches, 50–63; republished in Stanley J. Samartha 1996. *Between two cultures: ecumenical ministry in a pluralist world*. Geneva: World Council of Churches, 187–202.

—— 1991a. *One Christ—many religions: toward a revised Christology*. Maryknoll, NY: Orbis Books.

—— 1991b. "In search of a revised Christology: a response to Paul Knitter," *Current Dialogue* 21 (Dec), 30–37.

—— 1994. "The promise of the Spirit" in Stanley J. Samartha, *The pilgrim Christ—sermons, poems and Bible studies*. Bangalore: Asia Trading Corporation, 43–49.

—— 1996. *Between two cultures: ecumenical ministry in a pluralist world*. Geneva: World Council of Churches.

Sanders, E. P. 1991. *Paul*. Oxford: Oxford University Press.

Schreiter, Robert J. 1991. Review article: David Bosch, *Transforming mission*, *International Bulletin of Missionary Research* 15/4 (Oct) 181.

—— 1998. *The ministry of reconciliation: spirituality and strategies*. Maryknoll, NY: Orbis Books.

—— 2004. "The theology of reconciliation and peacemaking for mission" in Howard Mellor and Timothy Yates (eds.), *Mission, violence, and reconciliation*. Sheffield: Cliff College Publishing, 11–28.

Schweizer, Eduard 1989. "On distinguishing between spirits," *Ecumenical Review* 41/3 (Jul), 406–15.

Selvanayagam, Israel 1998. "Components of a Tamil Śaiva bhakti experience as evident in Māṇkkavācakar's Tiruvācakam" in David Emmanuel Singh (ed.), *Spiritual traditions: essential visions for living*. Bangalore: ISPCK, 418–38.

—— 2000. "When demons speak the truth! An Asian reading of a New Testament story of exorcism." *Epworth Review* 27/3 (Jul), 33–40.

Sepúlveda, Juan 1993. "Pentecostalism and liberation theology: two manifestations of the work of the Holy Spirit for the renewal of the church" in Harold D. Hunter and Peter D. Hocken (eds.), *All together in one place: theological papers from the Brighton conference on world evangelization*. Sheffield: Sheffield Academic Press, 51–64.

Shenk, Wilbert R. 1996. "The mission dynamic" in Willem Saayman and Klippies Kritzinger (eds.), *Mission in bold humility: David Bosch's work considered*. Maryknoll, NY: Orbis Books, 83–93.

Soares-Prabhu, Georges M. 1991. "From alienation to inculturation: some reflections on doing theology in India today" in T. K. John (ed.), *Bread and breath: essays in honor of Samuel Rayan*. Anand, Gujarat: Gujarat sahitya prakash, 55–99.

Society for the Propagation of the Gospel in Foreign Parts (SPG) 1703. Accounts (facsimile available from USPG, London).

Song, C. S. 1988. "Building a theological culture of people" in Jung Young Lee (ed.), *An emerging theology in world perspective: commentary on Korean minjung theology*. Mystic, CT: Twenty-third Publications, 119–34.

Special Commission on Orthodox Participation in the World Council of Churches 1999. Background materials for the first meeting of the Special Commission, Morges, Switzerland, December, 1999, http://www.wcc-coe.org/wcc/who/morges-00-e.html [accessed 7/24/06].

Stamoolis, James J. 1986. *Eastern Orthodox mission theology today*. Maryknoll, NY: Orbis Books.

Staniloae, Dumitru 1981. "The procession of the Holy Spirit from the Father and his relation to the Son, as the basis of our deification and adoption" in Lukas Vischer (ed.), *Spirit of God, Spirit of Christ: ecumenical reflections on the filioque controversy*. Geneva: World Council of Churches, 174–86.

Stendahl, Krister 1976. *Paul among Jews and Gentiles*. Philadelphia, PA: Fortress Press.

—— 1990. *Energy for life: reflections on the theme "Come, Holy Spirit, renew the whole creation."* Geneva: World Council of Churches.

Stibbe, Mark W. G. 1994. "Jürgen Moltmann's *The Spirit of life: a universal affirmation*: a British appraisal," *Journal of Pentecostal Theology* 4 (Apr) 5–16.

Suh, Nam-dong 1975. "The third age of the Spirit" (Sŏngnyŏng-ŭi chesam shidae), *Christian thought (Kidokkyo-sasang)* (Oct) 39–52 & 83.

—— 1983a. "Historical references for a theology of the minjung" in Commission on Theological Concerns of the Christian Conference of Asia (ed.), *Minjung theology: people as the subjects of history*. London: Zed Press, 155–82.

—— 1983b. "Towards a theology of *han*" in Commission on Theological Concerns of the Christian Conference of Asia (ed.), *Minjung theology: people as the subjects of history*. London: Zed Press, 55–69.

—— 1999a. "Eschatology and revolution" (Chongmallon-gwa hyŏkmyŏng) in Chukchai Suh Nam-dong moksa yukojip p'yŏnjip-wiwŏnhoe (comp.), *Suh Nam-dong shinhak-ŭi isak-chupki*. Seoul: Taehan-kidokkyo-sŏhoe, 307–15.

—— 1999b. "The Korean church's understanding of the Cross" (Hanguk kyohoe-ŭi shibjaga ihae) in Chukchai Suh Nam-dong moksa yukojip p'yŏnjip-wiwŏnhoe (comp.), *Suh Nam-dong shinhak-ŭi isak-chupki*. Seoul: Taehan-kidokkyo-sŏhoe, 126–136.

—— 1999c [1979]. "The question of theology of the *minjung* in Korean theology" *Hanguk-shinhak-ŭrosŏ-ŭi minjung-shinhak-ŭi kwacha*; debate held in 1979 including Suh Nam-dong and Yu Tong-shik, in Chukchai Suh Nam-dong moksa yukojip p'yŏnjip-wiwŏnhoe (comp.), *Suh Nam-dong shinhak-ŭi isak-chupki*. Seoul: Taehan-kidokkyo-sŏhoe, 356–90.

—— 1999d. "The unification of socio-economic reality as the theme of *p'ungnyu* theology" (Sahoe, chŏngch'ichŏk hyŏnshil-ŭi t'onghapi p'ungryushinhak-ŭi gwache) in Chukchai Suh Nam-dong moksa yukojip p'yŏnjip-wiwŏnhoe (comp.), *Suh Nam-dong shinhak-ŭi isak-chupki*. Seoul: Taehan-kidokkyo-sŏhoe, 411–12.

Suurmond, Jean-Jacques 1994 [1984]. *Word and Spirit at play: towards a charismatic theology* (trans. John Bowden). London: SCM Press; first published in Dutch in 1984.

Tacey, David J. 2004. *The spirituality revolution: the emergence of contemporary spirituality*. Hove: Brunner-Routledge.

Taylor, John V. 1963. *The primal vision: Christian presence amid African religion*. London: SCM Press.

—— 1972. *The go-between God: the Holy Spirit and the Christian mission*. London: SCM Press.

Thangasamy, D. A. 1966. *The theology of Chenchiah with selections from his writings*. Bangalore: CISRS.

Thomas, M. M. 1970. *The acknowledged Christ of the Indian renaissance*. Madras: Christian Literature Society.

—— 1990. "The Holy Spirit and the spirituality for political struggles," *Ecumenical Review* 42/3–4 (Jul/Oct), 216–24.

—— 1997. "Indian theology" in Karl Müller, Theo Sundermeier, Stephen B. Bevans and Richard H. Bliese (eds.), *Dictionary of mission: theology, history, perspectives*. Maryknoll, NY: Orbis Books, 202–212.

Thomas, Norman 1995. *Classic texts in mission and world Christianity*. Maryknoll, NY: Orbis Books.

Tillich, Paul 1951. *Systematic theology*. Vol. 1: *Reason and revelation. Being and God*. Chicago: University of Chicago Press.

—— 1963. *Systematic theology*. Vol. 3: *Life and the Spirit, history and the kingdom of God*. Chicago: University of Chicago Press.

Times Online 2005. "Obituary: Father Jacques Dupuis," 12 January, http://www.timesonline.co.uk/article/0,,60–1435781,00.html [accessed 6/28/05].

Tomko, Cardinal Josef 1990a. "Missionary challenges to the theology of salvation" in Paul Mojzes and Leonard Swidler (eds.), *Christian mission and interreligious dialogue*. Lewiston, NY: Edwin Mellen Press, 12–32.

—— 1990b. "Christian mission today" in Paul Mojzes and Leonard Swidler (eds.), *Christian mission and interreligious dialogue*. Lewiston, NY: Edwin Mellen Press, 236–62.

Tso, Man King 1991. "Theological controversy in Canberra: a reflection," *International Review of Mission* 80/319–20 (Jul–Dec), 355–60.

Ukpong, Justin S. 1990. "Pluralism and the problem of the discernment of spirits" in Emilio Castro (comp.), *To the wind of God's Spirit: reflections on the Canberra theme*. Geneva: World Council of Churches, 77–86. Also in *Ecumenical Review* 41/3 (Jul 1989), 416–25.

Van Butselaar, Jan 1992. " 'Thinking locally, acting globally': the ecumenical movement in the new era," *International Review of Mission* 81/323 (Jul), 363–73.

—— 1998. "The Gospel and culture study: a survey," *Exchange: Journal of Missiological and Ecumenical Research* (Leiden: Brill Academic Publishers) 27/3 (Jul), 236–47.

Vandana 1975. "From death to life: a reflection on an Upanishadic text in the light of the Johannine gospel" in Christopher Duraisingh and Cecil Hargreaves (eds.), *India's search for reality and relevance of the Gospel of John*. Delhi: ISPCK, 25–40.

—— 1981. "Indian theologizing—the role of experience" in M. Amaladoss, T. K. John and G. Gispert-Sauch (eds.), *Theologizing in India*. Papers of the seminar in Poona (Pune), 1978. Bangalore: CBCI Commission for Seminaries/Theological Publications in India, 81–115.

—— *Mataji* 1987. *Jesus the Christ: Who is he? What was his message?* Jaiharikhal: Vandana *Mataji*.

—— 1988 [1978]. *Gurus, ashrams and Christians*. 3rd edn. Bombay: St. Paul/Delhi: ISPCK; first edn London: Darton, Longman & Todd, 1978; 2nd edn Madras: Christian Literature Society, 1980.

—— 1989. *Waters of fire*. 3rd edn Bangalore: Asia Trading Corporation; 2nd edn New York: Amity House, 1988; first published Madras: Christian Literature Society, 1981.

—— 1991a. *And the mother of Jesus was there (John 2.1): Mary—in the light of Indian spirituality*. Jaiharikhal, UP: Jeevan Dhara Ashram Society.

—— *Mataji* 1991b. *Find your roots and take wing*. Bangalore: Asia Trading Corporation.

—— *Mataji* 1992a. "The Word as '*Vac*' and the silence of joy: a feminine interpretation," *Journal of Dharma* 17/3 (Jul–Sep) 220–32.

—— 1992b. "A way to world peace—as an Indian sees it," *Vidyajyoti: Journal of Theological Reflection* 56/7 (Jul), 337–46.

—— *Mataji* (ed.) 1993a. *Christian ashrams—a movement with a future?* Delhi: ISPCK.

—— *Mataji* 1993b. "Introduction" in Vandana *(Mataji)* (ed.), *Christian ashrams —a movement with a future?* Delhi: ISPCK, 6–7.

—— *Mataji* 1993c. "The Christian ashram movement today" in Vandana *(Mataji)* (ed.), *Christian ashrams—a movement with a future?* Delhi: ISPCK, 75–85.

—— *Mataji* 1993d. "Response II: from the perspective of an ashramic spirituality" in Dominic Veliath (ed.), *Towards an Indian Christian spirituality in a pluralistic context*. Papers and statement of the fourteenth annual meeting of the Indian Theological Association. Bangalore: Dharmaram, 99–117.

—— (ed.) 1995a. *Shabda shakti sangam*. Bangalore: NBCLC.

—— 1995b. "Introduction" (to Part IV) in Vandana (ed.), *Shabda shakti sangam*. Bangalore: NBCLC, Hinduism section, 190.

—— *Mataji* 1995c. "Towards an Indian Christian spirituality" in Vandana (ed.), *Shabda shakti sangam*. Bangalore: NBCLC, Christianity section, 235–39.

—— *Mataji* 1995d. "Introduction to yoga" in Vandana (ed.), *Shabda shakti sangam*. Bangalore: NBCLC, Hinduism section, 93–94.

—— *Mataji* 1995e. "Saraswati" in Vandana (ed.), *Shabda shakti sangam*. Bangalore: NBCLC, Hinduism section, 29–31.

—— 1995f. "God as mother in the Hindu and Christian traditions" in Vandana (ed.), *Shabda shakti sangam*. Bangalore: NBCLC, Christianity section, 50–59.

—— *Mataji* 1997a. "When I celebrate His birth, I think of His death, Part I," *The New Leader* (Dec) 1–31.

—— *Mataji* 1997b. "A fruitful life of wondrous happenings," *The New Leader* (Jun) 16–30.

Vassiliadis, Petros 1998. *Eucharist and witness: Orthodox perspectives on the unity and mission of the church*. Geneva: World Council of Churches.

Verstraelen, Frans J. 1996. "Africa in David Bosch's missiology: survey and appraisal" in Willem Saayman and Klippies Kritzinger (eds.), *Mission in bold humility: David Bosch's work considered*. Maryknoll, NY: Orbis Books, 8–39.

Vischer, Lukas (ed.) 1981a. *Spirit of God, Spirit of Christ: ecumenical reflections on the filioque controversy*. Geneva: World Council of Churches.

—— 1981b. Preface in Lukas Vischer (ed.), *Spirit of God, Spirit of Christ: ecumenical reflections on the filioque controversy*. Geneva: World Council of Churches, v–vi.

—— 1981c. "The filioque clause in ecumenical perspective" in Lukas Vischer (ed.), *Spirit of God, Spirit of Christ: ecumenical reflections on the filioque controversy*. Geneva: World Council of Churches, 3–18.

Volf, Miroslav 1996. *Exclusion and embrace—a theological exploration of identity, otherness and reconciliation*. Nashville, TN: Abingdon Press.

Vroom, Hendrik M. 1989. *Religions and the Truth: philosophical reflections and perspectives*. Editions Rodolpi/Grand Rapids, MI: Wm B. Eerdmans.

Wagner, C. Peter 1989. "Territorial spirits and world missions," *Evangelical Missions Quarterly* 25/3 (Jul), 278–88.

Wainwright, Geoffrey 1997. "The Holy Spirit" in Colin E. Gunton (ed.), *The Cambridge companion to Christian doctrine*. Cambridge: Cambridge University Press, 273–96.

Ware, Timothy 1993. *The Orthodox church*. 2nd edn. London: Penguin Books.
Welker, Michael 1994. *God the Spirit* (trans. John F. Hoffmeyer). Minneapolis: Fortress Press.
—— 2002. "Modernity and post-modernity as challenges to Christian theology," *Swedish Missiological Themes* 90/4, 435–47.
Wenk, Matthias 2000. *Community-forming power: the socio-ethical role of the Spirit in Luke-Acts*. Sheffield: Sheffield Academic Press.
Wilfred, Felix 1998. "Towards a better understanding of Asian theology: some basic issues," *Vidyajyoti: Journal of Theological Reflection* 62/12, 890–915.
Williams, Peter W. 1990. *America's religions: traditions and cultures*. New York: Macmillan.
Wimber, John 1985. *Power evangelism*. New York: Harper and Row.
Wink, Walter 1984. *Naming the powers: the language of power in the New Testament*. Minneapolis: Fortress Press.
—— 1986. *Unmasking the powers: the invisible forces that determine human existence*. Minneapolis: Fortress Press.
—— 1992. *Engaging the powers: discernment and resistance in a world of domination*. Minneapolis: Fortress Press.
—— 1998. *The powers that be: theology for a new millennium*. London: Doubleday.
World Council of Churches (WCC) 1956. "Christian witness, proselytism and religious liberty in the setting of the World Council of Churches," *Ecumenical Review* 9/1 (Oct), 48–56.
—— 1991a. *Confessing the one faith: an ecumenical explication of the apostolic faith as it is confessed in the Nicene-Constantinopolitan Creed (381)*. Faith and Order Paper No. 153. Geneva: World Council of Churches.
—— 1991b. "Giver of life—sustain your creation!" Report of section 1 in Michael Kinnamon (ed.), *Signs of the Spirit*. Official report of the seventh assembly of the World Council of Churches, Canberra, 1991. Geneva: World Council of Churches, 54–72.
—— 1991c. "Spirit of unity—reconcile your people!" Report of section 3 in Michael Kinnamon (ed.), *Signs of the Spirit*. Official report of the seventh assembly of the World Council of Churches, Canberra, 1991. Geneva: World Council of Churches, 96–111.
—— 1991d. "Holy Spirit—transform and sanctify us!" Report of section 4 in Michael Kinnamon (ed.), *Signs of the Spirit*. Official report of the seventh assembly of the World Council of Churches, Canberra, 1991. Geneva: World Council of Churches, 111–21.
—— 1991e. Report of the Report Committee in Michael Kinnamon (ed.), *Signs of the Spirit*. Official report of the seventh assembly of the World Council of Churches, Canberra, 1991. Geneva: World Council of Churches, 235–58.
—— 1995. *Spirit, gospel and cultures: Bible studies on the Acts of the Apostles*. Geneva: World Council of Churches.
—— 1998a. "Authentic witness within each culture" Report of section 1 in Christopher Duraisingh (ed.), *Called to one hope: the gospel in diverse cultures*. Report of the conference on World Mission and Evangelism, Salvador, Brazil, 1996. Geneva: World Council of Churches, 30–39.
—— 1998b. "Local congregations in pluralist societies" Report of section 3 in Christopher Duraisingh (ed.), *Called to one hope: the gospel in diverse cultures*. Report of the conference on World Mission and Evangelism, Salvador, Brazil, 1996. Geneva: World Council of Churches, 53–64.

World Evangelical Alliance 2000. "The Iguassu affirmation" in William D. Taylor
    (ed.), *Global missiology for the twenty-first century: the Iguassu dialogue.*
    Papers from the Iguassu missiological consultation, Brazil, 1999. Grand
    Rapids, MI: Baker Book House, 15–21.
Wright, N. T. 2003. "New perspectives on Paul." Paper presented at the tenth
    Edinburgh dogmatics conference, 25–28 August at Rutherford House,
    Edinburgh.
Yi, Mahn-yŏl 2004. "The birth of the national spirit of the Christians in the late
    Chosŏn period" (trans. Ch'oe Ŭn-a) in Chai-shin Yu (ed.), *Korea and
    Christianity.* Fremont, CA: Asian Humanities Press, 39–72.
Yong, Amos 2000. *Discerning the Spirit(s): a Pentecostal-charismatic contribution
    to Christian theology of religions.* Sheffield: Sheffield Academic Press.
—— 2003a. *Beyond the impasse: toward a pneumatological theology of religions.*
    Grand Rapids, MI: Wm B. Eerdmans.
—— 2003b. " 'As the Spirit gives utterance': Pentecost, intra-Christian ecumenism
    and the wider oikoumene," *International Review of Mission* 92/366 (Apr),
    299–314.
Yu, Chai-shin (ed.) 1996. *The founding of Catholic tradition in Korea.* Mississauga,
    Ontario: Korea and Related Studies Press.
—— 2004. "The relationship between Korean Catholics and Protestants in the
    early mission period" in Chai-Shin Yu (ed.), *Korea and Christianity.* Fremont,
    CA: Asian Humanities Press, 7–37.
Zizioulas, John D. 1985. *Being as communion: studies in personhood and the
    Church.* Crestwood, NY: St. Vladimir's Seminary Press.

INDEX